About the Author

Entrepreneur, politician and philanthropist Dinesh Dhamija created and built the pioneering online travel agency ebookers during the 1990s internet boom. Selling the company for $471 million in 2004, he founded two major Indian charities and supported the Liberal Democrat party's anti-Brexit campaign, becoming an MEP in 2019.

Today Dinesh Dhamija is developing a major solar energy project in Romania, along with several property investments. He lives on the Wentworth golf course in Surrey with his wife Tani, close to their two sons and one granddaughter.

To my wife Tani, gatekeeper and true believer

Dinesh Dhamija

BOOK IT!

How Dinesh Dhamija built and sold online travel agency
ebookers for £247 million

AUSTIN MACAULEY PUBLISHERS™

LONDON · CAMBRIDGE · NEW YORK · SHARJAH

A CIP catalogue record for this title is available from the British Library.

ISBN 9781398427235 (Paperback)
ISBN 9781398427303 (ePub e-book)
ISBN 9781398427297 (Audiobook)

www.austinmacauley.com

First Published 2021
Austin Macauley Publishers Ltd®
1 Canada Square
Canary Wharf
London
E14 5AA

Acknowledgements

The following people kindly contributed their time to help compile this work:
Tani Dhamija
Sanjiv Talwar
Tikka Kapurthala
Prashant Sahni
David Nicholson provided invaluable advice and expertise.

Table of Contents

Introduction

Everyone is unique. Wherever you start in life, you're always going somewhere that nobody else has been. Your experiences will be your own. It's up to you what you do with them and where you end up.

That was my feeling, arriving in England in 1968 at the age of 17, an Indian boy coming into a country grappling with its loss of empire, just weeks after Harold Wilson withdrew Britain's troops from east of Suez. Like birds coming home to roost, we members of the old colonies were drawn to the mother country, in search of an education, wanting to speak like the Queen, to wear smart clothes and seek our fortune.

After getting an education and mixing with the English at study, at play and at work, I faced the biggest choice of my life. Do I stay in this post-colonial society where I'm at best treated as a curiosity, a smartly-dressed young Indian man with a nice English accent, at worst as a second-class citizen who is told to go back to where he came from? Or do I retreat to India where my family owns property? I'm well-connected and could slip into a mid-ranking managerial, civil service or military job and play bridge in the Delhi suburbs.

For some reason, I took the harder route. There were few obvious paths to take in 1970s London for a BAME immigrant, none of which appealed to me, or for which I was qualified. Indians became bus drivers, accountants or shopkeepers. I had a law degree, but wasn't interested in joining a law firm. I had no money, so I didn't think I could start a business.

Whatever was going to happen, I was determined that it would happen in England rather than India. Even though I could live an easy life back home, the persistent corruption repelled me. English society, for all its prejudices and its class-based elitism, struck me as fair. People could succeed based on their talents and hard work, rather than by paying bribes or cheating. It felt like a greater challenge, with higher risks and the promise of higher rewards.

Staying in England made me feel unique. Despite the Indian population of Britain rising between 1960 and 1970 from 80,000 to 375,000, as Gujuratis and Punjabis emigrated from East Africa and from India itself, we were still outnumbered by 150 to one across Britain.

To start my own business was more unusual still. I got a strong feeling that banks wouldn't lend money to someone like me. This narrowed down my options: what kind of business can you start without money? As I'll explain in this book, travel is one of the few industries where you can (or could, 40 years ago) get credit, if only for a short time.

Once I'd started up, as one of the only Indian-owned travel agencies in Europe, my singularity became even more pronounced. I wasn't catering to the Indian market in Britain, who bought their travel tickets from their local grocery shops, or especially selling flights to India. My market was more concerned with Australians flying home from London and people with disposable income flying to other long-haul destinations.

As you'll see in these chapters, I've never been afraid to be different. Whether it be at ebookers, which became one of the first UK-based companies to list on the American Nasdaq stock exchange, buying other travel agents all over Europe, or running my back office from India, or taking Europeans out to work in the Indian offices. Entrepreneurship is about overcoming fear, whether fear of standing out from the crowd or losing everything you have.

What I hope to do by setting down these memories and the story of my life is to inspire others who may be thinking of starting out in business. Whatever barriers and challenges you face, take heart: they can be overcome through persistence and hard work, imagination and a bit of luck. Every successful business is a strange land at first: you just need to work out how to get there.

Creating a business is in my view one of the most useful things that any of us can do. It means we turn our unique skills into something of value, that benefits all of society, bringing jobs, wealth and welfare, changing the world for the better.

I hope you enjoy this book.

Chapter 1
Early Memories and Education

In June 2000, just after celebrating my 50th birthday, I was terrified. Unless I raised $45 million within a week, the business I'd spent 20 years building from scratch would collapse. My mind flashed back to childhood tales of my Sikh warrior ancestors being 'bricked alive' – sealed into underground rooms until they died. How on earth could I escape?

My life story has been one of frequent close shaves like this, punctuated by times of great fortune and growth. To find out more, read on…

*   *   *   *   *

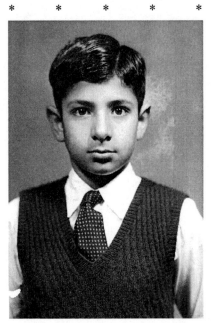

Dinesh Dhamija at 9 yrs, 1959

India, as we know it today, was just three years old when I was born in 1950. Partition in 1947 had torn the subcontinent apart, especially that area between the Himalayas and the plains of Rajasthan where millions of Hindus and Muslims had lived side by side for centuries, together with the partition of Bengal to create Bangladesh, to the east.

My parents' families were both from the Punjab, set in the hills above Delhi, where, in the not too distant past, maharajas had built palaces and fortresses to defend themselves from tribesmen and armies invading southwards. While both families were Punjabi, they were from opposite sides of Lahore; my father Jagan Nath Dhamija and his family came from Kamalia, a village near Lyallpur 100 km to the west in Pakistan, and my mother – Devika Sarabjit Singh – was from Kapurthala 100 km to the east, over the present-day border in India.

My father and Bobby Riggs at Centre Court, Wimbledon in 1939

My father was born to a liberal, middle-class family. His father, my grandfather, was a civil engineer and encouraged him to follow in his footsteps, so he studied for a Bachelor of Science degree at the D. J. Singh College in the 1920s, while the family were living on Manora Island in Karachi. During this time, my father would take long walks along the seashore, developing a love of solitude and introspection, along with a determination to study literature. After taking a Master's degree in Lahore, he was accepted by Emmanuel College, Cambridge University where he studied English for two years before graduating with a law degree in 1939.

My mother came from an aristocratic, royal family, who had owned vast swathes of the Punjab in the 18th century. Her ancestors included Jassa Singh, whose Sikh armies conquered cities from Lahore to Kashmir and Kashmir to Delhi; Maharaja Ranjit Singh, who created a unified Sikh state and pushed back the frontiers of the Punjab; and her second cousin was Maharaja Jagatjit Singh of Kapurthala, whose palaces became known as the Paris of the Punjab.

My mother in 1949, when she got married

My father had had a hectic escape from Pakistan in 1947 on a bullock and cart, with security men to protect him from the threats of violence and theft all around. He told me later about the trains that would rumble through northern India and Pakistan in both directions, full of headless bodies. Indeed partition was a trauma for the whole region. It was imposed by the British, who had outstayed their welcome and felt they had to divide the Muslim and Hindu communities in their wake. In a panic they drew random lines through the east and west of the Himalayas to create West and East Pakistan (later Pakistan and Bangladesh). Despite not experiencing partition itself, I could feel its impact throughout my childhood. Some of my earliest memories are of my father's mother, who lived with us until she died in 1957 when I was just seven. She would talk about how terrible partition had been, how there were so many refugees who were forced to leave behind all their belongings and property.

(More than 60 years later, when I was a Member of the European Parliament, these memories came back to me. In the 21st century, more than a million non-Muslims suffered persecution in Pakistan, fleeing to India to escape. And yet India is often portrayed as a villain in this situation. I told fellow MEPs that my own family were refugees from Pakistan and yet were accepted by India – and that it's best not to criticise those who accept you.)

Indira Gandhi and Nehru at my parents wedding 1950

My mother and father, 1967

At the time of my birth my parents were living in Australia where my father was working for the Indian Foreign Service as second in command at the High Commission. Despite being so far from India, I feel that my arrival in the early years of Independence might have felt like a resolution, for them, of the turmoil of partition. Within a couple of years of my arrival, my parents decided to move back to India, and we were soon joined, in early 1952, by my younger brother Sumant.

From the age of four I'd go with my father to Delhi Golf Club. One of the caddies taught me how to play and by the age of five, I was playing nine holes. Delhi Golf Club was extremely popular and it was quite a thing to be a member. Today there are 1,100 members and people are on a waiting list for 30 or 40 years. It was and is like the Marylebone Cricket Club (MCC) in England.

Even before I was born, my father had been active at both the Golf Club and the Gymkhana Club; there's a commemorative photograph of a board meeting in 1949, showing my father among the group who changed the name of the Gymkhana Club from 'Imperial' to 'Delhi'. Most of the board members were English, but since he'd graduated from Cambridge, I guess he was accepted by them. It was certainly a privilege to be a member and it was a tight society – everyone knew each other.

My first school was St Columba's in Delhi, an all-boys, Christian Brothers foundation, which has produced some remarkable people including the philosopher Deepak Chopra; the CEO of Diageo, Ivan Menezes; and an entrepreneur called Deep Kalra, who founded MakeMyTrip – the most popular Indian online travel agency. Deep and I actually agreed a deal in the 2000s – my company acquired his back-office systems.

My father's career meant we were soon off again, this time to Mauritius, where, from 1958 to 1960, he worked at the Indian High Commission. I remember very vividly two nights in early 1960, when cyclones swept over the island. Arriving in January, Cyclone Alix was bad enough, with 200 km/h winds that blew down hundreds of homes, but Cyclone Carol, which followed in February, was absolutely terrifying. Water streamed through the ceiling of our wooden house and in the middle of the night we heard a colossal noise. Out on our veranda were huge teak pillars, which had crashed to the ground. We were unharmed, but it was an exceptionally frightening experience. I found out later that it was the worst storm on record at that time, with winds above 250 km/h. It killed 42 people on the island and left thousands homeless.

Other than these storms, Mauritius was a lovely place to live; very relaxed and beautiful, with some of the world's best beaches. It has a unique mixture of African, Asian (particularly Indian) and European (particularly French) cultures, so the cuisine is fantastic. By the time we left, I could speak fluent French, thanks to the primary school I attended there.

By the age of eight, when we moved to Mauritius, I was a pretty accomplished golfer. I won an under-16 tournament on the island and used to love going to the Dodo course at Vacoas, near Curepipe, up in the central hills. At the time this was just about the only one on the island, whereas today it has many fine courses.

For the next few years, from 1960 to 1967 I went to boarding schools in India while my parents lived overseas and I'd visit them during the school holidays. This meant I studied with some quite privileged Indian boys.

The first of these schools was Mayo College in Ajmer, Rajasthan, a prestigious boarding establishment that modelled itself on an English public school. It was founded in the 19th century by Lord Mayo, who was Viceroy of India from 1868 to 1872. During his tenure he came to Ajmer and declared that he wanted to set up a college 'devoted exclusively to the education of the sons of Chiefs, Princes and leading Thakurs [noblemen]'. Indeed, its first pupil, when it opened in 1875, was Raja Mangal Singh, the sixth Maharaja of Alwar. Notable fellow pupils from my day include Vijayender Badnore, who is now the Indian Governor of Punjab, and Indra Sinha, who became a novelist.

Our headmaster was an Englishman called Jack Gibson, who had studied at Cambridge University and taught at several reputable schools. He'd also climbed some of the world's highest mountains, including Bandarpunch in Uttarakhand, more than 20,700 feet (6,300 metres) high, with Tenzing Norgay. He was an inspiration to us boys as we marched around in the cadet force and played in the sports teams.

My brother Sumant also went to Mayo College. All through my childhood, I was close to him and while we were both at the college we spent our spare time together. Sometimes when we were on holiday from Mayo College, we would go to India Gate in the city to buy ice cream, or to Delhi Golf Club for chips and Libby's ketchup. Or else we'd play tennis together.

The idea behind Mayo College was not only to provide high academic standards, but to produce 'men fond of field sports and outdoor exercise'. I played for my house cricket team as an opening batsman, which is a sort of 'field sport' I suppose. In any case, it gave me a lifelong love of cricket, like many millions of my fellow Indians, even though I never played a great deal after those teenage years.

I remember being very impressed by a Caribbean player of Indian heritage, Rohan Kanhai, who batted for the West Indies team in the late 1950s and 1960s, just at the time I was striding out at Mayo College on the fields of Rajasthan. In fact, he had made an early impression on me at the age of eight, when he scored 256 for the West Indies against India in Calcutta – the first batsman to make a double century at Eden Gardens. He played alongside some of the great West Indian cricketers like Gary Sobers and Alvin Kallicharran and inspired many later Indian cricketers. 'Rohan Kanhai is quite simply the greatest batsman I have ever seen,' Sunil Gavaskar once said. I have to agree. Gavaskar named his own son Rohan, in his honour.

Some of my other favourites were Farokh Engineer, who played for India in the 1960s and then for Lancashire in the 1970s. He was a dashing batsman and a very agile wicketkeeper. And Sachin Tendulkar, the most prolific batsman ever, with his 100 centuries and 10,000 one day international runs. I loved watching his cover drives and meticulous attention to detail.

Of the English players, I particularly remember bowler Derek Underwood. He once took 19 wickets on a wet pitch, where he was almost unplayable. He had a slow, left arm action which mesmerised batsmen and often caught them leg before wicket – Bishan Bedi without the turban. And of today's players, watching Ben Stokes is just pure pleasure.

During the holidays at Mayo College, I'd travel to Kabul in Afghanistan where my father was Indian Ambassador. He became close to the king at the time, Mohammed Zahir Shah, and to the king's uncle, Field Marshal Sardar Shah Wali Khan, who was commander-in-chief of the army that captured Kabul in 1929. Shah Wali loved Indian food and would attend dinner parties hosted by my father. Of all the ambassadors, I think my father was able to get closest to the seat of power in Kabul.

The king's son was a keen tennis player, so my father arranged a tennis tutor for him, but the person he found was no ordinary coach. He'd taught the Indian champion Ramanathan Krishnan – a two-time semi-finalist at Wimbledon, in 1960 and 1961, with a top ranking of world number six. Krishnan was the first Asian player to win the boys' singles title at Wimbledon and once beat the legendary Rod Laver while playing for India in a Davis Cup match. When he wasn't busy giving the king's son tips on his backhand, Krishnan's coach taught me and my brother to play, which was a tremendous asset to us later in life. What he always emphasised was to use touch, angles and finesse. Other players would try to hit the ball as hard as possible, but he preferred consistency and a good feel for the ball.

My father could call on this coach's services partly because he, too, was an excellent tennis player. He played for the university while studying at Cambridge and then played at the Wimbledon Championships in 1939, stepping out onto Centre Court to play the number two seed, the American Bobby Riggs, who eventually won the tournament. For our whole family, Wimbledon was a very big deal. For an Indian player to make the tournament was so unusual; once my father played there, he had the feeling he'd be guaranteed a job. He kept on playing at a high standard for many years –

indeed, he was in the final of the Mauritius Open Championships when we were there, at the age of about 50, still using touch rather than power.

I think that having studied at Cambridge University and been a competitor at Wimbledon did actually help my father get his first job, in the Royal Indian Navy. He joined just at the start of World War II in 1939 and sailed round the Cape of Good Hope three times. He had some close shaves; a ship sailing just ahead of his exploded and sank, hit by a German U-boat.

A few years later, in his letter of recommendation to the High Commissioner for India, my father's old tutor at Cambridge, Edward Welbourne, wrote: 'As a man, he had qualities of judgment, capacities for decision, courage in life, ease in personal encounter, which made him in my opinion admirably fit for Government service, that he was of high character, a man of great self-control, though of energy and ambition.' He concluded: 'If it is possible for him to be given an appointment in India, I feel sure he would be found to be a devoted and profitable servant.' Sure enough, he was appointed to the Indian Political Service in 1944 and was posted to northern India (now Pakistan), to look after the population on the border with Afghanistan. I'm sure this experience was a key reason for his later appointment as Indian Ambassador for Afghanistan.

During one of my trips to Kabul, I actually met the Afghan king. He was a very tall man. He had been in power since 1933 and in the early 1960s, around the time of my visits, he introduced a new constitution, with free elections, a parliament, civil rights, women's rights and voting for all. The king was close to the Italian Ambassador and when he was deposed in 1973, after ruling for 40 years, he went into exile in Italy. I always felt that it was a sad story, with two of his cousins usurping power and then allowing the country to fall into ruin.

I have such great memories of Afghanistan: going to see the 6th century Bamyan Buddha statues; driving everywhere in a big car with an Indian flag on the bonnet; all the lavish entertainment at our house, with servants and cooks and chauffeurs. I remember going to visit Mazar-i-Sharif, close to the border with Uzbekistan, with its blue-tiled mosque and shrine to Ali, son-in-law of the Prophet Mohammad. It was a few hours' drive away from Kabul, through the valley of Puli Khumri, along the Kunduz river, through orchards and wheat fields and up on to the high plain.

Once we saw a game of buzkashi played in Mazar-i-Sharif, where a goat carcass is pulled along by horsemen who try to throw it into a central spot. It's a wild, chaotic sport with dozens of players all charging around in the dust. There are few rules, no timings, no defined pitch and no teams, just a mass of men and horses fighting over a dead goat. The victors – who manage to put the goat in the right place – can win rugs, cars, even houses.

The next stage of my education began at the age of 14 when I moved to St Xavier's School in Delhi. This was a different kind of school, a Jesuit foundation started in 1960 in a former hostelry, called Hotel Cecil, which had more than 100 rooms, a swimming pool and lovely gardens. As with my two earlier schools, this was a place for the Indian upper classes, with lessons in English, and supposedly more of an emphasis on religion, although I don't remember them insisting on this particularly. Father Kunnunkal was the headmaster at the time; an impressive figure who was later awarded the Padma Shri, one of India's highest honours. Our tutors were monks, dressed all in white flowing robes, and I remember they used to beat us quite a bit. I can't remember exactly why though I suppose we must have been doing something wrong. Anyway, in spite of this, or perhaps because of it, the school was high-performing academically, and the exam results were always good.

Attending Christian schools as I grew up opened my eyes to a whole new religion and nurtured an acceptance of faiths other than my own. While I'm Hindu and have an attachment to Hindu spirituality, I feel comfortable in churches, mosques and any other religious buildings. I'm so grateful for an upbringing that gave me this tolerance of, and familiarity with, other people's faiths.

At St Xavier's, instead of boarding, I lived at the home of Mohammad Hidayatullah, who at that time was a judge in India's Supreme Court. He later became chief justice, then vice-president and then (twice, briefly in 1969 and 1982) acting President of India. This was a really important time in my life, living with his family and absorbing lessons from them. Whereas up to this point I'd coasted through school, getting average grades and paying more attention to sport, once I was with the Hidayatullah family, they stopped me playing sport and said: 'You've got to study.'

I learned a lot just eating with the family every evening. Their son, Arshad, was my age and was really into classical music, which was new to me. Mohammad Hidayatullah had studied law at Trinity College, Cambridge University, and at his home there would be a constant flow of politicians, writers and businesspeople talking about commerce between India and Britain, new laws, current affairs and the arts. It was a very high-powered environment; one of Hidayatullah's brothers became foreign minister of Pakistan and his daughter married the Crown Prince of Jordan. The family was also inter-religious – Mohammad was Muslim and his wife Pushpa was Hindu – which showed me how the two sides could work together in harmony.

All in all, it was a very positive experience for me; it gave me confidence in my abilities, inspired me to study hard and opened my eyes to a world of possibilities. At the end of that year, I earned 'first division' marks in my senior exams for the first time.

One of my outstanding memories from these years was when I met my mother' father – my grandfather, Prince Sarabjit Singh. He studied at Eton in the early 1900s while his father was busy in India and excelled at sports. I've seen cups with his name on for boxing and I think he played golf. He even tried jujitsu. Eventually Prince Sarabjit met his father for the first time at the Savoy Grill in London in 1920, when my grandfather was 18, and they returned to India together.

During the school holidays at this time my brother and I would often go along with our parents to ashrams for spiritual retreats. They didn't mean much to us at the time, but I expect they laid the foundations of an interest in spirituality and healing, which I've pursued later in life. As a young man, my father showed a keen interest in spirituality. He wrote in his book 'A Quest for the Eternal' about how he began his spiritual journey at the age of 18, visiting shrines and ashrams in search of knowledge and enlightenment.

In 1952, when I was just two and the family had just moved from Australia to Delhi, my father met the spiritual leader Shree Anandamayee Ma, who in the 1940s had established renowned ashrams in Calcutta (now Kolkata) and Delhi and welcomed visitors including Indian Prime Minister Jawaharlal Nehru and – later on – his daughter Indira Gandhi. For aspiring civil servants who wanted to progress up the ladder, it was a good career move to say you adored Shree Anandamayee Ma.

From a very early age, Ma had inspired worship and adoration from strangers. She was reputed to have performed miracles of healing and to have supernatural powers, radiating an aura of calm and happiness. Whether or not it helped his career, my father was utterly transfixed at her 'darshan' (an Indian concept, meaning a vision of a holy person). "Her beauty and her divine grace engulfed my being with an overpowering love," he wrote. "I knew that the great moment of my life had arrived and that I had found the One whom I had been seeking for years."

From this point onward, he and my mother would visit Ma whenever possible, whether at Vrindavan, along the road from Delhi to Agra, during holy festivals or at Modinagar, to the northeast of Delhi. He adopted the mantras and performed the daily rituals that Ma recommended, which brought him closer to eternal truth. He also took on her quest for self-realisation and pursued it for the rest of his life. When Shree Anandamayee Ma died in 1982, my parents bought a property close to her 'samadi' (tomb) in Kankhol on the

River Ganges in Uttarakhand. They made it into a nice, clean guest house and we still have it, welcoming travellers and pilgrims.

The final stage of my secondary education was at another Christian establishment, The King's School, Canterbury, in the southeast of England. This is the most important city in the country as far as the Church of England is concerned, since the Archbishop of Canterbury is its head. The school was in the precincts of Canterbury Cathedral.

Tennis 1st VI at King's School, Canterbury 1968

When I arrived in January 1968 I wish I could say that my fellow pupils had a Christian attitude to new boys fresh out of India, but sadly some of them were more like the bullies of 'Tom Brown's School Days' or 'Lord of the Flies' than the saintly choirboys you might hope for. They picked on me for my Indian accent and unfamiliarity with English customs. Plus I arrived at the age of 17, so while most everyone else had known each other and been friends since prep school I was a comparative outsider.

What made the biggest difference was my sporting talents. Within a few months, I was selected for the first tennis six, which improved my status at the school. Then the economic history teacher arranged a golf outing to Sandwich, on the Kent coast. I went along and won the 'long drive' competition. My peers were impressed with my 284-yard drive and I started to have a better time. I was gradually becoming accepted!

By the time school started again in September, after the summer break, most of the best tennis players had left to go to college, so I became captain of the team. This meant that I could sit with the prefects at the top table at mealtimes and was allowed to walk on the grass in the school grounds. It was a further stage of acceptance.

When you arrive in a new country as a foreigner, you perceive it through a distinct lens. In my case, I could sense that as far as my fellow schoolboys were concerned I didn't have the right demeanour for a school that was clearly towards the upper end of the British class system. They didn't understand, and why should they? I understood this so I found it easy to disregard the way people behaved towards me in school because I was from a different country. Fortunately, once I was an adult and went to university my experience was totally different.

King's is one of the oldest schools in the world, dating back to the 6th century. According to the history of St Augustine he founded an abbey at this time where teaching took place. From many points of view, it was an excellent school. It had a tremendous musical tradition, with its King's Week music event held annually in June. It was very good for rowing, and produced a lot of strong sportsmen. When I was there, David Gower was a younger student, doing well at cricket before going on to captain England as one of the most elegant batsmen in the sport.

King's also produced a succession of wonderful writers, starting with the dramatist Christopher Marlowe in the 16th century, through to W. Somerset Maugham in the early 20th century (who incidentally was teased for his French accent when he arrived at the school), to the travel writer Patrick Leigh Fermor and Michael Morpurgo, who wrote 'War Horse', his novel set in World War I. Indeed, you could spend an enjoyable few months reading nothing but the works of these men.

During the holidays from King's, I'd go to Prague where my father was Indian Ambassador and vividly remember the day in August 1968, when Soviet troops invaded the Czech capital to depose the government of Alexander Dubček. Dubček had ushered in the Prague Spring and liberalised the country, much to the annoyance of the Russian government of Leonid Brezhnev.

It was a lovely sunny Sunday and the first thing we noticed was that all our Czech neighbours were staying inside. We didn't understand what was going on, but we soon found out. Massive Russian Antonov planes began landing at the airport and military trucks rolled out of them, drove across the airport and out into the city streets. Troops rounded up people from the countryside to help fight the resistance, which was largely based in the cities.

My father was in an interesting position. He knew the British Ambassador and was on good terms with him, and he also got along well with the Russians. As the British and the Russians were on opposite sides of the Cold War and refused to speak directly with one another, they would pass messages through my father. I think that his extrovert personality was an advantage in these situations: he liked hunting, fishing, tennis and golf; there was always a cocktail party and at dinner there would be six glasses at each table setting: white wine, red wine, champagne, water, brandy and port. You can imagine how, dining every day like this, the ambassadors got to know each other very well.

Another event that stays with me from that time occurred later in 1968 when the Czechoslovakian team played the Russians in the final of the ice hockey world championships. Czechoslovakia won by four goals to three and I couldn't believe the excitement that night, as everyone ran out of their houses. There were people on top of cars, a million people in the streets chanting: 'We beat you!' My brother and I walked around Wenceslas Square in utter amazement.

In 1970 I managed to get four 'A' levels from King's: in economic history, history, British constitution and Hindi, but apart from Hindi (which was naturally pretty easy for me), my grades weren't fantastic, so I took a year off and went to a crammer in London, to improve them. This proved enough to win me a place at Fitzwilliam College, Cambridge, where my education moved up a gear and I could follow in my father's footsteps.

Jagatjit Singh – my mother's second cousin – and the Paris of the Punjab

Although he died just a year before I was born, stories of Jagatjit Singh's life stayed fresh in our family's minds, because he was such a remarkable character. He inherited the title of Maharaja of Kapurthala in 1877, at the age of five, and began ruling his kingdom in 1890. Unusually for the time, he was a hugely adventurous traveller, circumnavigating the world three times. He particularly loved Paris, and on his return from each visit, would introduce another innovation: a modern sewerage system, a telephone network, a better judicial system, an improved army and police force. He was also a social reformer; he introduced free primary education and agricultural cooperative societies.

Fluent in Persian, Urdu, Sanskrit, English, French and Italian, Jagatjit Singh had a passion for European culture, particularly French. He hired a notable French architect to design Jagatjit Palace in Kapurthala (now a military school) and its stately gardens, which were based on the Palace of

Versailles in Paris. He built another French-inspired home, Château Kapurthala in Mussoorie, based on the castles of the Loire valley. And just to complete the French theme, he brought over a celebrated chef from Paris, even offering to fund the chef's mistress to keep her happy. He was awarded the Grand-croix de la Légion d'Honneur by the French nation in 1926 and Kapurthala became known as the Paris of the Punjab.

In India, Maharaja Jagatjit Singh was regarded among the most important royals of his day, particularly in diplomatic circles. He represented the country three times during important political summits at the League of Nations in Geneva in the 1920s.

Outside his civil responsibilities and diplomacy, Jagatjit Singh led a colourful private life. He became infamous in Spain after marrying a penniless dancer called Anita Delgado, wooing her with precious jewels and inviting her to Paris, where she was greeted by 'his secretary, a dozen slaves and half a dozen automobiles' (as she later wrote in her memoirs). She was housed in a luxurious palace, where she was told that the maharaja would only see her once she had learnt French.

Anita Delgado was actually one of six wives, the last of whom – an aristocratic Czech actress called Evgenia Grosupova – suffered from a nervous disposition and eventually committed suicide by throwing herself from the top of the Qutub Minar tower, 240 feet (70 metres) above the Delhi streets, with her two beloved poodles tucked under each arm.

According to my uncle Brigadier Sukhjit Singh, Jagatjit 'enjoyed the company of interesting and attractive young ladies and he brought many back from Europe to stay in Kapurthala as his guests and personal friends, some of the most beautiful women I have ever seen'. Sukhjit wrote a biography of Jagatjit titled 'Prince, Patron and Patriarch', in which he called him 'a remarkable ruler whose reign was a period of eminence, culture, expanding horizons and notable public service'.

He was clearly a hugely influential and vibrant personality. Sometimes I think I inherited from him a similar passion for travel, innovation and social reform. But whatever similarities I may have with Jagatjit Singh, I'm relieved to say that my married life has been far less tumultuous!

Jassa Singh – the Hero of the Punjab

My 18th century ancestor Jassa Singh grew up in turbulent times, when Mughal emperors ruled northern India and sought to convert the population to Islam. Being 'bricked alive' (sealed in a small brick room until you died) was a common punishment. In 1718, the year he was born, the Emperor Farrukh Siyyar issued an edict: "Every Sikh was to be executed after arrest. Their families were to become the property of the state and the women and girls to become concubines or forced into slavery," wrote my brother Sumant in his biography of Jassa Singh, 'The Forgotten Hero of Punjab'. A year later Farrukh Siyyar himself was captured, blinded, tortured and finally strangled.

My ancestor, 1858

Growing up in Delhi, Jassa Singh understood the brutality of the Mughal emperors. As a Sikh, he venerated Gurus, who revealed God's purpose for mankind. A generation earlier, Emperor Aurangzeb ordered the murder of a succession of these Gurus, displaying their severed heads around the city. This only increased support among Sikhs for the movement and convinced Jassa Singh to avenge these outrages.

Sikhs like Jassa formed into fierce armies, committed to a strict code of behaviour and practices: they must never cut their hair, never smoke tobacco and never molest women. After training with the military leader Kapur Singh and becoming an expert archer, hunting wild boar and tigers, the teenage Jassa lived with other Sikhs in the jungle, feeding on roots and berries. Even at this young age, he stood out for his courage and skill. In 1732 he helped ambush the emperor's guards and steal a great cache of treasure.

In the years to come, Jassa Singh came to command his own forces, numbering thousands of Sikhs, as they battled the Mughal emperors and carved out their own territory in the Punjab, conquering the iconic cities of Lahore and Amritsar. At the age of 30 he was named Sultan-ul-Quom – King of the Sikhs. He benefited from invasions of Northern India by the Persian leader Nadir Shah and his successor Shah Abdali, who weakened the Mughals and left a power vacuum for Jassa Singh's forces to occupy.

In 1783, he finally overcame the Mughals and conquered Delhi, ushering in a new era in Indian rule. He established the state of Kapurthala where his successors then ruled and he laid the foundations for the Sikh Empire, which lasted for the first half of the 19th century. He was a giant of a man, physically, emotionally and psychologically. His legacy remains to this day, in the gurudwaras he built, in the pride of Indian people in their self-determination and in the example of his instinctive and inspiring leadership.

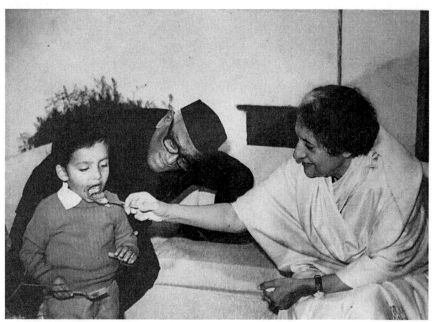

President Sanjiva Reddy and Indira Gandhi with my son Biren, 1980

Tani and me, 2003

With my son Darun, 2011

My Family, 2015

Chapter 2
Cambridge Days

For my family, Cambridge University has been an enormous influence on our education, our careers, our friendships and our lives. For my father, it opened the doors to an entire world of possibilities, from sporting triumphs to his work in the Indian Foreign Service. He was tremendously keen that my brother Sumant and I should enjoy the same opportunities that he did.

The roots of this attachment go back deep into Indian history. Several aristocratic, wealthy and well-connected Indians studied at Cambridge in the 19th century, like Sir Dorabji Tata, who helped to build an industrial dynasty, or Prince Ranjitsinhji, who played cricket for Sussex and England.

For my father's family, the star Cambridge graduate was Jawaharlal Nehru, who studied sciences at Trinity College from 1904 to 1907 before leading India to Independence in 1947 after a long struggle against British colonialism. Nehru's story became almost mythical in India's early years: Cambridge was a magical source of enlightenment and political wisdom.

Soon after Nehru's return to India, the self-taught mathematical genius Srivasa Ramanujan was accepted as a student and later elected as a Fellow of the Royal Society. This showed that even working-class Indian students could thrive at Cambridge, based on their natural intelligence and talent.

When my father travelled to study science and law at Emmanuel College in the 1930s, Indian students were still an uncommon sight in Cambridge, but he was generally treated well and excelled at tennis. At one point he was refused a place in the doubles team "because Indians don't combine very well". Without playing doubles, my father would have been denied a full 'blue' – the Cambridge accolade given to those who compete against Oxford in certain sports. His apparent lack of team spirit was overlooked in the end, thanks to a Greek Davis Cup player called Nikolaides, and he won a full blue in his final year.

In his work at the Indian Foreign Service, my father certainly found that it was helpful to have a Cambridge education. When he would speak with British diplomats around the world, many of them (I would say the majority) had studied at Oxford or Cambridge, so he could more easily relate to them. His tutor Edward Welbourne's letter of recommendation to the High Commissioner for India noted his 'personal decision, that the European mentality was better studied by spending time among living men, than by over-much attention to examinations'.

This may be a diplomatic way of saying that he was having far too much fun and neglecting his studies, but it is nicely phrased. My father put his Cambridge experiences to good use for the rest of his life, even if he did spend a lot of time playing tennis.

Once I had retaken my A-levels at the Davies Laing and Dick College in Notting Hill, west London, to get good enough grades for Cambridge, my father started badgering another of his old tutors, Dr W.W. Grave, on my behalf. Grave had been a Fellow of Emmanuel College in the 1930s and was appointed Censor (head) of Fitzwilliam House, as it was then known, in 1959. Once Fitzwilliam gained full college status in 1966, Grave became its first Master.

For me, as for my father, life at Cambridge was utterly different and better than before. The petty racism I'd experienced at boarding school in Canterbury was absent. We students of Indian or other ethnic minority heritage were treated with respect and curiosity, almost like a novelty. Since my father's time, there had been many more exceptional Indian students, such as Jayant Narlikar, who was at Fitzwilliam ahead of my time, and developed a new theory of gravity based on Einstein's work, or Amartya Sen, who studied economics at Trinity and won a Nobel Prize for his work on poverty and development. Nehru's grandson Rajiv Gandhi was also a student in the early 1960s, before serving as India's youngest Prime Minister in the 1980s.

In the time between school and university, my father found me a job in Cambridge for the technology firm Pye (owned by Phillips, a company in the Netherlands, where he was ambassador at the time). So I was already familiar with the 'town' side of Cambridge. I knew the places where young local people liked to go, the bars and cafes. It made my transition to student life a bit easier.

University was a liberating experience. I would spend time at the first wine bar, called Shades, that opened on King's Parade – the street which passes next to King's College and its vast gothic chapel. I would visit the Whim coffee shop, the Halepi Greek restaurant where for 35p you could get a fantastic moussaka with chips and peas. I'd even visit discotheques like Kambar on Wheeler Street next to the Corn Exchange.

Fitzwilliam College (previously House) was already 100 years old when I joined in 1971. It was originally for less well-off students, who would lodge with local families rather than live in a college. Then after 1963, it had much grander premises in the grounds of The Grove, a regency building up Huntingdon Road to the north of the city centre. The main hall, designed by Sir Denys Lasdun, opened in 1966, just a few years before I arrived.

Despite the fancier buildings, the ethos of the college remained: it attracted more grammar schoolboys than the more class-conscious colleges like Trinity, where Charles, the Prince of Wales, was a student just before I arrived in Cambridge, along with half of Eton. I don't remember any snobbism at Fitzwilliam, people were more down to earth and welcoming.

Just as at King's School in Canterbury, I threw myself into sports at Cambridge, playing tennis, table-tennis, squash and golf at every opportunity. The remarks from my father's tutor could pretty much have applied to me too. On Saturdays and Sundays I'd play golf for the University team at various members' clubs around the country, like Hunstanton and Brancaster, Royal Norfolk, or Roehampton in London. Then on Wednesdays we'd practise at Royal Worlington, about 25km into the Suffolk countryside. Leonard Crawley, a sportswriter for the *Daily Telegraph*, said that Worlington had the best nine-hole course in Europe.

My fellow golfers were people like Phil Edmonds, who could strike the ball for miles, with his cricketer's arm. He and I spent a lot of time together and I enjoyed his company, even though he could rub people up the wrong way. He was in the university rugby club and said something flippant to the club captain, who dropped him for the Varsity Match and he never played again – consequently failing to win a 'blue'. I guess he made up for that with his 51 England Test caps and five wickets against Australia on debut. He carried on winding people up through his whole career. In 1984, while fielding at square leg for England against a dour Indian batting pair, he took out a copy of the *Daily Telegraph* and began to read it. Since retiring from cricket, he's enjoyed an equally colourful career as an entrepreneur and investor in African mining companies, along with his flamboyant and scurrilous wife, the writer Francis Edmonds.

If I wasn't playing golf, I'd be on the squash courts, playing for Fitzwilliam alongside David Leakey, who was ranked number five in the university. One year we won 41 out of 42 matches. David then represented Great Britain at squash before becoming a Lieutenant General in the British Army, senior British negotiator at the Bosnia Peace Talks in Dayton, Ohio, and finally Black Rod in the House of Lords. David is one of the people I've stayed closest to through the years. We have a similar taste in food and joined the same clubs after university when we were in London.

I played tennis and table tennis for Fitzwilliam, and we generally did well. For years before I was there, Downing College dominated the college tennis tournaments – they would recruit the best players from schools like Millfield, which turn out fantastic sportspeople. Downing had won the annual 'Cuppers' tennis competition for 14 years straight, but when I was at Fitzwilliam we won it, narrowly beating them 5-4.

There was a community of Indian students at Cambridge, but I didn't really spend time with them because I felt I should assimilate with English people and English culture. My view was 'When in Rome...' And in any case, there isn't a homogenous Indian culture; there were so many different groups, the Gujuratis, the Tamils, the Punjabis and so on. Although there was an Indian Society, there wasn't a Pakistani society: for someone like me, who was an Indian Punjabi, with friends who were Pakistani Punjabis, it didn't make sense to define myself by a specific country.

At Fitzwilliam, there was one student that I bonded with over our ethnic roots: Ken Olisa. We didn't move in exactly the same circles – I was more into sports – but we'd meet at drinks parties. He was black and I was brown. After working at IBM (like me), he founded two technology merchant banks (unlike me) and was the first British black director of a FTSE 100 company and then the first black Lord Lieutenant of Greater London in its 500-year history. We served together on the Fitzwilliam fundraising committee and it was fantastic that he donated so generously to the college, giving it £2 million for a new library which bears his name. He's done an incredible job supporting young people, especially from BAME communities.

For a small and not-so-grand college, Fitzwilliam has produced a remarkable crop of people over the years. Sir Vince Cable was there in the 1960s, studying economics before working all over the world for governments, companies and organisations like the Commonwealth, then leading the Liberal Democrats to their best ever local government and European election result in 2019, going from one to 16 seats! He was an intellectual politician who understood how to win votes and influence people and I was sorry to see him stand down as leader.

Sir Peter Bazalgette was another contemporary of mine, who worked his way through the television industry, from a researcher to the Chairman of Endemol, in charge when it was sold for €3.2 billion in 2007, thanks largely to his creative and management genius. He's now Chairman of the Arts Council and I'm really proud of what he's achieved. He and I founded a dining society at Cambridge called Snails and we're still in touch.

We must have had some brainy students in those days, because we won University Challenge in 1973, in my second year, beating fellow Cambridge college Gonville and Caius.

I made a few friends outside Fitzwilliam too, like Firdaus Ruttonshaw, who was at Jesus College. He was an exotic and charismatic figure, born and raised as a Zoroastrian in Burma, taught at a Jesuit school in India and then accepted at Cambridge. He and I kept in touch and I made him Managing Director of Flightbookers in the 1990s. We still meet for lunches at good restaurants near where he lives in Kensington where he entertains me with his sharp tongue and indiscrete stories.

Cambridge has continued to be a much-valued part of my life, all the way through my career. I joined the Oxford and Cambridge Club after graduating and still go there every so often. If you want to host a dinner for 10 or 12 people, it's the easiest place to have it. The club is like a home from home. It's the sort of place where I'd arrange to meet Tim Dickson, another Fitzwilliam colleague and golfing partner, who worked as a journalist for the *Financial Times* and McKinsey, then started *Golf Quarterly* in 2010, which he still edits. He and I were paired at Cambridge for the Stymies – the university second team – against the Oxford second team, the Divots. Tim was recently elected captain of Royal St George's Club in Kent.

Later on, I was invited to play for the Hawks Club, established in the 19th century for people who have won a full blue competing for Cambridge against Oxford in a certain sport (golf being one of them). It was an honour to join this club, despite not having a blue. My wife Tani and I led a Hawks tour of India in 1984, visiting Bombay, Delhi, Calcutta and Goa, hosted in corporate guest houses by the local Indian golf clubs. We took a Hawks flag with us, together with golf balls printed with the club name: it was a nice 19-day tour.

Tani made friends with three of the other players' wives and the four of them had a riot. At the Tollygunge Club in Calcutta – one of the smartest country clubs in the world – they were determined to watch some horse racing and pestered the president of the Golf Club (who was also the head of the Jockey Club) for some betting tips. He took 10 rupees from each of them and put it on six horses. Five of them came in and they collected 1,500 rupees each! So then they decided to donate their winnings to Mother Theresa, who was famous at the time for her work in the city slums. They visited her and each received a blessing. Soon we discovered that all three (other than Tani) had become pregnant on the tour.

In Delhi, we played against the Army Golf Club: we turned up early in the morning. Once we'd finished playing, we found three brass bands in full uniform serenading us, playing *Que Sera Sera,* and a tent laid out with drinks.

Peter Green was one of our team and he thought he'd entered a time warp and gone back to the days of the Raj, as he sipped his gin and tonic.

*   *   *   *   *

Occasionally during my time as a Cambridge student, I'd get an urge to make some money. With two friends, Dhanu and Vikran, I once hired a trailer, complete with hamburgers, buns and boiled onions, for £25. We set off for the Notting Hill Carnival and sold our burgers at a profit of £65: I took the largest share because I put up the deposit for the trailer.

We were very naïve, we didn't realise how violent the carnival could become. I looked after all our cash because I was the biggest of us three, not even dreaming that someone might come at us with a knife and try to take all the money. My friend remembers us being threatened, though we escaped any injury and kept hold of the money.

I'd go down to casinos in London with friends and bet on the roulette tables, taking advantage of the free food and drink to attract customers. One was called the Apron Strings and membership was only £5, with nice dinners after 7pm if you were gambling. So we'd split into two groups, one putting £5 on red and the other £5 on black, then break after half an hour for a meal or a drink. Everything would be fine until the '0' came up and we'd lose all our money.

Sometimes me and Firdaus Ruttenshaw would go to a club in Park Lane and bet on either black or red, doubling our stake until it came up. Then one time the croupier hit red nine times in a row! We lost all our money on that occasion.

People often compare the skills that an entrepreneur needs with professional gamblers and I'm sure there are similarities. If you're betting on horses or on the financial markets, you have to study form and have a well-developed understanding of probability. For me, though, gambling was just a bit of entertainment with my friends, not something that I did to make money.

As for the serious business of studying, I spent a year on the Oriental Studies tripos, then decided to switch to law. I took an exam on the English legal system over the summer vacation, then joined the law faculty and studied for another two years. For me, the point of studying law was training the mind to think logically and succinctly, plus it was my father's subject. I wasn't planning to become a lawyer, just aiming to get an honours degree and play tennis and golf for the university.

What interested me was international law, especially when it was taught by Professor Elihu Lauterpacht. He was a very impressive lecturer and eventually founded the Lauterpacht Centre for International Law in Cambridge. My tutor, David Pearl, was an expert on Muslim law, which was an interesting choice for the son of a rabbi. He later became a high court judge and wrote about the legal systems of India, Pakistan and Bangladesh – a subject that I've spent a lot of time considering over the years.

I think a law degree prepares you for business and for life in various ways. English law is based on common law, and the great thing about it is that it's fair. People understand it and it's based on case law, so you can always connect it with real life. The disadvantage is that since there is a constant stream of cases, the law changes a great deal over time. You can't expect to come back to the law after any long gap and know everything. In fact it proves the expression 'a little knowledge is a dangerous thing' because in time, as more cases are decided, your knowledge goes out of date, and you can get into trouble.

The fairness of English law means that London is one of the most popular places in the world for arbitration. You're much less likely in London to have a case decided on the basis of political influence, as happens in other European countries. This also means that England is a very good place to base your business. The legal system is one of the greatest strengths of the UK, no matter what the *Daily Mail* might say about our judges. They're very fair.

From my point of view, since I wasn't an upper-class white man, I had disadvantages relative to some of my peer group. I think studying law helps to fortify you: when you're from a BAME background, you're working against the odds, so having a knowledge of the law is some protection. And studying at Cambridge gave me confidence because it's one of the two premier universities in the country: if you go through that system of tutoring and gaining knowledge, people are more likely to listen to you, because you might be talking sense. This gives you even more confidence and means that society appreciates you even more. In the years since Cambridge, this legal training has helped me out many times. When I left university, it gave me the confidence to face the world. When you start a business, you have to be outward looking. Employees need you to represent the company and speak for them.

During my time running Flightbookers, I had to fight one major court case, when the Nepalese government cancelled our contract with a couple of years still to go, without compensation. I sued them in the International Court of Arbitration, paying £1 million in fees to my lawyers Herbert Smith, who threatened to have Royal Nepal Airline's jets impounded at Heathrow unless they settled with me. They branded me as a thief, we felt threatened by them, and it took months to sort out because the documentation was hard to find, but we won the case.

In politics, I had another court case, this time suing my own party for discrimination in its selection procedures. This time I lost, but in the end it didn't matter because I was selected and won the election to become a Member of the European Parliament.

The more I travel, the more I realise how lucky Britain is to have its legal system. I've lived in 13 countries, and spent time in some of the redneck states in the US, in Japan, in Asian and European countries. The UK is one of the best-educated countries in the world, people are less discriminatory, more welcoming and more understanding. I've not seen any other country that would allow someone from any religion to come in and set up their own temple, mosque, gurdwara or whatever, with so much tolerance as there is in Britain.

Karan Bilimoria, King Cobra

When I first met Karan Bilimoria we discovered we had plenty of things in common: besides Indian heritage, we'd both studied at Cambridge and had relatives in the Indian armed forces – he came from a line of brigadiers and generals who had trained at Sandhurst. Since he'd played polo for the university, I proposed him for the Hawks Club; then to help his business career, I introduced him to the Young Presidents Club.

I love the adventurous, imaginative story of Cobra Beer, emerging from this one man's frustration that neither gassy lagers nor heavy ales suited Indian food. It takes a lot of guts to try to resolve that problem by yourself!

Like me, he dabbled in an import business, selling Indian-made polo sticks, fabrics and fashion goods to the upmarket Harrods department store in Knightsbridge in London. Then, from a small flat in Fulham, just around the corner from my early base in Earls Court, Karan borrowed money to start Cobra Beer, importing it from a brewer in Bangalore and touting it around English curry houses in an old Citroen 2CV. He struck commercial gold thanks to hard work, energy and the early 1990s rise of curry houses as the location of choice for large groups of young men, particularly late at night after drinking in pubs. They needed exactly Cobra's combination of refreshment and drinkability. The packaging, design and name –a snake with a deadly venom –all helped, as did an understanding of supermarket shelves. When the product is placed at eye-level, you're in business. Too far down, nobody sees it.

I invested in Karan's company and even though it collapsed in 2009, he rescued it by selling half of the shares to Molson Coors and I didn't lose any money. Doing a 'pre-pack' insolvency deal isn't my favourite way to resolve these problems, because quite a few creditors did lose out. But you can tell that he's still well-respected in Britain since he's just been voted chair of the Confederation of British Industry (CBI). And of course I share his passionately pro-European political views.

Chapter 3
Making a Living

My first venture into the travel business was, let's say, unconventional.

Just after leaving Cambridge my friend Ashok (with whom I'd already shared various hare-brained enterprises) managed to get an order for 50 saddles from a horse farm in East Anglia. He hired a Bedford van to transport them and I came along for the ride.

Once we'd dropped off the saddles and were on our way back to London, we discovered that there was a rail strike. So I persuaded Ashok to drive through Cambridge and see if we could pick up any stranded passengers at the rail station. We put 10 people into the back of the van, and they paid £1 each. It was like a 1970s version of people smugglers. When we got back to London with the profits, we went straight to Pizza Express for our favourite American Hot for £1.25 each.

In 1974, it was the era of peace and love, hippies and beatniks wearing kaftan coats, flared trousers and flowery print shirts. With another friend, Haran, I decided to import Pichwai paintings from India – typically traditional scenes of Lord Krishna's life, made by artists in northern India. The Beatles had visited Rishikesh in Uttarakhand in 1968 (virtually next door to the ashram where my parents' guru Shree Anandamayee Ma's ashes were laid), which set a trend for Indian culture and fashion.

We made a bit of money and the enterprise was taking off. But then one day we delivered some of these paintings to Selfridges in Oxford Street and the glass covering a picture smashed all over the floor. We were turfed out of the store and told that our goods were a safety hazard. That was the end of that business venture.

I briefly thought about joining the military, or going to look for work in India, but whenever I went back, the corruption appalled me. The whole economy seemed to run as a black market. Whenever you needed any kind of service, you'd have to pay a 'baksheesh', which in the West would be called a bribe and would get you into legal trouble if it was found out. In India it was considered acceptable and normal. The currency market ran on a dual system:

one official rate, say 10 rupees to the pound, and a black-market rate of 15 rupees to the pound for unofficial exchanges, because sterling 'hard currency' kept its value better than the depreciating rupee.

Later, once I'd married, my father-in-law was second in command of the Indian Army. When people knew this, the only jobs I was offered were from arms dealers, wanting to use my connections to the military to sell guns.

In London, there was a lot less corruption, but even so things were tough. The 1973 oil crisis had put the world into recession, particularly the US and Great Britain, whose economies depended upon cheap oil. There was political as well as economic chaos, with a miners' strike, power cuts, a three-day working week and Ted Heath's Conservative government declaring a state of emergency. He lost the February 1973 election to Harold Wilson's Labour Party and the country staggered on in a pretty dismal way all year.

With social collapse and falling incomes all round, what job did I fall into? Selling insurance from door to door in a rundown part of West London – an area known as the World's End, on the borders of Chelsea and Fulham. Actually I was selling a kind of 'assurance' savings plan rather than straight insurance, so my customers could feel they would get something in return.

These were council estates, with white working-class communities who weren't naturally friendly to immigrants. In 1974 when an Indian knocked on their door, they would give them racial abuse. So you just accepted it. The only thing was that by this time I had an English accent, thanks to two years in a public school and three years at Cambridge. The moment I started talking, their attitude would change.

It was very character-forming. If I could sell three policies during my shift, from 6pm to 10pm, the group leader would give me a free meal. But the structure of the work was self-employment: they gave me an advance, and I believed that I had the ability to sell. I had to prove to myself, even in the depths of a recession, in a tough neighbourhood.

While I managed to sell quite a lot of policies and made a bit of money, I only did it for six weeks. It proved to me that I could pay for myself and didn't have to depend on anyone else. At the end of the six weeks, I developed shingles on my shins, which is a measure of how nerve-wracking the work was. I was only getting a third of one per cent commission on the policies, whereas other insurance companies paid two per cent.

When you're short of money, whether you go to the high or low end of the social or commercial spectrum, it doesn't really matter. The important thing for me was that if it didn't work out, I would have had to go back to India. That was the last thing I wanted, even to join the Civil Service.

My next job was at a trading house called Associated Services. It owned wholesale warehouses in Nigeria and this company was set up in London, so that they could get banking services including letters of credit to buy goods overseas. It was owned by an Indian and the top management was all Indian. Whereas I'm Punjabi, they were Sindhis – people who lived in the Sindh area of what is now Pakistan until partition, then migrated to India and around the world. They're very good traders, you learn from the Sindhis the value of a penny, how to save a penny. We wouldn't use letter-headed paper to make notes, because it cost more than plain paper. In every single thing, it's keeping costs down to the bone. I learnt a lot from them.

My job was to confirm goods had been sent to Nigeria, with letters of credit. I was negotiating with 13 or 14 banks, using credit from China and trading in wholesale goods, sent by boat to Nigeria. Once the goods arrived in Nigeria, they could get £50-£100,000 in credit. So for two years I was dealing with banks, traders, boat owners and wholesalers in Nigeria, at a time when there were deep political problems in the country. In July 1975 there was a military coup against the ruling government: General Yakubu Gowon was overthrown by Brigadier Murtala Muhammed.

The awful Biafran War, based around Port Harcourt, had ended five years earlier, but it was still a tough place to do business. The ships we were dispatching over there would be blockaded and have to hire smaller vessels to offload their cargo on to the food wharves. Sometimes they'd put a layer of sardines over the real goods, like timber, as a disguise.

It was all about human ingenuity and doing deals with people. We had to keep a sharp eye out for where the company's bread was buttered, where the money was. For example, in Nigeria, women kept all the money because the men were always going out and getting drunk. They would pad their bras with cash.

In my spare time, I'd go to nightclubs and casinos in London with my friends, particularly the ones which offered free drinks and food if you were gambling. We'd put money on red or black and manage to survive without losing anything until the number 0 came up and we'd lose it all. The chips only cost 25p so we weren't playing for high stakes. If we were lucky we'd make enough for an American Hot pizza. The Playboy Club in Park Lane had a deal where you'd get a sirloin steak and fries for 10 shillings (50p in today's money) as an inducement to get you on to the casino tables. It was a fun place to spend an evening, in the days before I was married.

While I was working for this Nigerian trading company, my diplomatic passport (thanks to my ambassador father) lapsed, so I was left with a normal Indian passport. This caused a minor problem, because it meant I needed a visa to visit mainland Europe. But in 1976 the Home Office asked: "Would you like a British passport?" and I said: "Yes, please." I was naturalised, it was very easy. I filled out a form and they looked at my background...King's School, Cambridge...I've now lived in England for more than half a century and feel British in every way.

It's hard to know whether my education made any difference to my passport application. Indians in England had been arriving in numbers for a few decades already, before I arrived. The first wave in the late 1950s and 1960s came from villages in the Punjab and the majority of them worked in transport, driving buses or on the railways. People such as the parents of Sajid Javid, the former Chancellor of the Exchequer or Sadiq Khan, the Mayor of London. They weren't businesspeople; they took whatever manual jobs they could find.

Then in the 1970s there was a second wave of Indians into Britain who had migrated to East Africa, to Uganda and Kenya, but then had to leave when the political establishment of Idi Amin turned against them. They brought business talent and a lot more money. Many of these were Gujuratis (often called Patel) and they took over the nation's corner shops.

Meanwhile there were people like me, who came to educate ourselves and then stayed on. Many Indians of my generation came to train as chartered accountants, because you could be an articled clerk and earn money while taking the exams. Many of them remained in England and some have become tremendously successful. People such as Surinder Arora, who came to England when he was 13 from the Punjab and worked day and night in three jobs until he had built a hotel business, now with 6000 five-star bedrooms. He started with nothing and he's now a billionaire. Very driven, living near me in Wentworth, nice family. I respect him a lot.

In the late 1970s, I was living with some friends in Inverness Terrace in Bayswater, just between Notting Hill and Paddington. They had a contract to build a sugar factory in Iran, in the town of Shushtar on the Karun river. They'd hit a problem because the Iranians they'd hired to build the factory were refusing to work, knowing that if they finished the job, they'd be unemployed. So my friends hired 220 Indian workers and asked me to go out there and be their spokesman. The Nigerian trading business paid me £2,500 a year, or £50 a week, whereas this job offered £3,000 a year tax free, so it was a little better.

On top of the salary, I discovered that Iranians are very fond of snakeskin. So I borrowed some money from my father, bought 400 snakeskins in India and packed them into a bag. Once I arrived in Tehran, where I was staying with the Indian military attaché, I walked down the road and at the first leather shop I came to, I offered them to him and agreed a deal for three times the amount I'd paid. So that was one early enterprise that worked. Today you'd probably get into trouble with customs.

Just at this time, in 1976, my parents wanted to introduce me to a potential wife. They picked half a dozen that had been to the debutante balls – similar to the ones that you find in London. In Delhi I met three or four girls, but they were very protected, not at all mature. So I thought I'd better go to Bombay and see the couple they'd selected there. One had already got engaged and the other was Tani. I met her in December 1976, we married in October 1977 and have been together ever since.

Tani was an air hostess for Air India, which at the time was a very high-status job. Thousands of girls would apply for the positions and Tani had to represent the company – and by extension, India – in public. She did a lot of promotional work. For most Indians, travelling the world was a distant dream – it was far too expensive. As soon as we met, we recognised a fearless, adventurous spirit in each other: she had flown to Africa, to the United States! Completely different to the sheltered girls I'd met in Delhi.

The Indian government had just bought Air India from the Tata family and taken it into public ownership, so they would recruit the daughters of Indian VIPs. Even so, the law said that she had to leave the company when she married. She was 25.

Back in London after I'd finished the Iranian job, times were still tough. It was really hard to find work of any kind. Both Tani and I were used to pretty good standards of living – my father was an ambassador and her father the chief of the Indian Army. We had grown up in great houses, with lots of servants, cars and drivers, platoons marching up and down morning and evening. Guests were invited to lavish dinners. A few years before, in the early 1970s, my father was living in Wassanaar near The Hague in the Netherlands. There were 4,500 residents in this village and 4,000 of them were millionaires, including the Dutch Queen Juliana and Prince Bernhard.

I thought about joining the diplomatic service myself, and had a look at it, but then I thought back to my parents' life. Even though they lived in grand homes, a civil servant's salary didn't stretch very far. I thought of my mother asking: "How can I put food on the table?"

Things were so tight that, at first, we left our oldest son in India when he was very young, being looked after by Tani's mother. Britain was a difficult place to live: James Callaghan was the Prime Minister of a Labour government which didn't seem capable of governing: the 'winter of discontent' in late 1978 and early 1979 was a low point for the whole country: the unions weren't happy with the government and neither were the rest of us. Inflation was too high and there were problems in Ireland, Rhodesia, with Welsh and Scottish nationalists and disagreements over the Common Market.

By the time Callaghan was forced to hold a general election, after losing a vote of no confidence from Conservative leader Margaret Thatcher, his chances of winning were slim. Sure enough, Margaret Thatcher secured a 43-seat victory on 3 May 1979 and set about dismantling as much of the state-controlled apparatus of Britain as she could. Despite her victory and dramatic new direction for the country, Thatcher couldn't stem the tide of economic and social bad news. Inflation reached 20 per cent in 1980 and unemployment carried on rising for years, hitting 3.3 million in 1984, even though the economy was growing.

I started working at IBM as an assistant in the sales department. The old saying "Nobody ever got fired for buying IBM" also made it feel like a dependable, solid company to work for during a recession. They paid me £7,250 a year, which was more than I'd earned before, but I had to pay 50 per cent in tax – 40 per cent in income tax and 10 per cent in National Insurance – so there wasn't much left over to pay the mortgage on our £20,000, two-room flat in Shepherd's Bush, West London. It was hard to make ends meet.

Our office was in Leadenhall Street, in the City, and I would go to meetings with companies to try and sell them computers like the IBM System/32, which had come out in 1975 and became its best-selling model. It was popular with accounting companies and larger firms, with its 32 kilobytes of main memory. To put this in perspective, today people are walking around with smartphones which have eight million times more memory than this. At the time, the System/32 was a miracle of miniaturisation, compared with the giant IBM machines that preceded it, taking up a whole room and needing an air conditioning unit to function.

Getting through IBM's interview process was an achievement in itself, so I was at least pleased about that. I felt I needed a full-time, respectable job to support my wife and pay the bills. Although I got on with everyone at IBM, I didn't do really well. If I had flourished, and they'd patted me on the back, I would have stayed. In a way though, seeing the difference that a computer could make to a business, doing mundane tasks more quickly, accurately, more easily and at lower cost, gave me a taste of the transformation I'd later experience in ebookers.

Tani could see that I wasn't really content at IBM. Her view is that I'm congenitally incapable of taking orders: I have to lead in my own fashion. A highly-structured company like IBM robbed me of freedom and creativity. I became frustrated and lost interest in the work. "There's no point in having a frustrated husband," she would say. "If you don't like the work, there's no point." What she also spotted was my flair for selling and marketing. Even though her family wondered how we would manage if I didn't have a regular income, she was convinced by my persistence, energy and drive. "He doesn't even have a job!" her parents complained. But she much preferred the thrill of adventure and risk to the prospect of an unfulfilled, irritable husband. "We had no fear of failure," Tani remembers. "When Dinesh wants something he doesn't stop until he gets it. That's what I remember about him from the first time we met. Because he wanted me!"

Equally, I've always been able to rely on Tani's business instincts. She has a great feel for what will fit in with our business plans, whether in hiring people, taking new office space or outsourcing work to India.

Without any sort of formal business plan – because we didn't know how to make one – I convinced myself that if I could make at least £7,250 a year from my own business, and write off 50 per cent of it as allowable expenses, then I'd have doubled our standard of living.

So that's how and why we went into business. How hard could it be?

Chapter 4
From a Kiosk to a Continent

In 1979 I was working for IBM, reluctantly paying half my salary to the government, when Thatcherism suddenly appeared.

At her first speech to the Conservative Annual Conference as Prime Minister in October of that year, Margaret Thatcher laid out her vision for the country. Militant unions had been holding the country to ransom over wages and conditions, and she identified the problem: "The key to prosperity lies not in higher pay but in higher output," she said. "The future of this country depends largely on the success of small businesses." Thatcher's mission was to create wealth and employment through productivity and enterprise.

Like thousands of others, I took this speech as a rousing call to action. It told me that the Conservative government would support entrepreneurs who had the balls to start new businesses. By implication, regulations and taxes would favour us. And perhaps just as importantly, there was a sense that the country wanted this. Enough moaning about wages and working hours, it was time to do something for ourselves.

My entrepreneurial instincts came to life. Over the years, I'd sold paintings, snakeskins and burgers, but these were small-time efforts, rather than anything sustainable. What kind of real business could I start?

As a Punjabi, I didn't like the idea of being a shopkeeper, which was more associated with Gujuratis. On the way to work, I used to walk past a newspaper kiosk and chat to Jim, who told me he had five kiosks in different rail stations. His daughter had a small kiosk in Earl's Court but he said she wasn't enjoying it so how would I like to take it over? I had to overcome my initial reluctance – and the disapproval of my father, who said "I didn't send you to Cambridge to become a shopkeeper!"

Jim wanted £3,000 for the 'key' money, and my friend Freddie, who had made some money from investing in the stock market, offered to lend it to me in two instalments – an initial £1,500 and another four months later. Freddie said: "You're sitting at IBM doing nothing, why not have a go?"

I didn't know anything much about travel, but in early 1980 I made a sandwich board to put outside the kiosk and started selling theatre tickets from this little shop, which was no bigger than a box room, maybe 80 square feet altogether. There was a good deal of pedestrian traffic along Warwick Road in Earl's Court as people came to and from the station. We earned the £1,500 fairly quickly and paid Freddie back. But we weren't making much, we had to scrimp and save for months. We called the company Dabin, an amalgam of Darun and Biren, our two sons.

The site of my first travel office, 1980

My first shop, 80 square feet, 1980

Looking back, there was no strong reason for picking travel, except that Earl's Court was full of Australians who were looking for air tickets. It could have been anything really – shoes or computers or even cars. If I could sell it and make a profit, then I would have done it.

Things were going well and we had a couple of people working for us in the kiosk, but we noticed that the toilets we shared with the neighbouring kiosk were always filthy. It became a real nuisance, so we bought up the lease to this kiosk and started a sandwich shop! I took a real interest in creating top-of-the-range sandwiches; I'd go to the City and inspect what Birley's were selling, then come back and make them for half the price. Our travel agency staff liked them, some of our customers bought them, and it meant we could keep the toilets clean.

However, it almost landed me in jail. We hired someone to run the sandwich shop from 7pm to 2am, catering for late night shoppers and revellers. One day, the police summoned me to the station and said our employee had been caught dealing drugs from the shop. Special sandwiches indeed. Luckily, they didn't accuse me of any wrongdoing, but we lost our late licence.

Within a few months, our landlord Jim proposed taking us to London Transport where we could sign a year's lease for £4,000. By this time, I was becoming a little more confident and thought I could sell tickets to my friends, so I signed the lease. We began to find ways to get discounted tickets: Keith Prowse would sell us theatre tickets and pay us a 10 per cent commission, offering us a month's credit. This was very helpful, because it meant that we had cash in our bank account to use during the month.

We also agreed a deal with Mayflower Travel. This was an International Air Transport Association (IATA) registered agency based in Mayfair, central London, which could call on a month's credit and in turn offer me the same terms. They agreed to split the IATA commission with us on air fares that we sold. Between Keith Prowse and Mayflower, it meant we had enough money in our cash float to pay our electricity bills and our staff salaries. It was a delicate balancing act: we had hardly any money of our own, but if you can find out who has credit, there's always scope for negotiation. Once you get to know a business, you'll find that there are many places where credit is available.

I remember feeling grateful for the support of our friends and families at the time. This wasn't in the form of financial support, but just the way that they would come and visit us, maybe bring us some stationery supplies, or tell us what they'd seen going on in the travel business. They were our ears and eyes in the marketplace.

One day in 1981 a man with a beard came in and offered us Bob Dylan tickets for £5 each. I said they wouldn't sell in Earl's Court and told him to buzz off. But he promised me that I'd make £500 a day if I took them, so I gave it a go. Soon we had queues around the block and were making £1,500 a day, thanks to the bearded Harvey Goldsmith. I was knocking on heaven's door.

To become a travel agent, I took a British Airways correspondence course, so then I too could become IATA registered. At the time, Earl's Court was full of Australians on working visas, who came to London for a couple of years, earned some good money because the pound was strong against the Australian dollar, travelled around Europe and went home. We would quote them an air fare and they'd tell us they'd seen something better elsewhere, so we'd offer them tea and coffee and find out what prices they were willing to pay. It was our first attempt at market research.

There were thousands of Australians wanting to get home every year. We managed to find some pretty big discounts: I had a friend called Varjee, who was the Air India manager in Denmark. He sold Air India tickets out of Frankfurt, Paris or Amsterdam £100 cheaper than you'd pay in London. People would buy tickets to Australia and go via India. So we would put them on a coach or rail service for £50 and keep the difference. This rapidly caught on among the Earl's Court Australians – they told each other how to pay less to get back to Perth or Sydney. We made £20,000 before Air India caught on to the trick and put a stop to it by offering a London-Bombay-Sydney route with a two-hour layover. They only discovered this situation because Varjee's sales were 300 per cent higher than usual, while everyone else had lost out, including Air India's General Sales Agent in London.

We made hay while the sun shone. And it was ironic, in a way, that I started out in business selling airline tickets back to where I was born in Australia, 10,000 miles away.

Making money as a travel agent means constantly seeking out these types of deals, where you can get a reasonable margin. It was no simple matter, however. As an Indian, I wanted to sell to the Indian community, but the Indian, Bangladeshi and Pakistani market was already catered for by greengrocers in places like Southall, where they were only concerned about cashflow – they would sell air tickets for as little as 50p profit, whereas I was looking for £5 minimum.

Then I thought: "Why am I going for Indian customers who are 2 per cent of the population, when I could be going for the other 98 per cent? Why not go for English people who want to travel the world?" Suddenly the margin was £20 and I was much happier.

There was a similar problem with European holidays, because of a price war between Thomson, Airtours and a few other operators. You could get a week's holiday with full board in Spain, including flights, for £25. Travel agents would take 10 per cent of this, meaning they'd get just £2.50 for selling a holiday. It was impossible for a small agency to survive on this. So I focused on the long and mid-haul business instead, which had higher margins and wealthier customers, mainly flying to Australia, the Far East and the United States.

The Association of British Travel Agents (ABTA) offered me membership for £1,200 a year and my initial reaction was to tell them to take a jump. Then two or three people came in and asked "Are you members of ABTA?" and when we said no, they left. So we looked at the terms they were offering and saw that we were paying 3 per cent interest on our credit card payments, whereas ABTA had a deal with a credit card company offering 1 per cent. We were such a small team in those days, Tani and I did almost everything, even the accounts. So we joined ABTA and within two months we'd earned back the membership fee, looking after the pennies.

We had some scary moments too. One day a guy asked me for 25 return tickets to Hong Kong, costing £15,000. He offered me half the money and promised the rest later. We gave him the tickets but never received the balance. This loss meant we were so close to bankruptcy that I chased him all the way to Miami, where he offered to let me stay on his boat, but still didn't pay us what he owed. It took me days of pursuing him, wearing just the clothes I'd flown in, before I managed to get the money from his bank.

Another time, a well-dressed Indian gentleman with a trimmed white beard came in and paid £900 for a ticket to the United States. When he came back the next week, I took him out for dinner. He asked for a ticket for his daughter and promised to give me £900. But he vanished and I discovered that he was a wanted man: Interpol were looking for him. After that I told our consultants that if they ever offered credit, I'd take it out of their salary.

Very early on, we invited a friend's wife to come and work with us. Things were going really well, we were making money and she became an important part of the team, but after 10 months she announced she was going to a larger firm in the West End. Our world fell through, we couldn't believe it. But as time went on, we built it into our psychology. We didn't like people leaving, but it didn't hit us as badly as that first time.

After we'd been trading for a while, I had a visit from our landlord's agent. He was very friendly and we chatted for a while. He asked how our business was doing and I was pleased to tell him that it was going well. "We're making quite a lot of money," I told him. Big mistake! A few days later I received a letter informing me that our rent was going up by 100 per cent. All I was doing was telling the truth. That was a lesson in being more cautious, when dealing with landlords.

One of the biggest prizes in travel in those days was to be appointed General Sales Agent for an airline. I was desperate to get the GSA job for Air India and when the 1984 Indian general election, caused by Indira Gandhi's assassination, brought her son Rajiv to power, I thought the new government could give me a chance. So I decided to sell Air India tickets at the same price as the GSA, but without the commission, which meant we made no money. Air India did indeed sack its GSA but didn't appoint me! That was another disaster.

Instead of Air India, I got a privileged contract for discounted fares with Malaysian Airlines in 1984 and then won the GSA position for Royal Nepal Airlines (RNA) in the same year. A few years later, in 1993, the Nepalese gave me responsibility for the whole of Europe. This was a big step up. It meant that I looked after all of the airline's flights out of London, Frankfurt and Paris; and I could appoint my own GSAs in each of 12 different European countries, to support RNA's sales and marketing efforts. This turned out to be a great asset in the future, when I wanted to acquire agencies around Europe.

On top of the Royal Nepal job, I was appointed GSA for Air Botswana, which could then treat my office as its London base, Zambia Airways and Air Tanzania. These came along mainly through personal contacts: I knew the lady in charge of Air Botswana, I played golf with the manager of Zambian Airlines and I'd travelled many times to Dar es Salaam in Tanzania, so I spoke to the airline bosses and persuaded them to fly into Gatwick.

GSA jobs were highly prized. You had a kind of monopoly on flights on the airline, because you could offer discounts that weren't available to anyone else. You would get the distressed inventory and could undercut rivals. The agent who had the Air India GSA job was making upwards of £1 million a year from it.

Some people would resort to incredible tactics to win GSA contracts. I heard of a case where the Philippine Airlines GSA was set up by a rival with a call girl in London. The rival secretly filmed the encounter, unsuccessfully tried to blackmail him and then sent the tape to the airline. The airline stood by the GSA and refused to sack him: in fact they praised him for refusing to be blackmailed.

When there was a change of government in Nepal, the new aviation minister cancelled my contract and announced a new GSA. This was devastating news to me, so I went to see the son of a former Indian Prime Minister and asked for help. He knew the Nepalese Prime Minister and said he'd try and sort it out for me. To secure the contract I needed to find £80,000, which was way outside my budget at the time. Then on the way out to Nepal I stopped in Dubai and bought a lottery ticket in the airport for $140 for the chance to win a new Mercedes SE 500 costing £52,000. I won the car and they offered me £47,000 in cash. Then I borrowed the rest of the £80,000 from my father and father-in-law and we kept the Royal Nepal contract for another couple of years, until the Communists took over Nepal and we were all kicked out.

We didn't leave without a fight, however. I had taken on an office to service the airline, so I sued the Nepalese authorities in Paris at the Court of Arbitration. I held back £2.8 million in payments and engaged the law firm Herbert Smith to represent us (which cost us £1 million). If we'd lost the case it could have bankrupted us.

Our relationships with the airlines changed over time. At first, when we were starting out, I felt that airline managers looked down on us: their attitude was that agencies needed them, not the other way around. But after a while, we grew to such a colossal size, we were more on their level: we could relate to them and agree deals with them.

The bigger you became, the better prices you would be offered. Trailfinders was much bigger than us at the time and the airlines would offer them special deals, say reducing a £1,000 fare to £400. Some agents would operate as 'consolidators', meaning that they could sell tickets to a large pool of other agents, getting themselves higher discounts, maybe 50 per cent off the standard fare. After a while, I knew all the consolidators.

Of all the other agents, Mike Gooley of Trailfinders was the one I looked up to most. He was way ahead of us during the first 18 years of my career as an agent, from 1980 to 1998. Up until the pandemic he was making £25 million a year and owns the whole company 100 per cent. He's now in his Eighties. Mike also started in Earl's Court, but 10 years earlier, after a career as an SAS captain trekking through the jungles of Borneo and the deserts of the Middle East. Like me, he went to a Jesuit boarding school which taught him that his word is his bond. In business, that has been a great asset to us both: Trailfinders has a tremendous reputation for treating its customers properly and standing by its promises. It puts your deposit in a trust account and doesn't touch it until you're back from your holiday, unlike many tour operators who use deposits to fund salaries. He has a very good sense of how to survive in the volatile and unpredictable travel business, based around customer service. In an interview published in May 2019 he warned that tour operators who buy airlines often put themselves in danger. Four months later, Thomas Cook – the world's oldest tour operator, with its own airline –

collapsed into bankruptcy, prompting the largest peacetime repatriation exercise in British history.

Apart from Mike Gooley, I always watched the progress of people such as Freddie Laker, whose Skytrain budget airline went bust in 1982, soon after I started Flightbookers, and Richard Branson, who continued where Laker left off. Branson was like a cat with nine lives: selling Virgin Records for billions, his debut flight having a bird strike which cost him £600,000, British Airways pulling out all the levers against him, getting a massive investment from the Middle East and Singapore Airlines.

Entrepreneurs like Branson will always try to push the envelope with employees, to make them better, rather than become like the Civil Service. If you're working for the government, there's no penalty for making mistakes, no learning, because an older person always makes the decisions. There's no financial incentive or promotion prospect for doing anything different. Having come from IBM with its 'you'll never get fired…' motto, that was the opposite of the attitude I wanted for my company. I think the United States is the best example of entrepreneurship: they don't mind if you go bankrupt, as long as you're honest. You're promoted to the top if you're good and killed if you're bad. It's the purest form of capitalism, but it's reached its limits now because Trump's given it a bad name. Capitalism has to grow old and die, like a person, I guess.

Receiving an award from Richard Branson, 1993

Some of the airline owners in the 1980s and 1990s were pretty thick. Some were intelligent. As an agent, we thought the Far East carriers like Singapore Airlines or Cathay Pacific were very good. Then later the Middle Eastern carriers like Emirates and Etihad became very good. None of us thought very highly of the UK, European or US airlines. Qantas was a good airline. One day my friend Firdaus Ruttonshaw flew first class from Sydney to London (with a stop in Bahrain). As he left the plane in London, he was given a voucher for £200. They said: "We upgraded two people from business to first class, so we deemed that everyone in first class should get £200." Similarly, on Singapore Airlines another friend asked for a newspaper and when they brought the *Daily Telegraph* he turned straight to the sports pages. A few minutes later, the hostess came along with three more papers, all ironed (so that the ink doesn't come off on your fingers) and turned to the sports pages.

Personal relationships were important all the way through this period, as we built up Flightbookers. In 1993 I joined a group called the Young Presidents Organisation, which introduced me to dozens of people running businesses all over the world. I'd go to academies and universities, picking up ideas and discussing problems and opportunities with people. To get to know my peers, I joined the Travel Industry Golf Society (TIGS), which was very difficult to get into – they had a 'one-in-one-out' policy, but because I was a bit above average as a player, they let me in. Golf is a very good way of getting to know someone. You get three or four hours with them, then a drink afterwards. You learn a lot from the way they do things.

Teeing off at a travel industry tournament, 1994

Tani and I would go on 'familiarisation' trips, basically holidays organised by the airlines or by national tourist offices. These were ostensibly for travel agents to find out about places, so they could sell more flights or holidays – that was the official purpose – but they were also a good chance to meet other agents and find out what they were up to. There would be 10 or 12 agents from the UK; this made it easier to communicate with them.

It was a nice way to combine business and pleasure. We went on trips to Tanzania, watching the animal migration in Arusha, then visiting the Ngorongoro crater – the ancient caldera of a massive volcano, 12 miles wide, with an ecosystem of lions and Masai tribespeople armed with sticks to protect themselves. In the Serengeti Game Park, on the border with Kenya, we saw lions walk up into a tree and go to sleep. And nearby in Lake Victoria there were thousands of pink flamingos.

To survive as a travel agency you need to build up privileged relationships with the airlines, hotel and car companies, so that they offer you 'merchant' fares which translates to discounts of up to 75 per cent off standard prices. Travel suppliers only grant these fares to people they can rely on, so I had to meet them all and gradually build their trust.

After 15 years of running Flightbookers, I was finally offered a merchant deal with British Airways in 1995. Tani and I were on a familiarisation trip to Queensland in Australia and got to know the BA person. We were staying in a floating pontoon over the Great Barrier Reef, which was a tremendous privilege. Getting that contract was quite good for our profits and our business.

Tani was 100 per cent employed in the business, looking after the administration while I had more of a helicopter view and was the public face of the company. She had a keen eye for anything that wasn't right. For example, one time she found that a cheque hadn't been banked, but had been filed away instead. So she decided to look through the last six months of documents and found cheques worth thousands of pounds. I think it's always good to have a woman's point of view in a company.

Everyone reported to Tani except for my PA and the Finance Director, who reported to me. It was a joint effort and the business definitely benefited from having both of us. She was much more down to earth than me and more risk averse, which saved us many times. The sales side was more down to me, and ticketing was her side. She would say: "Let me run this, because it gives us our profits. We don't know what's going to happen."

Early in our business career, I bought a 1962 Rolls Royce Silver Cloud II for £6,000, which wasn't a very down to earth decision, but I persuaded Tani it was a worthwhile deal. Nobody in the UK wanted such enormous gas guzzling cars at the time, after the 1970s oil crisis, so I decided to take it to

Hollywood in California and sell it for a profit. I shipped it across the Atlantic to my cousin in San Francisco and agreed to exchange it for a Los Angeles travel agency called Happy Bookers, owned by the 1966 Olympic pole vault champion Bob Seagren and his wife Kam Nelson. In the end she ran off with another man and the deal fell through, so I sold it to a budding actress. The lesson is, if you try something like this, you generally don't make any money.

Tani's parents were very helpful to us in those days, when we were madly busy with the business. Her father sent a Gurkha soldier to help us and her mother came to look after our baby sons. In 1983 we were stuck in Delhi airport, trying to fly back to London and Air India wouldn't let us on to the flight, saying it was fully booked. We were sitting there for three hours before the chap who was looking after us got up and said: "I'll come back". He disappeared into the Air India office and straight away the manager came running out with our boarding cards. I asked him how he did it and he said he told them: "Mrs Dhamija is the daughter of the governor of Punjab." I would never have done that, having been brought up in England.

We sent our boys to private schools in London from an early age, first to a Montessori school on Kensington Gore next to the Royal Albert Hall, then to St James School in Queensgate, then Wellesley House boarding school on the Kent coast in Broadstairs and finally to Harrow School, one of the top private schools in the country, where Winston Churchill and Jawaharlal Nehru studied. It meant that we could concentrate on building the business. It gave them a good English upbringing and helped make them both gentlemen, who would never try to jump the queue by dropping names in an airport.

So let me drop some names on their behalf. When they were at Harrow, they were friends with two Thai princes called Vacharaesorn and Juthavachara Mahidol. Their father was Crown Prince Vajiralongkorn of Thailand and their mother was an actress called Sujarinee Vivacharawongse, who was the king's consort for 18 years. Together, they had four sons and a daughter, despite Vajiralongkorn being married to Soamsawali Kitiyakara (his first cousin) at the time.

One day, the boys' housemaster at Harrow rang me and asked if the princes could come and stay at our house over the school holidays. This was fine with me, although I thought it was a bit funny, because normally royal children would stay with the Thai ambassador. Later we found out that Vajiralongkorn had disowned the boys' mother and her children, taken away their diplomatic passports and royal titles and accused her of having an affair with a 60-year-old Air Marshal. The family all had to go and live in the States, so that was a shame, but my sons stayed in touch with them. Vajiralongkorn was crowned King of Thailand in 2019, three days after marrying wife number four, having survived a scandal some years previously where he was pictured in a video cavorting with his topless third wife, celebrating the birthday of their pet poodle Fufu, which had been granted the title of Air Chief Marshal of the Thai Air Force.

*   *   *   *   *

I never read books about entrepreneurship or deal making. I just fell into running a business because I wanted to put food on the table and was pushed into a corner. But once you set up in business, you find out that the freedom is very rewarding and enjoyable. As Steve Jobs put it, it's more fun to be a pirate than to join the navy. Between us, Tani and I worked out our strategy for the future, with her doing the administration and me as the statesman.

Sometimes we'd stumble across new ideas, or inspiration to grow the company. In 1994 we were on a trip to Tokyo and on a bus, talking about our strategy for the next year, whether we should increase our profit target by 20 per cent or 40 per cent. An American stranger across the aisle from us said "Have you tried 100 per cent?" I didn't think that he knew my business – he made gears for planes – and I told him it wouldn't work. But when we got back to our hotel room, I thought: 'Why not go for 100 per cent? It's a stretch, but we can do it.'

So we reduced the desk size per person in our office by 60 per cent, so we could fit more people in, bought computers and put the screens inside the desks, under a glass cover, and the servers underneath, which gave us more room and our staff could see whoever came to meet them. Then we introduced a sliding scale of bonuses for sales commissions: 3 per cent for flights, 5 per cent for car hire, up to 9 per cent for hotels and insurance, because we made more on those than on the flights. We started automating our processes. And at the end of 1995, we'd made 40 per cent more sales and 60 per cent more profits. That was a good result for Flightbookers and something we'd never have achieved if it weren't for a stranger on a bus in Japan.

Although it might seem like a minor event in the whole story of Flightbookers and ebookers, Tani and I both look back at this event as a business epiphany. As Tani remembers it, the encounter meant that our thinking changed completely. "It got us out of prison, we began working towards this target of 100 per cent growth, we started growing much faster, our margins rose," she says, thinking back. "When our growth reached 60 per cent, airlines started coming to see us, because we were taking market share away from other agencies. It really expanded our thinking."

Despite this rapid growth, we always had to keep a careful eye out for fraud. At one time, we had customers who would ring our office in Tottenham Court Road and make a booking on their American Express card, usually for business or first class tickets. They'd promise to come in and pick up their tickets. Our staff hadn't asked these customers to sign a form and show the card they'd used for the booking, as they should have done. Altogether we lost £25,000 on cards that were unauthorised by Amex and they refused to refund us any more than £8,000. We had to fire the people who took these bookings, because we were worried they were part of a conspiracy (and in any case, they hadn't followed the right procedures).

It was just at this time that I started looking in earnest at various new business models. Automation was one possibility: computer systems were becoming more sophisticated and replacing or easing the arduous back office work of filing and storing documents, managing accounts and dealing with payroll. We invested in the latest software to reduce costs and improve efficiency, but there was a limit to what this could achieve.

Some large companies were establishing call centres in Eastern Europe and the Far East, including India, which appealed to me, but we weren't large enough to benefit from this, and initial feedback was poor: British people couldn't understand Indian accents and the technology was unreliable.

Then I started to hear about a new invention called the internet, which academics were using to transfer documents to one another. You had to plug your computer into a phone socket and wait until a little box stopped squeaking and then you might be able to see some green writing on a black background, with lots of symbols like >>>>> and ///// and words that meant nothing to you like DOS and HTML.

Most people that I spoke to thought it was rubbish. They decided it was a waste of time and would never catch on.

Chapter 5
Going Online

For more than a decade, we'd built up Flightbookers, signed deals with airlines and expanded into Europe. Yet I felt that we could do better. The 1990s was the decade of globalisation: the Berlin Wall fell in 1989 and Communism, with its limitations on travel and freedom, was in retreat; people were keen to explore the world for business and leisure, in far greater numbers than ever before.

Part of my own globalisation was to join the Young Presidents Organisation in 1993. It had quite selective membership criteria: you had to be under 45, turn over $50 million a year and have at least 50 employees. Once you were a member, you could go to events all over the world, meet the heads of big companies, or study at YPO university courses.

It was at a YPO event in San Francisco in 1997 that I was first struck by the huge potential of the internet. A guy who owned Sun Microsystems said to me: "When I'm sleeping I make money." I asked him how. He told me he'd paid £500,000 for his company's servers. I asked him how I could do it in the UK. I'm no software geek, never mind guru, but I could see the bigger picture. If I'm making money day and night, that has to be good. So I was determined to get this idea going back home.

The US was three years ahead of Britain in this technology, and in its development of internet businesses. But the technology was really still in its infancy: the World Wide Web and HTML had only appeared in 1990, along with the first internet service provider. The first web page was created in 1991 and then Marc Andreessen wrote the code for the Mosaic browser, followed by Netscape Navigator. Amazon launched in 1995 as another browser. There were clearly big things happening over there, everyone was excited by the possibilities.

In 1998 I went to another YPO meeting, where all the giants of the internet congregated, other than Bill Gates. Jeff Bezos of Amazon and Larry Ellison of Oracle were there – Ellison had his own private fighter jet. I was like a wide-eyed fan, seeing what was going on. The founders of Kleiner Perkins were there, guys who were earning $210 million a year, who had financed America Online (AOL) and Yahoo! It was quite amazing to see the valuations of the companies they'd invested in.

At another event around this time, William Sahlman – a professor at Harvard Business School – made a telling comparison. He said: "Ladies and gentlemen, the GDP of Zambia, Kuwait and New Zealand is equal to the market cap of Amazon, Yahoo and AOL." We all looked at each other. To have a market cap as big as that...with millions of people working in their companies. I had to see if this internet could help with our business.

I signed up for a six-day course at the Massachusetts Institute of Technology (MIT) run by Professor Jeff Sampler and others. Jeff was and is one of the top experts on how new technology will influence business. For years, he's been lecturing on e-commerce, digital transformation and new business models.

What excited me, besides the energy and potential of the Silicon Valley pioneers, was how little attention my peers in the British travel industry were paying to these developments. I don't think many of them were entrepreneurs in the way that I was. I'd lived in many different countries, I felt very European rather than British. My father was a diplomat, so I'd moved around. My background gave me an ability to think laterally, in a way that my peers couldn't. If I saw something good, I could bring it back home, rather than saying "not in England".

For example, British travel agencies at that time used to expand in Northern Europe, but not Southern Europe. They'd say: "We don't understand these Mediterranean types." It was like the difference between the Britain of the 18th century, when people went out and discovered the world, to the late 19th century, when all the wealth came to Britain and the country became more insular. Of the main travel agencies, all were run by British people, except me, from India.

First Online Steps

By 1996, Flightbookers had grown to a reasonable size: it was in the top 10 largest UK travel agencies and from an international perspective, it was larger than the top three Indian travel agencies put together. I'd become aware of the internet through the Young Presidents Organisation, but hadn't yet worked out how we could apply it to the business. Then a German friend called Rudi Weissmann came to visit me in London to tell me about his new interactive flight booking system. It was based on a computerised flight reservation system called Sabre (Semi-Automated Business Research Environment), developed in the US by my old employer IBM for American

Airlines in the late 1950s and early 1960s. Travel agents began using the system in the 1970s and then it migrated online in the 1990s.

Rudi's version of Sabre would provide us with seamless confirmation of online ticket bookings. He was a young guy, had a small team based in Stuttgart and had set up a European travel agency group, hosting industry conferences in exotic locations, where we'd discuss the future of the business. I went to a couple of these, in Saipan (a US-owned island near the Philippines) and in Costa Rica. He was a forward-looking guy, and his software system was the first of its kind in Europe, possibly the world.

The thing Rudi did differently was to put consolidated fares on to the Sabre system – normally you'd only get the regular published fares from the airlines. They never wanted to advertise their consolidated fares because their corporate customers would query why they had to pay full price.

Historically, consolidated fares were more of a European than an American phenomenon. In the States, it was more first-come, first-served, whereas here, you had ethnic communities such as the Indians, Pakistanis, Bangladeshis and Sri Lankans. Each airline wanted to access these markets, so they would reduce their prices so that – for example – they'd sell 50 seats out of 300 on a plane. It was about slicing and dicing the fares based on supply and demand.

Rudi Weissmann tried to sell his version of Sabre to travel agents all over Europe, including many in the UK, but they weren't interested: they dismissed the internet as a fad and said that Americans didn't know what they were talking about. The staff at Flightbookers were really not keen at first. They saw the internet as an alien technology which was threatening to automate the office and take their jobs. Even from my point of view, I trod carefully. Rudi wanted me to pay him DM100,000 (equivalent to £30,000) to use his version of Sabre. So we negotiated for a couple of weeks and I offered him DM8 (about £2.50) per booking instead. I wasn't optimistic that he could achieve any kind of scale very quickly, but he was happy with this offer. He said he would cover everything at this price: we would get a computer-generated message every morning at 8am to say how many bookings had come through, then again at 12pm.

Every day, I'd check the messages and there were zero bookings. I started to think this had been a waste of time. For two or three weeks, just zero, zero, twice a day. Then one day we got two bookings. I was so sceptical of the system and I thought Rudi was doing his own bookings to make it look good. The office checked them out and told me they were real. The next day there were three bookings, then zero. Then four bookings. By September 1997 we were getting 1,000 bookings per month.

I wanted to create a new team to handle the internet bookings, so I asked each of my eight sales team leaders to give me one of their people. Because they were so scared of machines taking over their jobs, six of them gave me their worst salesperson. But what happened was that, since the internet had sorted all the flight booking details, these people had spare time to ring up customers and sell them hotels, hire cars and insurance. All the good stuff that makes us money. So they became the biggest-earning salespeople in the company.

When any new technology comes along, adoption takes the form of a bell curve. The edges of the bell are the 5 per cent at each end, with a parabola that moves up and down. You can divide the whole bell in half, with the first 50 per cent being more in favour of new technology and the second half against it. The first 5 per cent will always be willing to try new things. They're the geeks. The next 45 per cent, once they see the benefits, will go for it. Then it will take the next 45 per cent a long time to adopt the new technology. And the final 5 per cent will never do anything new. That's how it works for all new tech innovations.

In the travel industry, our main competitors owned businesses where they sold long haul flights which they could combine with hotel bookings. They weren't selling package holidays. When the internet came along, these people could see the same bell curve as me, but because they were quite successful, they weren't in the top 5 per cent for new tech adoption, they were in the 45 per cent who waited to see how it worked. They were making money, so why try something new? To expand, they acquired other companies, rather than investing in new technology. Some of them were pretty aggressive. They'd say to me: "You're really stupid. How is the internet going to make any money? Just because Americans do it, doesn't mean it's right."

In those days, around 1997, there were more and more internet-related conferences in London. I used to go and speak at them. At first I found that almost all the delegates were American. Then some British people began turning up. But hardly any Europeans. Soon, there was more acceptance of what I was doing. I became an evangelist for the internet. The more people came up to me and said: "Bugger off", the more convinced I became. What was especially gratifying was when a group of travel industry CEOs approached me and said: "We're really sorry, we missed the boat." This was a couple of years after we had gone online, and they were finally looking around for software.

After agreeing the DM8 per booking fee with Rudi in Stuttgart, I then proposed buying his company outright and bringing the whole operation to London. Rudi and I agreed a price and I gave him 25 per cent of the fee as a down-payment. So he sent me a couple of people from his team – a marketing guy called Mirko and a developer called Tosti (short for Dirk Tostmann) who had been president of the computer club at Dresden University. I said I'd pay Rudi the remaining 75 per cent when he brought the rest of the team to London. This proved a step too far for Rudi: he wasn't persuaded that my company could really make it work, so I fell out with him. But we had the software, which was what we wanted. And I saved myself from having to pay the other 75 per cent.

As our business expanded, we had to re-engineer the software in any case. Every few months we would hit another point where the traffic was too high for our capacity.

The 24-hour nature of the internet really sparked my imagination. It set all sorts of thoughts racing in my head. Millions of people work hard in their offices during the day. It takes a lot of time and effort for them to drive into a shopping district, park their cars, find a travel agency and queue to speak to a consultant. Or what about night workers, who want to make bookings in the evenings, when travel agencies are closed?

For us, the time when people wanted to book their flights didn't make any difference. We could punch their tickets in Japan or the United States, any time of day. Now that we were the only UK company with a global distribution and booking system, with instant confirmation from our online system, ebookers went viral. Before, a travel agent would have to make a call or send a letter to confirm. For us, this happened automatically. All we were interested in was the 5 per cent at the front edge of the bell curve, who were embracing this new internet technology. The UK had a working population of around 30 million people, so 5 per cent meant 1.5 million people, and all of them would take holidays in some form or another, spending £600 or £700 per person on average. You can see how it added up, even though only a relatively small number of people were using the internet at the time, and even fewer were using it to shop.

In a nutshell, our target market was the 'cash rich, time poor' client who wanted to travel to a medium or long-haul destination. You're selling something to people that lets them go across the world – they book it so far in advance, they read up about their destination, it's something they look forward to and dream about.

Although I worked for IBM in the late 1970s, I wasn't a technology buff. I understood the basics – how faxes had replaced telex in the 1980s, how the internet was about to change commerce – but my expertise was in getting people together, leading from the front, not just sitting back and asking people to do things. In the travel industry, that meant organising our marketing and sales departments, making sure the back-office functions of accounts, human relations, administration, etc were running smoothly, and winning new business. The internet took care of the marketing and new business side of things in an absolutely transformative way. Suddenly we were marketing to the world, 24 hours a day.

The internet also promised to reduce prices and costs for the whole industry. Phone bills would be a fraction of their old level. No more postage costs to send out tickets. Staffing costs were far lower, because so much of the fulfilment process was automated. We still had to staff the back end, but that's cheaper and it's easier to recruit people. Winning new customers was always a combination of convenience and price. If you had both of these criteria, you were well ahead of the competition.

The rise of the internet was a perfect example of how entrepreneurship works. You had to be alert to new developments outside your own commercial ecosystem – in this case the United States, where widespread adoption happened much more quickly and aggressively. You had to balance the risks of investment in an untried business model, against the rewards of first mover advantage and semi-monopolistic conditions. You had to understand your target market and how demographic, social and economic change would impact those consumers.

Purely from an operations point of view, our office went through three phases: telephone, computer, internet. The transition was so fast that changes took place almost every day. Fortunately, between us, Tani and I were happy to embrace these changes: we weren't particularly attached to anything and we didn't fear new things. I think this is an important psychological factor in entrepreneurship, especially at times of rapid change. If you're scared of losing something, you'll miss out on opportunities in front of your nose.

The speed of change was both exhausting and exhilarating: our marketing plans would change from day to day. If we saw a good idea, we'd implement it immediately. If the competition did something smart, we'd do it too. There was no time to be tired or bored. Our job was to get the phones ringing, to raise the conversion rate, to keep people buying, work out whether our employees were good, average or poor and incentivise them on that basis. They also had to get used to constant change, so it became normal for them.

Flightbookers had already won a good slice of the market, through hard work and spotting the opportunities to reduce prices. Fearlessness and the internet helped us to capitalise on these existing advantages.

Budget Airlines Shift the Business Model

In November 1995, the first easyJet service took off from London Luton for Glasgow. In the same year, Ryanair celebrated its 10th anniversary by flying 2.25 million passengers around Europe: a no-frills, low cost, rapid turnaround service, based on the lessons of Southwest Airlines in the United States – the first true budget airline, launched in Texas in 1966. Between them, easyJet and Ryanair massacred the incumbent European carriers like Air France, Swissair, KLM, Lufthansa and SAS. Several went bust, like the Belgian carrier Sabina, and the others were forced to adapt, launching their own budget subsidiaries or slashing their fares. KLM and Air France merged, as did British Airways and the Spanish airline Iberia.

For the wider travel industry, the budget airline model also represented a big challenge. Ryanair and easyJet wanted their customers to book with them direct, by phone or, as soon as they could master the technology, online. This cut out the middle man (the travel agent) and put a lot of pressure on margins across the sector.

For Flightbookers, it was a less challenging development, because we concentrated on long haul bookings. But even so, it was a sign of the way the industry was going. Would there soon be long haul budget airlines, where you booked directly online? The writing was on the wall. We would have to sell more hire car, hotel and insurance bookings if we wanted to make any money. We also had to survive on lower profit margins for each booking: Ryanair and easyJet were threatening to eat our lunch.

Joining Clubs

Joining the Young Presidents Organisation was extremely positive for me: it gave me access to people and ideas that were just not available in the UK; it spurred me to take my business online, provided models for me to follow, fellow spirits to turn to for advice and countless events where I learned from others' mistakes and triumphs.

By the time that some ideas in business, like certain online innovations, have made it into the national press and on to television, it's already too late. And most of the financial press is about very large companies, not about smaller ones like ours. So by spending time with other entrepreneurs, you stand a better chance of discovering market-changing ideas and technologies ahead of the crowd. When your company is at an early stage, clubs like YPO are a fountain of knowledge, especially from your own peers. You can read real life case studies of other people's experiences.

YPO gave me a window into the world of American business. At one of the university courses in New York in 1995, I met Barbara Corcoran, a New York real estate broker who told me she'd just won a court case against a fellow property businessman called Donald Trump. She showed him a business plan that she wrote on a paper napkin and he took it away, saying "Thank you very much, I'm going to use it," without any compensation. By getting the paper tablecloth below it and shading the impression of her writing, she proved her case and a judge decided in her favour. That tells you about the culture of the guy. (Barbara later wrote a motivational book called 'If you don't have big breasts, put ribbons on your pigtails'.)

In 1996 I went to a YPO event at Washington University. It was election year and both Democrats and Republicans wanted to get businesspeople on side, so they all turned up and made speeches. Bill Clinton had already been president for four years, but 90 per cent of YPOers are Republican. When he came to speak, it was an extraordinary thing to experience. Clinton was head and shoulders above everyone. He could talk on anything. He could start a speech in such a way that it sounded good to Republicans. And of course he was re-elected in a landslide.

YPO was just one club among very many that I've joined over the years, which contributed to ebookers' success. After leaving university I joined the Oxford and Cambridge Club, which was a very good place to meet people, especially for a meal. Its wines are much cheaper than elsewhere. The RAC Club nearby had squash courts (and even better food). Elsewhere in central London I'm a member of the Conduit Club in Mayfair, which brings business and creative people together to promote ethical sustainability; for its food, I like the Arts Club – also in Mayfair – which has an arty membership as the name suggests – and Mossimans Private Dining Club; 10 Trinity Square in the City has a high-powered financial sector membership and is hidden away in the Four Seasons Hotel at the Tower of London; and I'm a member of the Ritz and the Claremont casino clubs (the latter, based in Berkeley Square was where Lord Lucan would often gamble before he mysteriously disappeared in 1974). These days, I barely ever go to these, unless I have friends over from India who are desperate to go, since India has banned casinos.

Since joining the Liberal Democrat Party a few years ago, I've been a member of the National Liberal Club, though I rarely go these days, so it's a bit of an extravagance. And for golf, I play at Wentworth, where I live, and Queenwood, a few miles down the road.

I suppose that the combined effect of all these clubs is that you do meet a lot of interesting and active people who are innovators in their field. Many of the places are good for hosting individuals or groups, giving them a treat. People love to go to the Arts Club for example.

When I was building Flightbookers and ebookers, I'd invite people to these clubs when I was trying to get an airline or online deal. It was a way of getting to know people.

How The Airlines went from Subsidies to Profit Machines

Together with a few other agencies, I'd pressurised the airlines over the years to introduce discounted fares. Since many of them were publicly-owned 'flag carriers', they had little incentive to maximise their profits: if they flew half empty, it didn't matter, because their governments would subsidise their losses. Slowly, though, we kept chipping away at this attitude until one by one, they began offering us negotiated rates on a certain route. For a while, they tried to protect their full market fares, calling these new offers 'ethnic fares', but that didn't last for very long.

Once the technology was available, the airlines began ever more sophisticated fare segmentation. An economy cabin would be divided into eight fare classes, Club and First Class into three. As a flight filled up, each class would be ticked off: first the 'air miles' customers, then seats at increasingly high cost, depending on how full it became.

Each of the airlines set up a 'yield management' team, to maximise profits from each flight. We worked with these teams, which became an important part of the airlines' business model. Eventually, low cost carriers like Ryanair and easyJet came in and cut out the agents completely by selling straight to the public (using the yield management tools that the flag carriers had developed). This forced agents like us further into the mid and long-haul sector, along with short haul package holidays. The travel industry changed an awful lot during the 25 years I was in the thick of it, sometimes playing a role in those changes.

Chapter 6
Listings and Search Deals

Once we were selling more than a thousand tickets a month online in late 1997, the rest of the travel industry and the investment community started to pay attention. I started getting invitations to speak at conferences run by companies like Jupiter and Forrester, who both specialised in how new technology could benefit corporate management.

After one speech I gave at a Jupiter event, a few private equity investors approached me. It was a time of internet fever – when a new online company listed, its valuation might rocket up to billions of dollars. These investors saw that I was doing something online, with a bookings and software engine.

These investors weren't interested in whether I had three years' accounts, they weren't even interested in whether I was making a profit. In most business cycles, the financial markets are cautious about young companies listing. But these weren't normal times, this was once in a blue moon.

In the end, I didn't take up their offers, but the experience made me feel that I could go on to the stock market. My accountant Sanjiv Talwar drew up a business plan. He's a very solid, down to earth, no nonsense guy and was later to become financial director and then MD of ebookers. He came to us with a sparkling CV, including a PhD in corporate finance from the London School of Economics and work for accountancy firm Coopers & Lybrand.

Our pitch was that since we had Flightbookers in the background, with its 18 years of trading, its consistent profits and its great collection of contracts with airlines, hotels and car hire companies, we were simply putting this business online. Other online travel agencies had to go out and get contracts, or buy competitors.

Sanjiv had been working with us for a few years already: he initially advised us on business plans in 1997, when we were expanding Royal Nepal Airline's operations across Europe and building a network. He was very sharp and perceptive; he could spot business opportunities and read balance sheets very well. Then when I wanted to launch ebookers, I invited him to join us full time. He had his own accountancy firm and tax advisory, so it was a struggle to persuade him to leave it behind. I could tell he was the best person to draw up our business plan, so I was persistent. After a while, he said he would work on his own business until 10.30 each morning, then come over to ebookers. As Sanjiv remembers it, he turned up at 10.30 am on the first day, saw how much work there was to do – and how exciting the prospects were – and came in at 8.00am from the next morning onwards. He really threw himself into the project, researching data for our business plan, looking at how Amazon and Expedia had built their enterprises and driven customers online and how to get statistics from publicly-available sources.

Sanjiv and I had a tiny room for ebookers, really too small to swing a cat. We sat either side of the same desk, writing our business plan while Flightbookers carried on, paying our expenses. All we needed was the software to do the marketing for ebookers, while we consolidated hundreds of new online travel companies into a larger entity. That's why it was so convenient for our value to be measured in sales and revenues: we were selling the services of other companies, but it counted as our revenue.

Besides the private equity interest, I began to receive regular offers of investment. British Airways came along with a proposal, valuing the business at £1.5 million including Flightbookers and offering to buy half of it. So did the accountancy firm Arthur Anderson, who thought it was worth £15 million. We listened to them, but turned them all down because they were attaching onerous conditions and undervaluing the business. Whenever we discussed valuations in the States, the numbers were far higher. I spent six months trying to make some headway in London, then within 24 hours of landing in the US, I was offered $5 million for less than 10 per cent of the business. This kind of investment would give us the possibility to progress and develop the company.

Even in the States, there was a big difference between the valuations we'd hear of on the West coast, in California, compared with the executives in New York, who were more worried that the internet was a bubble. Groups such as Kleiner Perkins realised that the internet meant you could sell things through media, 24 hours a day, worldwide. Anyone who's online can sell on the Isle of Skye, Seattle or Sydney. The whole world becomes a high street. These guys saw the advantages much quicker than elsewhere. Whenever they saw a new technology being developed somewhere outside the States, they'd invite them to the USA, give them a holding company in Delaware, then move them to California, coach them, mentor them and give them money. So many people made businesses like that.

At the same time there were academics at elite colleges like MIT in Boston saying that the internet was overblown and wouldn't change the fundamentals of business. I told them they were wrong. The evidence we were seeing at ebookers was convincing enough.

Many of my employees at Flightbookers were among the early sceptics. They would look at us with pity or condescension as Sanjiv and I settled into our tiny office. They couldn't see how an online business would work. If everyone can see what you're charging for tickets, surely your competitors will be able to undercut you and steal your custom, they reasoned. The overall mood was: "Let them indulge their fantasies and in a few months they'll come to their senses and realise that it's not a viable business model."

We needed an initial injection of cash. My first call, as so often, was to my great friend Firdaus Ruttonshaw. Since he'd already made a healthy return on a £140,000 investment in a technology start-up, he made the same offer to me. We couldn't do that much with £140,000, but it was a start. It showed that people had enough faith in our plans to commit real money. Then in May 1999 I took Sanjiv to meet a friend of mine called Sudhir Choudhrie at his home in London. Sudhir had built a hugely successful investment business, with interests in aviation, technology, healthcare and hospitality. He imported televisions into India and his uncle chaired Hindustan Aeronautics, one of India's major aerospace corporations, so he understood both the aviation world and the potential of revolutionary developments in technology. He immediately offered us $5 million, on a valuation of $55 million, to get ebookers off the ground.

Just visiting Sudhir's home was mind-blowing. He's a prolific art collector and his walls were hung with Andy Warhol and Damien Hurst prints, while Anish Kapoor sculptures stood in corners. One day I'd love to see his collection of antique cars, collected from the dusty neglected garages of India's maharajas and lovingly restored. Some of them are great investments too: he paid $3,000 for one Rolls Royce which is now worth $250,000. Later that year, Sudhir put another $3 million (at a company valuation of $160 million) into ebookers, bringing his holding up to 10 per cent.

This injection of funds helped us to build ebookers from the ground up. We hired marketing people, administrators, HR and accounts people, and moved the office from Tottenham Court Road to Warren Street half a mile north. We were really starting to accelerate at this point, but we recognised that, to achieve our ambitions, we'd need a great deal more money than $8 million. So together with Sanjiv, I set about pursuing a stock market listing which would – we hoped – bring in tens of millions of dollars that we could invest in the business.

Through studying the American market, I saw the dramatic difference between 'bricks and mortar' valuations and the online equivalent. It was one of the mysteries of the age: why should a well-established, popular company like Flightbookers with £49 million in annual sales have a relatively tiny valuation, whereas a fledgling online business like ebookers, with only a fraction of the sales (£1 million), barely any track record and an uncertain commercial future, attract a valuation into the hundreds of millions of pounds?

Of course, company valuations take into account future potential, but these figures were so out of proportion with one another, that you could forgive Flightbookers' staff for their doubts. The whole internet market was becoming a frenzy: companies were getting massive valuations solely on the basis of the 'clicks' they received on their websites, irrespective of turnover or profits. The theory was that these 'unique visitors' would, over time, turn into valuable customers, even if nobody truly understood how this was going to happen.

I was aware of these overblown valuations, based on little more than thin air, but they didn't deter me because I was confident that ebookers would thrive, genuinely creating value by providing more choice, lower fares, higher speed of commerce and reduced overheads. The internet was the perfect distribution channel for travel companies: it used technology to shrink the world, forming connections between companies, countries and continents that would previously have taken hours or days to achieve.

While I was confident in ebookers' prospects, the hectic pace of the internet boom meant that we had to act fast. Each year that went by was equivalent to seven normal years, so in 1999, with ebookers still just three years old, I decided that the time was ripe to go for a public listing. In May I hired JP Morgan to handle the IPO of our shares on the Nasdaq exchange. For the previous few years, JP Morgan had trailed Goldman Sachs and Morgan Stanley in embracing internet businesses: Goldman had spotted the potential early and offered its clients the chance to invest in some amazing opportunities. It was the lead underwriter of Yahoo's IPO in 1996, for example. JP Morgan was desperate to make up for lost time and its clients leapt at the chance to invest in ebookers.

Even so, from the initial agreement with JP Morgan to the moment of going public was a rocky road. There were many issues to address. First, we had to deal with a potentially explosive scandal in Nepal. For several years, I'd held the General Sales Agent position for Royal Nepal Airlines, but after the Communist Party took over the country, they sacked everyone who had been appointed by the previous government. The *Kathmandu Times* ran a story on its front page saying that I'd taken $50 million from the airline illegally. While we were in New York talking to JP Morgan about how to go public, Commerzbank found this story as part of their due diligence and JP Morgan said: "We can't go ahead. You have to prove this isn't true."

So I rang up my secretary in London and she found papers showing that we'd reached a settlement with the Nepalese authorities in 1996 in which we were awarded £2.8 million in compensation for our losses, rather than having taken $50 million. We sent this whole judgement and arbitration to JP Morgan. Fortunately, they accepted our argument, but it gave us a scare – what if they had taken a more rigorous approach, worried about reputational damage?

There were a number of people at JP Morgan, both in New York and London, who doubted that the IPO would work. Some thought that the markets would be suspicious of a 'foreigner' such as me. Once again, I felt that fortune was on my side: Andrew Wilson, the lead manager at JP Morgan in New York, had lived in London and had bought tickets from Flightbookers, so he was on our side. And in the London office there was an Indian guy called Nish Kotecha who could vouch for us. He was called up by his boss, who had major concerns. "Who the hell are ebookers?" he asked Nish. Luckily for us, he stood his ground and was told that the success or failure of the IPO was on his head.

We had meetings with JP Morgan's lawyers that would last four or five hours, discussing our presentations and documents in excruciating detail: where to put a comma; what word to use to describe a certain situation. Then, when it came to investor presentations, three of us from ebookers had to deliver our pitches in 15 minutes. The first time I tried to do this, I took 45 minutes just on my own. Sanjiv Talwar remembers that I managed to whittle this down to seven minutes within a week, which must have been a relief to everyone.

To attract investors in the flotation – and to reassure nervous markets – JP Morgan set up a roadshow all around Europe and the States in autumn 1999. We needed to convince investors of how the offering was unique: we were first in our class, we were pulling people from the offline world to online sales, our bookings were roaring. Lastly – and perhaps most importantly – our fares were as much as 60 per cent lower than our competitors and we had airline contracts and negotiated fares through Flightbookers, built up over 16 years.

To bolster our position with the financial markets, we realised that ebookers needed a presence in mainland Europe. Under Flightbookers, we'd worked with a whole string of companies in the main European capitals, so there were some obvious candidates for companies to buy. Others were part of the club that Rudi Weissmann put together, of which we were a member. We decided to buy companies in Germany and France – the largest and third-largest economies in Europe – which meant that, together with our home market of the UK, we covered more than half of Europe's population at the time. In France, we bought La Compagnie des Voyages in August 1999 and in Germany we bought Teletravel, a purely internet-based company, in October. Both of these companies were eager to sell. They loved the fact that we had negotiated fares, which was a big advantage in the industry. And the price we had to pay for them, based on a bricks and mortar valuation, was tiny compared to our own internet valuation. They haggled a bit on price, but we were happy to raise the fee a little. We wanted to keep the management and most of the employees so it didn't make sense to screw the owners to the floor.

We assembled a team, headed by JP Morgan Bank, together with Salomon Smith Barney and Commerzbank, to promote our shares on the Nasdaq exchange. Each of these partners compiled a brochure laying out the reasons why ebookers shares would be a great purchase, together with a rundown of the main risks. Reading these documents today, 21 years later, they still sound very compelling!

JP Morgan argued that, as a pioneer in offering interactive online travel bookings in the UK, we had 'significant first-mover advantage'. Together with our 18 years of experience with Flightbookers and our relationships with 47 airline suppliers and 64 airlines, the bank forecast that our revenues would soar by 285 per cent in 2000 and a further 213 per cent in 2001. It based these figures on the expected runaway growth of the internet across Europe, with e-commerce expected to jump by 94 per cent each year until 2003 and revenues hitting $20 billion in 2003. "We believe ebookers is poised to capture a good portion of this growth," wrote JP Morgan. Specifically, the bank forecast that online travel bookings would explode in the coming two years, rising by 111 per cent per year. The brochure added that Flightbookers' relationships with airline suppliers was a 'significant barrier to entry' for competitors and that our technology, such as sending flight updates through a 'standard GSM wireless telephone' (i.e. a mobile phone) meant that we provided a richer user experience than the competition.

On the downside, JP Morgan noted that we'd only just bought these companies in Germany and France, so it was hard to tell whether they'd work out for us; they pointed out that airlines might decide to offer discounted fares on their own websites (but they thought this was very unlikely, because it would mess with their regular business and affect their brands) and that competitors with similar products could become an issue, although for the moment, none of them offered the geographical and product range that we did. It conceded that we might not make a profit for a couple of years.

In its more detailed analysis of our prospects, JP Morgan looked at the competition we faced from Microsoft's Expedia and Sabre's Travelocity, concluding that ebookers would 'capture more than its fair share of the expected $7 billion online travel market in 2003'. It laid out our future plans, to acquire six companies across Europe by June 2000, so that we'd have a potential customer base of more than 300 million people, how we'd spend $40-50 million in a major marketing campaign over the next year, and how 59 per cent of our revenue would come from outside the UK in 2001, up from zero in 1999. Along with the hectic pace of European internet growth (25 million users in 1998 expected to become 84 million users by 2002), the document reminded readers that Europeans take far more holidays than Americans: 153 per cent more vacation days per year, to be precise. Whereas Americans fly easily and frequently across their country, for Europeans, almost every flight is an international one, making negotiated fares more valuable than they would be in the USA. To top off the positive impression created by the brochure, JP Morgan gave it a snappy headline: "Book It!"

The roadshow started in Rotterdam, with executives from the bank, plus others from our two other bankers, Salomon Smith Barney and SG Commerz. We buzzed from Rotterdam to Amsterdam, to Paris, Frankfurt and Milan, travelling by private plane, with limousines to pick us up. Although there was a good deal of curiosity about the internet, European investors had a very different attitude to Americans. They were kind of wide-eyed, asking: "What the hell's the internet?" and my impression was that they'd buy some shares then sell them at the first opportunity.

On Saturday, just as we were about to fly from Milan to London for the next stage of presentations on Monday morning, I heard that my father had died in India. As the eldest son, it was my duty to go and light the funeral pyre. So I immediately flew to Delhi, travelled to the cremation and washed my father's body with water from the Ganges river. At 4pm he was cremated and we had to greet hundreds of mourners. Then at midnight I set off back to London, leaving my wife to sprinkle my father's ashes in the Ganges four days later. I landed at Heathrow at 5am, ready for the first roadshow appointment at 8am on Monday morning.

JP Morgan were sympathetic and asked whether I'd like to delay, but we went ahead and had eight meetings that day – three in London and five in Scotland after a midday flight. Being so busy helped me to deal with my father's death because I could just concentrate on ebookers – it kept my mind off everything. Two days later we flew to New York on Concorde with British Airways (on free tickets, because BA were getting £40 million a year out of us) and arrived at 9am for the next round of meetings. My father was still on my mind, but there was no time for reflection: we had another few days of constant meetings – jumping in and out of a Gulfstream G4 private jet.

One of the stops was Minneapolis, where the temperature was -25 degrees: our overcoats were designed for the mild British winter, so when we tried to walk a couple of blocks to the next meeting, we almost froze to death! We quickly hailed a taxi.

Roadshows are managed on a cookie cutter model, like a production line. Bankers such as JP Morgan have tons of people coming through. We would take a jet three times a day, meeting two or three people, starting at Portland, Oregon, at 4am, because New York started at 7am, then clocking off at 3pm. Then going to Seattle, and down the coast, and moving, then going east, to Houston and Denver. It didn't matter which route we took, because we weren't on a scheduled airline and we'd leave all our luggage in the plane. We went everywhere by limo, then when we were ten minutes away from the plane, the driver would say to the pilot 'start your engines' and we'd run up the stairs, buckle up and take off.

After a week of US meetings, we ended up in Chicago before flying back to London. Altogether, we had visited eight countries in 12 days, giving the same presentation to 72 groups of investors without a break. Finally, I could sleep.

These roadshows happened every quarter: we had to tell the main shareholders how we'd done, as well as the European fund managers in Rotterdam, Amsterdam, Paris, Milan, Zurich and Geneva, where all the family offices are based. And we had to do all the press and TV interviews. That was my job – the media would come to our offices and interview me – plus trying to hire the best people.

Even after all these meetings and having generated acres of publicity, many still doubted that we could succeed in going public. Some of my friends told me I was wasting time on the internet. Traditional travel agency chains, with their hundreds of high street shops, dismissed the new technology and thought people wouldn't trust it with their money.

Despite these criticisms and scepticism, when I look back on this time my general feeling was of people trying to help, rather than being jealous of us. They must have thought the odds were against us, so our stock market flotation wouldn't really affect them. More than anything, though, was a feeling of mild confusion: what was the right thing to do or say? Who was for you or against you? We had no idea.

On 11 November, 1999, we made our stock market debut and JP Morgan took out a full-page advertisement in the *Financial Times* to tell everyone, using a picture of an airline captain's hat. In the travel industry, all hell broke loose! Travel companies were saying: 'How did this happen? This idiot is a millionaire!' We'd achieved a sky-high valuation, making the company worth $306 million. It was huge!

I remember just before the flotation going into JP Morgan's office and deciding that we'd go with an initial share price of $18. Once we started trading, it was $34, or a valuation of nearly $600 million– we were 24 times oversubscribed. We floated 20 per cent of the company and the company's share was $61 million, reduced to $53.9 million once costs had been deducted. Suddenly, I had the resources to invest properly in the business and turn it into something completely different from its origins.

Searching for Success

At various Young Presidents Organisation events and other tech conferences, I'd learned about the power of search engines. We were already using Rudi Weissmann's search engine for our confirmation process, so I understood how powerful they were. Of the main US-based search companies, I decided that AOL and Yahoo! were the two that could offer ebookers the best prospects, so I set out to do a deal with them.

AOL began life in 1985 as a computer data company called Quantum, which renamed itself America Online in 1991 just at the dawn of the internet. It soon introduced its own email addresses, an internet access engine that worked with Microsoft Windows, and then in 1997 acquired CompuServe (another large internet service provider), followed by Netscape in 1998. These deals made AOL hugely powerful in online search.

By the time of our stock market flotation, AOL was the uncontested global king of internet service providers. Its market cap was over $125 billion, it earned $9.5 billion per year and had more than 23 million subscribers – 64 per cent of the market. If we could get AOL to place ebookers at the top of its search results when its subscribers looked for flights and holidays, we'd be made.

Yahoo! was also in a strong position. It was a younger company – founded in 1994 by two Stanford graduates as 'Jerry and David's Guide to the World Wide Web' and then renamed Yahoo! Like AOL, it grew through a series of acquisitions, buying webmail service Rocketmail and web hosting provider GeoCities to compete with web portals such as MSN, Lycos and Excite. Its stock market valuation hit $118 billion in early 2000.

With $53.9 million (£38 million) in my pocket, I went to see AOL and Yahoo! and asked what they wanted, in return for top search position. Between them, they wanted half of what I'd just raised – £19 million. That was quite a shock to me. I left the meetings with my tail between my legs.

Then the next day I signed two cheques to them for £19 million – £15 million to AOL and £4 million to Yahoo!. It gave ebookers three years of virtual monopoly in online travel bookings. From annual revenues of $23 million in 1999, in the first year of the deal we made $100 million in sales. In the second year it was $300 million and in the third year it was $600 million. All without a competitor in sight.

In a nutshell, AOL and Yahoo! offered us 250,000 page impressions per year across the UK, Germany and France for travel bookings – every time someone booked a flight online, the sale would come to us for fulfilment. For them, the deal meant they were offering another service to their customers, helping to make their sites more 'sticky' (i.e. encouraging people to use them more often and for longer). Also, AOL and Yahoo! each wanted to set up travel divisions, with our booking engine behind them. So with AOL Travel, we fulfilled the bookings, adding to our sales and profits, and they gained an extra presence in the market.

We paid Yahoo! much less than AOL because I had a personal connection to the European head of Yahoo! at the time, through the Young Presidents Organisation. So this turned out to be a hell of a deal. I think that even AOL began regretting it in the third year, when they saw how much we were making. For us, it was a virtuous circle: customers who came to us via the search engines were much more *au fait* with buying products online, compared to those from offline channels, who would want to call up by phone.

At the time, the deals were purely an act of faith, based on my hunch of how important search engines were becoming to the online marketplace. As it turned out, both AOL and Yahoo! expanded rapidly over the next couple of years, in 2000 and 2001, making the deals even better value for us.

I might have been wrong. Maybe another search engine would spring up and put AOL in the shade. Sure enough, another pair of Stanford students incorporated a search company in 1998, calling it Google. Maybe you've heard of it.

Fortunately for us, since Yahoo! had signed a deal to license Google's search engine in 2000, we could benefit from that thrusting new entrant's technology too, although it was nowhere near as powerful as it would become in the mid-2000s. Google had the beginnings of machine learning and artificial intelligence, but it was very low quality at the time.

We had to stay on our toes all the time, responding to what customers demanded. They'd ask us: 'Why haven't you got this on the website?' And we'd have 50 people working on it, to improve the site's usability and functionality. We kept an eye on what Expedia and Travelocity were doing, our American cousins, who had recently arrived on our shores. They were three years ahead of us: we could copy their ideas and come up with our own innovations.

So from 2000 onwards, I had the premium online travel agency in the UK, Germany and France. It gave me first mover advantage in Europe over my British competitors Lastminute and ahead of Expedia and Travelocity from the United States. We had Flightbookers behind us, to do the fulfilment, and money in the bank. We brought Flightbookers in-house in 2000, to make them part of the business.

The biggest difference between us and the competition was that, through Flightbookers, I had been in the trade for 20 years. I had an office full of contracts, and all I had to do was put them online. The others had to go out and negotiate from scratch. Because Flightbookers was still turning a profit, we never needed more capital to expand ebookers and we never had to sell shares to keep the business afloat.

All these factors gave us tremendous momentum. Companies would clear their diaries to see us. The airlines were clamouring to do deals with us; they began offering us deeper and deeper discounts. When we messed up an occasional booking, or the customers cancelled and wanted a refund – which would normally cost £50 – the airlines forgave us and didn't charge anything.

Our biggest deals were with British Airways. We'd developed the relationship from the point where they'd offer us quasi-exclusivity on a particular route, say London to Sydney. If you played the game properly, they would give you more business every year, until they'd give you the whole world. It became a self-fulfilling prophecy: the more business they gave you, the better you would do and the more business you gave them.

With the internet, relationships with airline managers became even more important. As sales went up, we were giving so much to the airlines, their managers only had to look after online bookings to succeed. We were selling £600 million worth of tickets a year.

They had all understood the massive importance of the internet for the future of their industry. Online bookings meant lower costs, higher volumes and (for the moment) a higher social class of customer, with the income level to support high tech equipment and the sophistication to deal with online transactions. What's more, the airlines could see that ebookers understood these new commercial trends: that's why we were at the top of the search listings.

As Jack Welsh, CEO of General Electric, said: "You have to be number one or two in your industry. When you're number one, you control your destiny." You have a higher premium when the stock market goes up, and you get bashed less when it goes down.

It became important to keep track of our share price: it could be affected by all kinds of factors. For example we did a deal with the supermarket chain

ASDA, to become ASDA Travel's booking agent. Once this deal was mentioned in the press, because ASDA was owned by WalMart – the largest retail chain in the world – our share price doubled from $14 to $28. The stock market investors knew WalMart, so they reacted to the connection. On another occasion, someone sold a few shares with an asking price of $33 and the price dropped suddenly from $37 to $33. Although a fall of $4 may not seem very much, it actually made a huge difference to our business – in valuation terms it meant $60 million down the tubes. Our contacts at JP Morgan said: "Oh we're sorry, we weren't paying attention." (They should have quickly bought some of our shares, to maintain the price).

In 2000, our market cap reached $770 million, but then after the dot.com crash, it fell to just $60 million a year later. This was completely out of kilter with our sales, which were more than doubling from one year to the next. We just had to recognise that stock prices look to the future, and are based on market sentiment, rather than reflecting what you're doing at the time.

Besides the Nasdaq, we also listed in Germany, on the Neuer Markt based in Frankfurt. This exchange launched in 1997 as a European version of the Nasdaq, appealing to investors keen to profit from the technology boom. We listed there at the peak of its popularity, in early 2000, when its index hit 9,000, a sharp rise from 1,000 just two years earlier. We didn't stay on it for long, because someone sold some shares against the Neuer Markt rules and so we switched to a London listing instead. That turned out to be fortunate for us, since the Neuer Markt lost 96 per cent of its value between 2000 and 2002 and shut down completely in 2003.

It's important to keep good relations with the press, to assure your shareholders and investors. We had a couple of in-house public relations people who were very good, plus a couple of external agencies – one for the financial press and one for the consumer side. We had to report quarterly for the Nasdaq, so that always interested the press, and half-yearly for the London Stock Exchange, but generally we found that the UK and European press were quite welcoming and it was easy to get publicity. The internet was such a new thing, the public was keen to learn from internet entrepreneurs. We were at the cutting edge of technology and people started thinking: 'Why would I go down to the High Street and get a parking ticket when I can book at any time, from home?' It was a good deal for them.

Selling the Dream

Our product ethos was to sell a dream. People buy holidays well in advance, so it becomes a dream in their minds. When we went public in London in 2001, there were pictures of me carrying a palm tree, wearing dark glasses, then sat down in a deck chair with one of those big beach balls. It was about sunshine, holidays, warmth.

Launching ebookers at the London Stock Exchange, 2000

The message was different for different people. For the US market, we would get a lot of money from the marketing arms of cities like San Francisco, Miami, New York. So they would advertise with the airlines, or on their own. That was a different kind of marketing. The States was our largest market.

Consumers were ABC1s, under 45, the first 50 per cent of technology adoption. They were time short, asset rich, and they loved the idea that you could book holidays after you came back from work, talked to your wife, booked on a credit card which gave you payment protection. Plus the great thing about the internet was that it wasn't dependent on a region, or a high street, so it gave you a much larger market. When you make mistakes, they're hidden because your sales are always good enough to mask them.

Explaining the business to IPO investors was a bit like Covid-19. You have such a lot of scattered information coming from different places. The only thing you could say for sure was that instead of being open for eight hours a day, you were now open for 24 hours a day. So this by itself will mean that your sales will double or triple, reaching night workers, people who want to buy things in the evenings, etc. So you'll get fast growth. And for us, it was a duopoly, only one or two other agencies. We were going to take a lot of the market.

Traditional Versus Online Agencies

Our drive was to switch people from offline to online. But we had both sides, whereas the Americans like Travelocity, and LastMinute.com in Europe, only had online. The stock markets loved the idea of 'pure play', where your whole business model was online. This was the main reason for creating ebookers, so we could present ourselves to stock markets as a pure play operation, but people kept nit-picking about our status. They would say 'you're still printing tickets.' In reality, we were a 'bricks and clicks' model, like Amazon's relationship with Whole Foods.

There was a problem – as bankers and analysts in the city were at pains to explain. In the evolution from bricks and mortar to pure play, you can't have additional enquiries, chat boxes, etc. But at the time, seven out of eight shoppers would do their research on the internet then go out and buy things in shops. The city guys could not easily explain this – most of them tried to lump us with an online channel, because that's where the big valuations were.

Once we'd opened a new physical office for ebookers and could show the rapidly increasing sales, this demonstrated our pure play model. We were in Russell Square and Flightbookers was in Tottenham Court Road. Only about a mile away from each other, but once you're away, you're away.

The people I employed weren't from the travel business, which also helped distinguish us from our 'bricks and mortar' roots. The COO was Ian Reed. Sanjiv had nothing to do with the travel business. The CIO was from the Cern laboratory in Geneva. None of the senior management, apart from me, had anything to do with travel. I knew the travel side, I could ask them to do this and that. And after a while, all the fulfilment was done in our back office in India. Our sales figures triumphed in any argument. The internet meant we didn't have to be on the High Street, we could still sell $1 billion a year.

*   *   *   *   *

Throughout this time, from going online in 1996, through our stock market listing in 1999 and search engine deals into the 2000s, business models were changing at great speed. You have to adapt just as quickly, or else you'd go out of business. If you look at any 10-year period, there's a 50 per cent churn of companies in the FTSE 100. It was even more pronounced in the online world, with companies rising out of nowhere and disappearing just as fast. We had to innovate constantly to stay alive.

By 2003, within four years of listing, ebookers had broken into the FTSE250 list – the most valuable 250 listed companies in the UK. This was quite an achievement.

Chapter 7
Massive Growth and
Crashes in the Early 2000s

When you look back at early years of the 21st century, it was just one disaster after another.

Leading up to the millennium, businesses became terrified that their IT systems would crash at midnight on 31 December, 1999, unable to comprehend the next day's date. The phenomenon was known as Y2K (short for 'Year 2000') and it caused a global panic, with everyone trying to hire software engineers to correct this phantom problem. As an internet company, we felt pretty vulnerable to this.

There was the sudden dot.com crash of March 2000, just four months after we'd gone public, which destroyed everyone's confidence in internet companies. Then in 2001 there was the 9/11 World Trade Center attack which virtually halted the aviation industry, followed by the SARS epidemic in 2002 which put people off travelling to the Far East, and then the American invasion of Iraq in 2003 which further depressed travel and left the global economy in a state of shock. The following year, the Boxing Day tsunami of 2004 devastated huge areas of southeast Asia.

You would think it was a terrible time to run a travel business.

For some, it was. Many of the online companies that emerged out of nowhere in the late 1990s, fuelled by extraordinary stock market valuations yet with little or no profits, struggled or collapsed once the dot.com boom was over.

By contrast, ebookers was firmly rooted in a 20-year-old bricks and mortar enterprise – Flightbookers – which we still owned, and was profitable all the way through this turbulent period. With the revenue from our deal with AOL and Yahoo! deal flowing through the business, we could afford to acquire a string of European companies, broadening our reach to the continent's 300 million consumers – a market the size of the United States. This was my prime ambition at the time.

Since I'd been running Royal Nepal Airlines' European sales and marketing operations for a few years, I'd already appointed agents all over Europe – France, Germany, Spain… Having dealt with them, I knew that they were good at their jobs and that I could trust them. So when it came to buying companies, I knew which were the best ones. Each of them were quite small, and they weren't expensive to buy, because their value was calculated in bricks and mortar terms, whereas we had an online valuation, so our shares were much higher at that time. All we needed from them was their language skills and their expertise in negotiating consolidated fares. We bought seven over a period of six months, followed by three more.

We had companies in each of the three largest markets – UK, France and Germany – in the Netherlands which is a mid-sized market of 17 million people, and then in the smaller Scandinavian, Swiss and Austrian markets. On the website, you just clicked on a flag and it took you to the site for each country. Even though Switzerland was a smaller market, it was the most profitable: we had 70 people there and the Swiss paid the most money per ticket of any country.

Our search engine gamble was certainly paying off: in the first year, we made $100 million in sales, in the second year $300 million and the third year $600 million. All without a competitor in sight. Our stock market valuation more than doubled from $306 million in 1999 when we listed on the Nasdaq and German Neuer Markt to $770 million in 2000, which gave us a sense of superhuman powers. If the company's worth had doubled in just six months, then within a couple of years it would surely be worth $3 billion!

Of course, these were just idle fantasies. But they were real enough to me that when I was approached by three separate bankers, each with a proposal to 'collar' 5 per cent of the shares, putting them in a blind trust which I could then access later, I turned them down. Partly, it was greed, expecting the share price to continue defying gravity well into the future and partly it was my unfamiliarity with City regulations – I was worried that this was an illegal dodge, because I'd been told that I couldn't trade for six months after going public. If I'd taken their advice, I could have put away more than $100 million.

If you compare our history to that of companies such as Boo.com, which launched its website in November 1999, they had a very different experience. Led by flamboyant Swedish online entrepreneur Ernst Malmsten, it was valued at $350 million in early 2000, but misunderstanding its target audience led to dreadful sales and inadequate technology gave it a bad reputation. On top of that, wild overspending on everything from marketing to staff parties condemned it to an early grave. Boo.com went out of business in May 2000.

Our main (and only serious) rival in the European online travel business was Lastminute.com. Now I'm nothing like as good looking as Brent Hoberman or Martha Lane Fox, but I like to think that my balance sheets look a bit nicer. Since they didn't have any experience in the travel industry, compared with my 20 years, they had to start everything from scratch. Instead, they were experts in media strategy: this was a much-valued skill in the late 1990s, during the internet boom.

The financial press saw Brent as an innovator who could anticipate how young people would spend their money online. He was educated at Eton and Oxford and his father owned a large retail business in South Africa. And Martha was an attractive, persuasive leader who understood what consumers wanted. She came from an aristocratic English family and had also studied at a private school (Westminster) and at Oxford. She appealed to the new breed of thrusting young tech entrepreneurs, combining looks, brains, breeding and a valuable online business.

You could understand how the newspapers lapped up this story, with its photogenic leaders, novel technology and exotic market of long-haul holidays in the Maldives or the Caribbean. Lastminute certainly won more than its fair share of column inches in the media. Meanwhile, I was keeping a close eye on our sales, our costs, our revenues and our share price, as the two companies jockeyed for market share in the late 1990s and into the new millennium. Unlike party people such as Boo.com, Brent and Martha kept a pretty good check on their expenses.

Lastminute went public in March 2000, four months after us and just a few days before the dot.com crash. After that, its share price dived from 380p on listing to 190p a month later. Like us, they recruited City leaders to bolster their credibility with stock market investors, including Allan Leighton and Ed Kamm, former Chief Finance Officer of Travelocity. I thought about adding a Chairman or Chief Executive and discussed the prospect with Sir Stuart Rose, who later became CEO of Marks & Spencer in the mid-2000s, but decided against it.

I thought that Lastminute buying Holiday Autos for £16 million in 2003 was a shrewd deal: like us, I'm sure they made more from car hire than from flights, and Holiday Autos was a well-established, profitable business working in 40 countries. Some of their other deals, I'm not so sure about. They paid £59 million for a French online travel agency called Degriftour, which I thought was more about ego than economics: it made Lastminute the largest e-commerce company in Europe, according to Brent, but it ignored the problems of integrating many different cultures, technologies and markets.

Martha and I were set up in the media as competing rivals, contrasting her youth, beauty and appeal to the City with my more measured approach. An amusing feature in *The Times*, published in June 2002, describes Martha as the 28-year-old child of an Oxford don and the granddaughter of the 6th Marquess of Anglesey, set against me as the 52-year-old son of a diplomat – old enough to be her father. The writer contrasted the way that I promoted ebookers with Martha, who used her own persona as a marketing tool.

Similarly, Lastminute, with its flashy pink-themed website and banner advertising, went after a different market. Our website, according to this article, was rather 'dour'. But Martha didn't really understand travel as well as I did. "Dhamija had a head start, and prefers to keep within the realms of his knowledge – in other words, travel, rather than chasing the entertainment buck," wrote *The Times*.

These observations were all true. But the key difference came towards the end of the article, when it noted that in 2001, Lastminute had £18.4 million in sales, whereas we had £147 million. It concluded that "Dhamija may just succeed in gently beating Lane Fox to take his place in the spotlight." There was an ongoing rivalry between our two companies, which the financial press did their best to provoke, with stories like this. I remember going on one roadshow to the States, which went really well. At the time, the City was so enchanted by Martha that investors were using every opportunity to sell our shares and buy hers. Allan Leighton was cheerleading this effort, telling everyone to buy Lastminute. People started 'shorting' our stock, to profit from future falls in its value. But after our triumphant roadshow, our shares went through the roof, leaving these investors desperately scrabbling around for somewhere to buy them.

According to another press article I read, Lastminute had 13 different Chief Technology Officers in the seven years between its foundation in 1998 and its sale in 2005. And it took the company more than five years longer than us to outsource its admin functions, finally opening a BPO operation in Poland to handle back-office and customer fulfilment after 2006.

By the end of 2001, after 9/11, Lastminute's shares were down below 80p and the company announced a £54 million loss. They suffered from all kinds of problems, some of them similar to ours, and some different. They bought more companies than us, but didn't have the market knowledge to distinguish which would be the best fit. Once they'd overcome the dot.com crash and 9/11 and sales began rising, they were faced with 20 different financial ledgers and 27 different mid-office administrative systems, compared with our low-cost, centralised Indian BPO operation at Tecnovate.

When Travelocity bought the company for £577 million in 2005, Brent and Martha's shares were down to £26 million (Brent) and £14 million (Martha), because they'd diluted their holdings through new share issues, in order to buy more companies. Lastminute had never made a profit, and nine years later it was sold to another online travel agency for £76 million.

There were times where we almost did a deal. I discussed the idea of QXL buying us – they were a British online auction site which was thriving at the time, before eBay came along. I was pretty sure that we were about to go bust within a couple of months. In mid-2000 I had breakfast with Allan Leighton, chairman of Lastminute, and he suggested a share swap to merge ebookers with them. He said I should meet Brent Hoberman to discuss a merger, but when I saw him, Hoberman insisted that he should be CEO of the combined company. I said: 'I'm older than you, and I know the suppliers. I'll be CEO for two years then I'll leave.' But he refused that idea. I pointed out that since I would own 30 per cent of the combined company, it put me in a strong position. He responded that he'd need a 'very strong contract'. Anyway, he must have gone back to Allan Leighton and decided not to pursue the idea.

Often, I could sympathise with Brent and Martha's predicament. In June 2000, as internet stocks worldwide fell through the floor, we needed $45 million to become cash positive. If I didn't raise it, we were done for. I remember being interviewed by a CNBC presenter who said bluntly: "You need more money. Where are you going to get it? The internet is down the tubes, no-one cares." I said: "Can you give me a few days?" There was a website at the time which compiled a 'dot.com debts list', measuring companies' burn rates and predicting when each of them would go bust. We were on the list.

Our sales results, amid all this industry carnage, were still in great shape. So I sent them to JP Morgan and to the private bank Julius Baer in Switzerland. My accountant Sanjiv Talwar was really helpful at this point. He and our marketing director Glenn Trouse flew out to Zurich to speak with the Julius Baer executives to present our plans to them and convince them to invest $15 million. The bank listened to our presentation, then agreed to put in €15 million, on condition that we raised a further €30 million elsewhere. When the Julius Baer guys said 'euros', Sanjiv took a deep breath and said: "Could we have $15 million rather than €15 million?" – Euros would have meant a shortfall of around $2.5 million. Fortunately, they agreed and the deal was done. Sanjiv waited until the lift door closed before jumping in the air, then calling me with the good news. He describes this episode as the highlight of his time at ebookers, but also the most nerve-racking. We had the money three days later. But it was a close shave. I think they were partly reassured that both Sudhir Choudhrie and I had put our own money into the business.

Ebookers Team: Dinesh Dhamija, Glenn Trouse and Sanjiv Talwar, 1999

Apart from this momentary panic, things were going really well. We had the fantastic deal with AOL and Yahoo!, appetite for internet commerce had steadily risen, so that 15 per cent of the British public were now buying online. As ebookers, we went from one employee (me) to 2000 people in three or four years, from one company to 11 different ones across Europe.

It was a very steep learning curve. When we held our first Annual General Meeting (AGM) as a public company, I hired the Long Room at Chelsea Football Club, because we had hundreds of shareholders. We put in several drinks and food stations. But apart from our own staff, only one shareholder turned up! We really needed him, though, so he could second our agenda. After that, we really scaled down AGMs. I remember one time that a woman turned up late with her six children and straight away asked "Where are the biscuits?" I think she was touring AGMs for the free food.

We had to upgrade the board of directors, partly to make the whole company more efficient and professional and partly to reassure the stock markets and the financial press that we knew what we were doing. So we hired people like David Gill, who was the Managing Director of Manchester United and had negotiated a 10-year deal with Nike for £320 million. We thought he was amazing. And John Donaldson of Thomas Cook, who brought with him years of experience of the travel industry and was respected in the City, because he ran a public company. Incidentally, both Gill and Donaldson were over six feet six inches tall.

The 1990s Cadbury Report on corporate governance recommended that companies should split the roles of Chief Executive and Chairman, so I started looking for a CEO. I had a queue of senior people lining up for the job – a Who's Who of the City. The editor of the *Daily Telegraph*, Charles Moore, came to see what was going on. One of the people who applied was the son of the owner of Sea Containers House, a vast building on the Thames. He owned Harry's Bar in Mayfair, one of the most exclusive clubs in the capital. But I turned them all down, because all they were interested in was learning about the online sector, they wouldn't have offered us anything new.

I had to instil a sense of urgency in my colleagues, although they could see that the value of the company was increasing rapidly. Everyone could see it. We adopted a new brand image, with a 'dream' logo of two deckchairs on a beach, designed by our marketing guru, an American guy called Glenn Trouse. Our sales were growing like the clappers and putting small travel agencies around Europe out of business, which added to our monopoly status and made us increasingly attractive to our large US rivals. And for the airlines, it made a lot of sense to do business with us. They always want to deal with one large company if possible, rather than a load of smaller agencies.

Like many owners of fast-growing businesses, I had to deal with lots of personnel issues. You start with a handful of employees and you know all of them. Then you have 500 and it's impossible to have that same relationship, so you have to delegate and accept that people won't achieve things at the same pace or capability you set for yourself. My rule of thumb is that if someone can perform at 70 per cent of the best person in the company, that's fine. When you add a new person, look for an added 70 per cent.

We had all kinds of issues to deal with. At our Dublin office, it turned out that employees were using the computers to watch porn. They didn't realise that we had a piece of software which logged which sites they went to. I didn't know it myself. At the time I was hiring 15 people a week, so I didn't know these people personally. I had to take the IT department's word for it and we got rid of them.

Our Managing Director in the Netherlands ran a travel agency with his wife: we bought the business and kept them on. But they had a peculiar idea that they'd never sell travel insurance, and they'd never charge more than 7 per cent commission. We had to fire the wife, and then, one day when the husband was putting cash into an automatic bank deposit box, he said he was mugged and all the money was taken. At this point we parted company and I replaced him with another Dutch MD who put the margins up to 11 per cent, sold insurance and, instead of falling, our sales doubled. It was tough to get rid of the old MD but we had to do it.

In France, we had even more trouble. Basically, we had 45 people in the office and they just weren't producing. We looked at the productivity figures across Europe and the French office was bottom of the list: they turned up late to work and clocked off early. Basically, they were being French. I said: "Listen guys, I'm either going to close you down or I'm going to fire 30 people." They said: "You can't do that" and quoted French employment law at me. So I hired a French lawyer and found that I could fire 10 people. So I did. I fired 10 people every month for three months and moved the jobs to Dublin (warning them to stay away from naughty websites), where the Irish Development Authority offered us IR£7,000 for every job we created. We kept 15 people on in Paris and we didn't have any more problems after that. Moving part of the French operations to Dublin was an early example of ebookers using technology to work remotely, something we later expanded on a far greater scale in India. It was in keeping with our brand as an online business, where the physical place in which someone worked became increasingly irrelevant.

In Scandinavia, we had mixed fortunes. The Helsinki office in Finland worked really well. In Oslo, my flight over there was one of the scariest of my life. We were in the middle of a terrible snowstorm and the pilot only managed to land on the third attempt. Maybe it was an omen, because the company we bought caused us lots of problems. The management stole hundreds of thousands of pounds from us and I later discovered that they were known crooks, members of the Oslo Mafia. So we shut them down and started another operation.

In Sweden, we bought a Stockholm-based company and I really liked the manager, so I promoted him to MD and paid him more. But within a month he'd resigned and gone to Expedia to head their operation. That was quite shocking. I should have tied his hands with stock options.

In Denmark something similar happened: we bought a company owned by the footballer Brian Laudrup. The manager would come and meet us in a hotel, instead of at his office, which happened three or four times, he would turn up with his results, he was IATA-registered. His results weren't so good and, despite several attempts, we never saw inside his company. So in the end, we decided he was trying to hide something and closed the business down.

In retrospect, we could have bought more companies, especially in complementary areas such as insurance or car hire. We looked at some and turned them down, but they might have improved our profitability.

In the London office, we had to deal with various illicit romances and emotional crises. We had a Chief Technology Officer called Tosti from Heilbronn in Germany with a fixation on Lara Croft, which obsessed him to the point where we bought him a life-sized mannequin for his room. He was plagued by women troubles and was the only staff member who was allowed to smoke in the office – we gave him his own room with windows.

Everyone else was in an open plan formation, so if they wanted to smoke they had to go outside. One IT manager was forever dashing out for a smoke with a woman from the office. We soon found out that they were having an affair, despite him being married to a famous opera singer. One day, during a meeting, I asked this woman to take minutes. At the end of the meeting, I asked her to remind us what had been said and she'd not made any notes. So we had to fire her.

At the same time, we did know how to have fun. Twice a year we'd have big parties with a vodka fountain on a carved block of ice for hours, chocolate fountains, 300 or 400 people all getting drunk and we'd give away flight tickets and holidays. It's important to incentivise people and look after them, to get and keep the best people. We had some very high calibre people – one of our Chief Technology Officers, Andrew Weir, had a double first from Cambridge and a PhD and had worked at the CERN nuclear research centre in Geneva.

In fact, around this time I spent a lot of time in Geneva running the European operation from the centre of the continent. It meant I'd fly to London on a Monday morning, work there on Tuesdays and Wednesdays, then fly back to Geneva where I'd work on Thursdays. Every three months, I'd go to the States and to Frankfurt to visit our shareholders and investors. I bought an apartment in Trump International Tower on Columbus Circle in Manhattan (now sold) and took out a contract with Warren Buffett's NetJet for a private plane that I could use to make these brief trips around Europe.

If we delivered results, the share price went up. The shareholders were very pleased with us and the airlines were saying 'Marvellous!' and our sales kept rising. The staff also responded to share price changes: if the price was rising, they'd be in the office until 10pm. When it started falling, they'd all leave at 5.30. I knew that keeping sales volumes up was the main thing. Profits are great, but as long as your sales are getting higher, then the eventual value of the company is going up at the same time. Plus you have to keep a grip on costs.

My view is that you can only run a successful business if your costs are under control. And in my wife Tani, I had a world class cost controller. One of my closest colleagues, Sanjiv Talwar once told me: "Without Tani, your costs would be 150 per cent higher." She was an excellent confidante and had a better sixth sense about things than me. If I thought something was normal, she would think it was excessive. She was always holding the fort, sorting things out for me, dealing with people, but leaving the public-facing stuff up to me. She was happy to stay in the background.

Founder Dinesh Dhamija and Finance Director Sanjiv Talwar, 1999

Inside the company, Tani got suppliers to sponsor events for ebookers staff, motivating them without additional costs. For suppliers it was a cost-effective way of getting the attention of a captive audience comprising our main buyers and sales staff, a way to really "stick in their minds" and lead to more sales directed towards their products. For ebookers, it was a costless, motivational and fun evening, even more so if prizes were involved.

While this tactic worked very successfully on numerous occasions, once it did not. All the European managing directors were due for ebookers conference in Delhi, flying in from 10 different countries in Europe. One supplier in Delhi arranged cabs from the airport to our hotel. But the supplier compromised, having only one large vehicle for flights whose arrivals were spread over about eight hours at night. The MDs did not appreciate being made to wait for hours at the airport for other flights! Although it was amusing to hear Europeans curse the supplier, with vigour and colour generally known to come only from Punjabis, Tani handled the situation, calmed everyone down the next day, and the conference was a big success.

To help me with media appearances, JP Morgan flew out a woman from the States to train me, costing $5,000 a day. All I can remember is you should never cross your arms or put your hands out in front of you, because it looks defensive. After we went public, I had to face the press every quarter, appearing on Bloomberg, CNBC and CNN etc – sometimes on the BBC. As they say, 'every dog has its day'. In India, our story became quite well known. There were articles on the front pages of the newspapers about an Indian 'lad' who had gone to Europe and made good. When I went to India I was treated as a minor celebrity – not quite Bollywood, but a Delhi or Gurgaon version of it.

Back in Europe, we had to protect and promote the brand whenever we could, which wasn't always easy. We had earned our place as the first online travel agency in Europe and wanted to keep it. For example, Expedia registered the web domain 'ebooker.com' and therefore siphoning off some of our business. I thought: 'They're American, what do you expect'? but eventually we managed to stop them. (We once wondered, for a joke, about buying 'ehookers.com' since sex websites are so profitable. But when we looked, the website domain name had already been taken. And it was probably not the best way to impress shareholders).

After surviving the dot.com crash of 2000, and getting the business back on track, the New York terrorist attacks of September 2001 had a devastating effect on the global economy, especially in travel. Airline fleets were grounded, everyone wanted their money back, we were losing millions of pounds a week. After a few years of extremely rapid growth, we suddenly had to fire people – 140 across Europe, 60 in the UK and 80 elsewhere. We couldn't afford their wages. This sudden downturn, like the dot.com crash before it, gave the critics and doomsayers a chance to gloat over our misfortunes.

The impact of the attack was immediate. For the following four days, the only communication we had with anyone was people demanding refunds for flights. A minor salvation was that its timing could have been worse: on the 17th of each month, our revenue from the previous month would leave our bank account. Since this happened on the 11th of the month, we still had cash in hand to repay hundreds of customers. But when you come into work and lose your shirt every day, you soon realise you don't need so many people.

What amazed me was that, as soon as we announced the job losses, our share price jumped up. That was a big lesson for me: the stock market is always looking forward, taking things into account. It taught us to focus on the fundamentals. Our market capitalisation, which hit $770 million earlier in 2000 slumped alarmingly to just $60 million by the end of the 2001. If only

I'd accepted that offer to collar shares, when they were at their peak, I could have bought the rest of the company.

Instead, we had to tighten our belts and concentrate on the fundamentals of the business: were our websites functioning properly? Were our salespeople trained well enough to execute transactions, to direct people towards car hire or travel insurance deals? Were we keeping costs under control? And in each case, I'd say we were on top of the issues. Each week we hired students on an hourly rate to check our website usability, along with 40 or 50 tech professionals who would maintain, upgrade and operate the sites. We poured money into training, both in India and Europe, to maximise sales opportunities. And we certainly kept a lid on costs.

Despite rocky market conditions, people were not leaving us, because overall we were expanding. In fact they were applying to join us. It was an amazing ride, so exhilarating, learning new things every day. In marketing, I had more money to spend, with suppliers, offering all kinds of incentives, with goodies coming in from hotels and airlines, familiarisation trips to Dubai or Rome with free flights and hotels. The point is, in every field, in HR and legal, I had a huge learning curve, balancing expansion with keeping costs in check. For example, I used to go to lawyers in London for contracts, but the same firms charged far lower rates per hour out of London, so I learned to go to those, with a panel of lawyers. In every field we were learning and trying to save money as there was a tension between expanding and saving. We learnt how to assimilate and work with European offices, we found that we had 90 per cent in common with these businesses, although it hadn't been done before.

We still had the AOL and Yahoo! deals running at this point (they ran out in late 2003), so our quasi monopoly position on European internet travel search was secure, our bricks and mortar business Flightbookers – which was now a subsidiary of ebookers – was still making a profit and besides Lastminute, which had its own troubles, there was little sign of serious competition elsewhere.

It seems odd, from the vantage point of the 2020s, how little attention national or European regulators paid to what we were doing. There was no real discussion of competition questions, of anti-trust legislation or investigations by the Monopolies Commission, as there might have been if we were a traditional corporation. I was once asked to attend a Select Committee in the Houses of Parliament, but in general, we were left to ourselves. Things were happening much faster than the politicians could keep track.

Over in the United States, Microsoft faced a savage anti-trust case in 2000 which threatened to break up the company, and took a further 11 years to settle. It took the European Commission until 2004 to mount a similar case against Microsoft, fining it $611 million, with Competition Commissioner Mario Monti telling Bill Gates: "Dominant companies have a special responsibility to ensure that the way they do business doesn't prevent competition…and does not harm consumers and innovation."

At our level, at least in the search domain, there were no such concerns and we were happy to make hay while the sun shone. And once the global economy and travel industry recovered from 9/11, we really made a lot of hay. More and more consumers were prepared to book online, in 2002 sales roared back and we had upwards of three million people a month on the website.

In 2003 I was named UK Entrepreneur of the Year by *Business Management* magazine, followed by Asian Man of the Year in the GG2 Leadership Awards in 2004. These were gratifying plaudits, but I knew – from bitter experience – that in business you are never more than a few months away from a crisis, which could wreck your plans and dreams.

The next stage of the company's progression would be make or break.

Eight of My Heroes in Business and Politics

Elon Musk (1971-)

The Thomas Edison of the 21st century, Elon Musk is one of my heroes. What he's achieved in telecommunications, energy, transport, electronic payments, underground tunnelling and space exploration just boggles the mind.

Musk's own mind can seem boggled, when he follows the example of ex-president Trump and tweets about Tesla and the stock market late at night, but his vision of a world running on sustainable energy, travelling at unheard-of speeds, populating distant planets and communicating from mountains and deserts is pure science fiction made real.

Tesla is Musk's highest-profile venture and I'm a big fan – I own two of the cars – but his SpaceX programme is arguably more important and commercially valuable. Where some billionaires might dream of launching two or three satellites, Musk has launched more than a thousand, with a licence for ten thousand already granted. This has transformed access to telecommunications, whether you're on the top of Everest or in the middle of the Sahara. SpaceX has saved NASA huge amounts of effort and expense, meaning that Musk has the full support of the US government. His alliance with Donald Trump made sense from that point of view, despite the disgraced president's retarded views on the environment. I'm glad that Musk had the balls to sever ties with Trump after he withdrew the US from the Paris Climate Accord.

Where Musk has excelled is in research and development: nobody can match him on battery development, not even the biggest automakers, which is an astonishing achievement. For example, I can power my house from my Tesla car, if I need to.

Musk is a freak of nature, in a good way. He thinks differently, he's borderline insane – the archetypical mad genius – and he's bucked the whole stock market by taking on the short sellers and triumphing, hence becoming the world's richest man in January 2021. I admire that aspect of his career as well. You have to applaud when a company like Tesla, under huge international scrutiny, appreciates by 700 per cent in a year.

Jeff Bezos (1964-)

I like stories of people who start out with very little and make an impact. Jeff Bezos's mother was a 17-year-old high school student and he was raised by her and Mike Bezos, who had arrived in the States as a penniless Cuban immigrant. Bezos junior set up his first business as a teenager from the family garage.

Despite the lure of Wall Street riches, Bezos spotted the potential of the internet in 1994, moved to Seattle and put his computer science degree to use selling books online. Just as ebookers took off in 1998, I can imagine the adrenalin rush that Bezos must have felt in 1995 when Amazon.com sold books in 45 countries in its first month and turned over $510,000 in its first year, from nothing. The rest of Amazon's history, to date, is one of the defining commercial phenomena of the age. The hundreds of billions in revenue, the trillion dollar valuation in 2018, the domination of cloud storage with Amazon Web Services, the massive growth of its entertainment brand, the innovations of Kindle, Alexa, Prime Air deliveries and Blue Origin – Bezos's space exploration programme – and his multiple philanthropic foundations.

Amazon is the fulfilment of the American national champion model, where society and government actively promote a company, allowing it to snowball, acquire competitors, found new enterprises and boost them far beyond their original size and value. I wish European governments would emulate this model. It would do wonders for our economy.

What's extraordinary about Amazon is how it has transformed commerce so fundamentally. It has killed the High Street, saved millions of people countless hours of their time, delivering what they want faster than ever before, at cheaper prices. On a much smaller scale, this is what ebookers did for the European travel market, so of course I'm a fan. Much as people might decry the demise of town centre shopping, was it really the best use of our time? Driving through congested streets, queuing at tills, carrying goods home, wasting your journey because items were unavailable, getting parking tickets.

How much better to spend your leisure time with family, entertainment, sport, exploring the countryside. COVID isolation would have been much less fun without Amazon.

Lee Kuan Yew (1923-2015)

Of all the politicians whose careers I've followed, Lee Kuan Yew of Singapore stands out as the most phenomenally successful. After earning a double first in law at Fitzwilliam in Cambridge, where I studied, he founded the People's Action Party (PAP) and achieved independence from Britain, then from Malaysia. He turned Singapore into the most prosperous, modern, cosmopolitan, safe, highly-educated, stable nation in South-East Asia through force of personality and a shrewd combination of public and private investment.

Lee was a consummate diplomat. He maintained warm relations with the Chinese, hosted Deng Xiaoping in 1978 and prioritised socialist principles such as affordable housing, high employment and gender equality, while attracting multinational corporations through a generous tax regime and Western-facing regulations. Among democratically-elected world leaders, he was extraordinarily popular: under his guidance, PAP won seven consecutive elections between 1959 and 1990, making him the world's longest-serving Prime Minister.

Some of this longevity was down to his strict, almost autocratic approach, stifling media criticism and criminalising minor offences, but I'd say that it was mostly due to the adoring devotion of Singaporeans, who owed him their liberty from colonialism, their jobs, prosperity and status as the runaway success story of the region, if not the world. When people wish that Britain could become the Singapore of Europe, you can see how fundamentally the relationship has changed. From a 'cesspool of squalor and degradation' in the 1940s, Singapore is now described as an economic miracle and one of the foremost industrial powers in Asia.

Besides our common Cambridge background, I met him briefly in Delhi as a child when he visited in the 1950s and played golf with my father. Singapore's history under Lee is something I wish had happened in India, as the country similarly fought its way out of British control and sought to marry democracy with industrial modernisation. Perhaps there is still time for Lee's example to inspire the current generation of Indian leaders with his wise council and dedication to his people.

Sheikh Mohammed bin Rashid Al Maktoum (1949-)

A second nation-builder is Sheikh Mohammed Al Maktoum, official ruler of Dubai since 2006 and effective ruler since 1995 when he became Crown Prince. People think that Dubai must be swimming in oil and gas, like Abu Dhabi or Qatar, but actually its meagre energy resources were almost depleted in the 1990s when Sheikh Mohammed came to power.

Instead, with vision and imagination, he turned Dubai into a financial, tourism and business centre. He created free trade zones, founded Emirates Airline, completed huge building programmes and established Dubai International Finance Centre in 2006, with its rules based on English common law.

You can't say that Sheikh Mohammed started out poor, but you can admire his bravery and confidence. He trusted English and Irish executives to run his companies - like Sir Maurice Flanagan, Emirates Airline's first CEO - rather than keeping all the jobs for locals. In a matter of a few years, Emirates outstripped the incumbent elite of British Airways, Air France and other national carriers to become one of the world's finest carriers. From my vantage point in the travel industry, that was a massive achievement, in record time.

Dubai International Airport is one of the great modern-day hubs, the equal of Singapore's Changi Airport or Seoul Incheon in South Korea. Emirates won the trust and admiration of travellers and airlines, which made Dubai into a hugely popular destination, where before there was little but sand.

Outside the UAE, he also transformed the horse racing and breeding industry, boosting its finances and global esteem. As a long-naturalised Englishman, I'm a tiny bit jealous of anyone who gets to sit next to the Queen in the royal box at Ascot. Sheikh Mohammed's Godolphin stables is the largest in the world: it employed three-time Champion Jockey Frankie Dettori and the world's highest-paid trainer John Gosden, whose horses have won more than 3,000 races including the Arc de Triomphe and the Epsom Derby. John and I were friends at Fitzwilliam College in Cambridge.

Finally, in October 2020, he helped to negotiate the Abraham Accords, forging trade and diplomatic relations between the UAE and Israel. It was a long-awaited step towards peace and security in the Middle East.

Jack Ma (1964-)

Jack Ma's life is the stuff of legend. A poor kid from a Chinese backwater, he could smell opportunity from ten miles away and didn't stop running until he found it. When Alibaba raised $168 billion on its New York Stock Exchange debut in 2014, it was the culmination of decades of such opportunities, each one magicked out of thin air and turned into gold.

I love his persistence: he would stand outside Hangzhou hotels in the snow waiting to accost tourists and ask them to teach him English; he failed his college maths exams three times before finally winning a place; and when a business first offered goods on his Alibaba website, "We bought everything they sell. We had two rooms full of things we bought for no use, all garbage – in order to tell people that it works."

At 5 foot 5 inches high, Ma is a fireball of energy who spotted the potential of the internet in China, far ahead of anyone else. Like me, he studied the lessons of Silicon Valley, persuaded major investors to take a chance on him and saw the bigger picture. Against tremendous odds, he executed his plans with astonishing results, defeating Western giants like eBay through an intuitive understanding of what Chinese businesses and consumers wanted to buy, sell or finance.

Like many Chinese entrepreneurs, he had the tacit support of the state, though most of his funding came from Western companies like Yahoo! and an earlier stock exchange listing in Hong Kong. His vision and drive are tremendous: creating a large enterprise in China is enormously daunting, there are countless laws, people are constantly watching one another. To have developed a payments platform where mortgages are agreed within seconds, with an algorithm so good that it has brought in the entire Chinese hinterland...you have to raise your hat to him. Alibaba is like the Amazon of China and Alipay is its PayPal – it has the whole country of 1.45 billion people sewn up. Transaction levels are huge.

Jack Ma's runaway train came to a halt in late 2020 when the Chinese government pulled the IPO of his Ant Group finance business, saying that he was 'rich enough'. I hate to say it, but they may have a point.

Mo Ibrahim (1946-)

During a flight over Kenya, Sudanese-British businessman Mo Ibrahim was struck by Africa's economic paradox: "I looked out of my window. The country was so lush, so green," he said. "I wondered how the people there could ever be hungry. Looking at the spaces, huge, endless spaces, animals, water; everything was there. I came to the conclusion that unless you are ruled properly, you cannot move forward. Everything else is second. Everything."

With a PhD in telecoms from Birmingham University in the UK, Ibrahim developed cell-phone coverage for tens of millions of Africans before selling his Celtel company for $3.4 billion in 2005, the same year that I sold ebookers. He then set out to help the continent of his birth realise its potential.

To improve governance, he established the Mo Ibrahim Prize for Achievement in African Leadership: former political leaders receive $5 million plus $200,000 each year for the rest of their lives. It seeks to prevent them becoming autocratic as they cling to power, fearful of losing their wealth.

A second foundation, the Ibrahim Index of African Governance, ranks all 53 African countries according to human and economic development, political rights and rule of law. Since 2005, this index has given Africans the tools to measure their leaders' performance and to hold them to account, similar to the World Bank's Ease of Doing Business Index.

"We need a scientific, objective basis for the discussion," Ibrahim said. "We say 'OK, what exactly have you delivered? How many hospital beds, how many schools, for how many children? Are your people safe? How many violent deaths in your country? How many unemployed people?' The important thing is to get this information and disseminate it to the widest possible audience, so the citizens in every country know what the government is doing."

Ibrahim has done great things for Africa, partly because he can highlight governmental flaws and corruption with a clear conscience. He made his money without resorting to bribery or dishonest behaviour. "To do business in Africa, you don't have to pay bribes," said Ngozi Okonjo-Iweala, the former Foreign Minister of Nigeria. "My good friend Mo Ibrahim is living proof of that."

I admire Ibrahim for his business achievements, modernising a continent's telecoms, speeding up commerce and increasing transparency, but even more for how he used his wealth: his Foundation is political philanthropy at its finest, bringing new hope to millions of people who previously suffered in silence.

Bill Gross (1944-)

Since founding a solar energy project in Romania, I've paid attention to the latest thinking on renewable energy. One of the smartest entrepreneurs in the field is Bill Gross: he started IdeaLab in 1996 and has IPO-ed or sold dozens of companies for billions of dollars, including Tickets.com, CarsDirect and NetZero. But his central mission is to commercialise renewables.

His latest project is Energy Vault. It builds 75m-high cranes that lift heavy blocks to store kinetic energy – a solid object version of hydroelectric power generation. He's had $28 billion worth of orders already.

Gross points out that people originally depended on biology for power generation, using human and animal muscle. After the Industrial Revolution we switched to chemical-based energy, using oil, gas and batteries. In response to climate change, we must now embrace physics-based generation through sun, wind and gravity.

Not only are these elements cheaper, cleaner and more effective than hydrocarbons, they're evenly distributed around the world, meaning that we'll avoid the geopolitical conflicts of oil economies, while tackling climate change. The more energy a country produces, the more its GDP rises, so harnessing renewable energy should transform a host of nations in the coming years. IdeaLab also plans to capture CO_2 and store it underground.

Gross is a charismatic figure in the investment world. I like the way that he's persuaded people like Bill Gates of Microsoft and Steve Case of AOL to join him, investing in projects that sit outside the traditional venture capital or private equity model. He thinks big, talking about trillion-dollar opportunities - cornering the global hydrogen market for example, or solving the world's carbon emissions.

He's not a household name like Elon Musk or Jeff Bezos, but I think what he's doing is very exciting and important.

Sir Richard Branson (1950-)

My junior by three months, Sir Richard Branson redefined what it meant to be a British entrepreneur. Never has one individual built such an extraordinary collection of businesses under one brand, steeped in his flamboyant, irrepressible, optimistic, media-friendly, laid back character. He may have started off a Virgin, but he's got into bed with everyone.

Branson's entry into the airline industry was sheer chutzpa, one of countless examples of ignoring convention and precedent. So many had tried and failed, even with state backing. It took tremendous nerve to tackle British Airways and similar audacity to launch Virgin Galactic in 2004. He's been pushing through new frontiers ever since, amassing a fortune of $7.8 billion as of January 2021 as his stock rose sharply.

Like many of the great entrepreneurs through history, Branson is a showman at heart. He's never happier than when dressing up and playing the crowd like a modern-day Barnum with his circus of underwear, condoms, radio stations, mortgages, trains, planes and spaceships. When so many products are effectively interchangeable, it's important to add some character to your offering: somehow Branson even manages to make financial services sexy and exciting.

For me, touring the media studios and speaking to journalists about ebookers was always enjoyable, even when I had to defend disappointing results. I was associated with the brand, so how I performed had a material effect on the whole business. I think Branson, more than anyone else, showed us all how to do this. He wouldn't hide from the media (far from it), he came across as honest and open, cared for his staff and customers and transmitted his enthusiasm for his product.

Of Branson's many close shaves, my favourite is when, aged 16, he was boarding at Cliff View school in Sussex. He began spending time with Charlotte, the pretty 18-year-old daughter of the headmaster. One night a teacher spotted him tiptoeing out of Charlotte's room and the headmaster expelled him on the spot. Branson wrote a suicide note, gave it to another pupil and started walking towards the cliffs near the school. Teachers came running after him and the expulsion was rescinded.

High stakes, high rewards. That's how Branson has thrived.

Chapter 8
Tecnovate

At the turn of the millennium, India's economy was roaring. Its GDP rose by almost 9 per cent in 1999, as more multinationals were attracted by newly-relaxed regulations and the 20 million English-speaking graduates entering the workforce every year at wages 70 per cent lower than in the West.

I felt sure there would be a way for ebookers to do business in India. With my family background, I had a fantastic network of contacts at high levels in Indian society and business. But I wasn't interested in selling to Indian customers – the margins were too low, there was very little internet penetration at the time, and local travel agencies dominated the market. So I was looking for other ways to collaborate, to capitalise on this giant wage differential, set against the high quality and calibre of Indian employees.

At the same time, pressures were building in London: being a publicly-quoted company meant that every decision you took was closely scrutinised. If any part of the business showed a weakness, it would probably transmit rapidly to the share price, giving investors a reason for concern. The market demanded that you predicted what your results would be for the coming months and would punish you if you underperformed, for whatever reason.

At ebookers, we found that our margins were shrinking as the volume of our business grew. People were still coming to terms with using the internet and there were endless problems. Our phones were constantly ringing with customers wanting to know if their booking had gone through. We spent countless hours helping both staff and customers to understand the new technology, and there was always something not working properly.

My second cousin, Prashant Sahni grew up in India, then studied for a Masters in International Finance at the London School of Economics, before working as a chartered accountant for Arthur Andersen in London. In early 2001, he was back in India, working in venture capital in Bombay.

After we met by chance at a family event in New Delhi, I offered Prashant a job as head of business development at ebookers, hoping that he could identify some new European businesses for us to acquire. He came to London, took a look at our model and spotted that our back office was costing too much. "Your operating costs are out of whack with your scale of business," he said. The idea of transferring these operations to India started to seem like a great idea. Since labour costs were so much lower, we could invest in a far more intensive support network, with teams ensuring that no issues were left unresolved.

Whereas I was into a pattern of rapid acquisitions, buying companies all over Europe, Prashant urged me to look at India as a way to reduce our costs, which were threatening to cause us serious problems. He pointed out that dozens of multinationals had set up Business Process Outsourcing (BPO) operations in India, with call centres employing thousands of people answering customer calls and dealing with back office administration such as payroll or procurement.

We were a fraction of the size of a company like Barclays, IBM or Procter and Gamble, who invested many millions of dollars into Indian operations, often through BPO providers like Wipro Spectramind or EXL. Despite our size, Prashant figured that it could still make good business sense for us and set about finding a suitable deal for us.

We had in fact already tried using an Indian BPO company, Customer Asset in Bangalore. We carried out a pilot project in early 2001, outsourcing our telesales function. The results were disappointing: there was only a minor increase in its conversion rate of calls to sales, compared with our London office, which didn't justify the expense of the Indian operation. We cancelled the project.

Equally, we quickly ruled out building an Indian BPO centre from scratch. Getting the right permissions, telecom connections and employees would be an expensive and lengthy process, with uncertain rewards. On the other hand, buying an existing facility seemed just as fraught. Some of the valuations Prashant was offered were exorbitant, expecting us to pay a big premium for a lot of empty tables and chairs.

As a VC (Venture Capital) investor, Prashant had seen how BPOs worked in India. He figured that they involved three main expenses: people, IT and leasehold improvements. But his knowledge was purely theoretical, because he'd never built or managed anything of this sort. He freely admitted that he lacked the background for running a BPO. "I knew nothing about travel, IT or BPOs," he said recently, when we chatted about those days.

He began looking for a suitable company to acquire. First, he spoke to a traditional travel agent in India, but they were clueless about the internet. So then he approached online travel agencies and found that everyone was going bust. He finally settled on a company called Make My Trip which was owned by a VC called eVentures. Like so many others, Make My Trip was in a desperate financial hole. At first, its CEO Deep Kalra (who attended the same school as me, St Columba's in Delhi) was only interested in selling the whole business. After a short but intense bout of negotiation, he agreed to sell us the customer service operation for the cost of the fixed assets: $25,000 plus 81,000 shares in ebookers issued over the following six months. We kept on all Make My Trip's employees, in their original roles.

For this bargain price, we inherited a 50-seat facility, with all its staff and management, its technical and telecom systems, its know-how and customer care experience and an excellent knowledge of the local market – vital for staff recruitment. Prashant was thrilled by the deal: "We got the business for a throwaway price!" he told me. We definitely benefited from good timing, because Make My Trip badly needed the money, whereas we badly needed the computers, connectivity and staff. It meant we could start immediately rather than ordering hardware.

Make My Trip's owners fought us over the terms of the deal, which gave them relatively little in return for something that was of major value to us, but Prashant's shrewd negotiating skills won them over. He persuaded them that, by selling to us, they'd save the cost of retrenching their employees, taking these costs off their books. "We'll take them for free!" said Prashant, making it sound like he was doing them a massive favour. At least Deep Kalra was able to save the company. Years later, it became very successful.

The biggest saving to us wasn't the cost of the facility; it was the exceptionally close fit of the existing operation to our needs: trained professionals working in the online travel business, with all the relevant technology and management in place. This meant the deal was low risk and low cost – even the equity release was insignificant: it never diluted our share price. On top of that, we routed the deal through a company in my old home of Mauritius, to maximise tax advantages and make sure we could repatriate profits and speed up the registration process. Prashant picked up a shell company from his lawyers called Technovate, removed the 'h' and turned the middle 'c and n' into an infinity sign in the logo. I liked his inventiveness and energy, so I appointed Prashant CEO of the new company.

Within weeks, we'd outgrown this original site in Delhi and Prashant set about finding bigger premises. He found a prime spot near the city centre, arguing that the higher rental cost (compared with a more isolated location) was worthwhile, since we'd attract better employees and spend less on transport. Even so, Prashant still cut a tremendous deal with the building's landlords, getting a 60 per cent discount in return for a long-term agreement.

As a lawyer, I like to think that I'm a good contract negotiator, but Prashant always puts me in the shade. Maybe an accountancy background is the key: blinding people with figures and graphs. He pulled off the same trick with Tecnovate's telecoms and technology deals, winning us a sharp discount and a guarantee that any fall in their rates over 5 per cent would be passed on to us.

We signed the contract to launch Tecnovate in August 2001, promising investment of £2 million − £1 million to begin with, followed by a second million within the first year. The international travel industry was flourishing, ebookers was reaping the rewards of its agreements with AOL and Yahoo! and we were primed for a tremendous second half of 2001.

Then our world caved in.

Within a few days of the 11 September 2001 attacks on the World Trade Centre in New York, international air travel virtually ground to a halt. Nobody wanted to fly. The future of ebookers as a going concern came into question. Could we weather this unprecedented collapse of confidence? Was this the right time to spend £1 million on an untried operation thousands of miles from our home market?

We decided to go ahead anyway, confident that the crash in the market would be temporary and the eventual benefits of Tecnovate would justify the investment. The one big difference was that Tecnovate had to raise the second £1 million itself, through debt (but of course Prashant managed to negotiate a brilliant deal, borrowing in dollars instead of rupees, which lowered the interest rate).

While many Indian BPOs at the time were thriving, there were no guarantees of success. Some failed because − as with our experience with CustomerAsset − the sums didn't add up. Others found that the Indian accent put off customers who had trouble understanding it. In other cases, the technology proved unreliable or poor quality − it could be hard to hear what the Indian call centre operator was saying. So we trod carefully.

Another pitfall was the high turnover of BPO employees. New centres were opening with increasing frequency, leading to high competition for trained workers. In the early months of our operation, we suffered from this along with the rest of the industry. Turnover reached 80 per cent at one time, as rivals poached our staff − who were highly prized - with attractive wage offers.

I was keen to migrate as many back-office processes to Delhi as possible, but Prashant insisted that we start with modest targets, concentrating on entry-level work such as data entry and processing, or hotel email confirmations and correspondence. We ran the two systems − London and Delhi − in parallel for around nine months before we were confident to make the full transfer. This meant long work hours and constant shuttle trips back and forth, which was exhausting for Prashant and his team. Meanwhile, our business was still in crisis, with dozens of redundancies and severe spending cuts.

Prashant's approach was to make the BPO work financially, both for Tecnovate and for ebookers. Instead of charging per seat, as many BPOs did at the time, he charged per task. This meant that we could keep track of how the business was working for us, rather than making open-ended payments for unspecified rewards.

Gradually, conditions improved. Prashant developed Tecnovate's capacities over the months, adding email sales, online support (phone and email) and telesales to the mix. Tecnovate became the internal tech support for the whole of ebookers; Prashant also introduced reconciliation work – tackling large amounts of low-value transaction accounting. This work was uneconomic for our European offices, but Indian labour costs meant that it was worthwhile. Virtually no amount was too small for the staff in India to chase down and get a refund. Tecnovate's accounting function became a profit centre for ebookers overall.

India in the early 2000s had a growing reputation for digital skills. Western businesses began outsourcing their website development and production to companies like Infosys, Tata Consultancy Services and hundreds of others. We hired some talented IT people and Tecnovate took over our website and search engine optimisation work, which did wonders for our marketing and increased our sales ratios.

As Tecnovate matured, it added more and more central functions: internal audit, financial accounting, treasury, budgeting and management information systems. Within a couple of years, Prashant had assumed responsibility for at least 12 of ebookers' major business functions, spread across three categories: travel, IT and financial services. Apart from ebookers' Chief Financial Officer, who was based in London, all the company's finance staff were in India.

When we compared Tecnovate's results with those of CustomerAsset, our short-lived pilot scheme in 2001, and those of the London office, there were startling differences: CustomerAsset's best telesales conversion rate was 13 per cent; in November 2002, the London office recorded a 22 per cent rate; Tecnovate's telesales conversion rate at this time was 29 per cent. Its email conversion rates were equally impressive, reaching 24 per cent compared to just 4 per cent in the UK.

Prashant reckoned that these stellar results came from the enthusiasm of his team and their desperation to succeed, along with his strategy of hiring experienced salespeople from outside the travel industry. "You can teach a person about travel, but you can't necessarily teach a travel expert about sales," he reasoned. I'd agree with that: when he joined us, Prashant didn't know the first thing about the travel industry, but I taught him and he soon picked it up and was an excellent manager.

By the end of 2003, six of ebookers' top ten salespeople were in India.

From a logistical point of view, the time difference between Europe and India worked in our favour. People would make a booking in Europe during their business hours, the Indian BPO office would issue the tickets overnight and they would be ready for the customer in the morning. Prashant guaranteed us that his staff would respond to emails within two hours, which was far faster than our competitors could manage. This was yet another advantage: customers were delighted with the quick turnaround and were more likely to book with us. Then he promised that, if customers wanted to book a flight after working hours in Europe, Tecnovate would process the booking, whereas – once again – our competitors couldn't respond so quickly. He even promised to indemnify us against any losses from technical errors.

For me, the way that Tecnovate grew and prospered was pleasing in two ways. Of course I was happy to see its profoundly positive impact on ebookers' financial results and the improvements in administration, technology and back office efficiency. I was also delighted to play a part in bringing skilled employment opportunities to India, to contribute to the country's modernisation, the population's emergence from poverty and its growing reputation on the international stage.

The way that Prashant came up with new solutions and used technology to improve our speed, efficiency and reliability made a huge difference to our financial results. Our reputation as a cutting-edge high tech business grew: Tecnovate took over the customer service function and streamlined its own operations through smart use of automation software. He set up an analytics team to crunch through the data that we were collecting from our offices across Europe, giving each of our teams further competitive advantage as they negotiated with airlines, car hire and hotel companies and insurers. It was 'purchasing power arbitration' in action, in nine different languages. We became one of the top performing companies, from any sector, on the Nasdaq exchange.

In 2002, Prashant came up with another innovation which gave Tecnovate a further piece of international kudos and commercial advantage. He spoke to the managing director of our Finnish office at a meeting in London and she asked him how Tecnovate could improve its customer service for the Finnish market. Although many Finns speak excellent English, some have limited language skills and – in any case – they prefer to converse in their mother tongue.

On the face of it, hiring Finnish nationals to work at Tecnovate's offices in Delhi seemed prohibitively expensive and complex. Then between them, Prashant and the Finnish MD struck on a novel idea. Why not offer "the adventure of a lifetime" to the stream of European gap year students who flowed from Europe to India every year, employing them at local wage rates plus health insurance, accommodation, transport and subsidised meals in return for a year's work?

It was an untried model, maybe it was crazy. Would any Europeans really want to work for us in India? We started with an advertisement for five jobs, posted in a Finnish newspaper. Within hours, we had 150 replies. Soon we had Finns, Germans, Swiss and Norwegians flying out to Delhi and busily joining in with Indian colleagues at the BPO centre, before setting off on adventures around the country in their gap years.

They helped European customers in their native language and they learnt a bit about India rather than sitting on a hill smoking dope. (Some of them might even marry each other). It was a surprisingly successful business innovation, with positive benefits to both sides. Customers planning a trip to Denmark would be pleasantly surprised to find our phone operator at an Indian call centre could recommend a good restaurant in Copenhagen. German callers discovered that our operators knew the difference between a carnival and the Oktoberfest. Our Indian employees picked up some foreign language skills and learnt about European countries.

By the end of 2003, we had 70 Europeans at the centre in Delhi, just under 10 per cent of the workforce. Besides working well for us in terms of efficiency and the convenience of addressing customers in their own language, this model attracted a lot of press interest. There were stories on the BBC, in *The Economist* and in Indian papers *Financial Express* and *The Times of India*. Academics latched on to the story as well, putting it into case studies about the surprising cultural and economic advantages of outsourcing.

Some of our European employees stayed on beyond their year's contract and gained promotion inside the company. Others moved back home, studied, then went to work for us in our European offices. The high staff turnover that we suffered in the early stages was replaced by a stronger loyalty: our attrition rate in 2003 fell to 15 per cent, far below the industry average of 35 per cent. For some reason, our male Indian employees were no longer interested in looking for other jobs while there were blonde Swedish 18-year-old women in the office.

Each department held monthly parties, which were extremely popular. Groups of employees would head off on trips around India, for sightseeing at the Taj Mahal or to have fun in Goa. In the office, it was an exhilarating mix of cultures, young people learning from one another, learning new skills and discovering how to use the technology. There was an open, friendly atmosphere – working in the travel industry has an excitement to it in any case: the walls were covered in pictures of exotic locations.

Tani, who had mentored Prashant and overseen the set-up of Tecnovate, remembers that the whole staff were hugely enthusiastic and eager. They wanted to make things happen, to understand how the Western market worked, to learn new skills. Compared with her experiences working with the back office staff in London, things worked much faster in India, it was easier and more efficient to manage. People really respected the job they were in; they wouldn't leave at 5pm – working hours didn't mean so much to them, they just wanted to get the job done. By contrast, English employees in London had no real attachment to their work; it was just a way to pay the bills.

We ran a three-shift, 24-hour system, picking people up and dropping them back home, giving them furnishing allowances, holiday time to explore India and a smart working environment. Prashant's mother helped some of them to decorate their homes, picking out Indian drapes, rugs and lamps for them and making sure they were comfortable.

From the UK side, Tani spent a lot of time building Tecnovate and working with Prashant. He credits her with teaching him a great deal about the travel business and how to make sure the nuts and bolts of the company were in place. He and I also worked closely together. I invited Prashant on several road show tours of the United States and Europe. We would discuss the vision and strategy of the company and how we wanted to expand.

One unusual feature of Tecnovate was its relatively complex set of responsibilities: in contrast to the low value tasks demanded by many Indian BPO centres, we recruited and trained people in sales, marketing, IT and website production, accountancy and human resources. These skills were extremely valuable for people to use later in their careers. We set up our own training school, made sure that we were teaching an approved curriculum and turned our best employees into travel gurus.

Prashant's focus was on high quality, high end standards of service. Recruiting trained IT staff was a costly business, but he had a solution for this: he charged people to take courses at the Travel Guru training centre, making it a source of profit as well as a recruitment ground for Tecnovate. We tapped into a growing demand among young people to get into the travel industry. Once they'd trained with us, they could look for jobs at British Airways,

Virgin Atlantic or Thomas Cook. I think we were the first company in India to do online interviews: we'd ask questions on geography, we'd do role playing with them. We paid three times more than they would earn in airline offices, so we attracted high quality people. And the fact that they treated work in the travel industry as a career, rather than as casual work, also helped improve our retention rates.

Another advantage was how quick they were to spot opportunities. For example, if someone booked a flight to Florida, 90 per cent of the time they would also want a hire car. So our people at Tecnovate would call up the customers and offer them a car. We'd use these techniques to coach our staff in the UK. If they didn't listen to the training or the advice, we'd let them go.

Prashant kept people on their toes by rotating them around different departments, keeping them fresh and challenged. The ones that showed good potential were soon promoted. For example a young woman called Sabina Chopra joined Tecnovate as a customer service assistant. Prashant moved her around the company, finding that she excelled wherever he put her, until she was virtually running the whole business. In 2006, she set up a travel company with some partners. Yatra is now listed on the Nasdaq and is the second-largest online Indian travel agency.

Tecnovate emerged at an opportune time for us, just as India became capable of hosting businesses of this sort. Up until the end of the 1990s, the country just didn't have sufficiently reliable or affordable high-speed data connectivity. It routinely took months to get a simple phone line installed, never mind a whole datacentre. So just as going online gave ebookers a competitive marketing and price advantage over our UK rivals, Tecnovate delivered cost and efficiency advantages ahead of our peers. I would give Prashant much of the credit for this performance. He spotted the opportunity to develop a semi-autonomous operation, connected by service-level agreements and an incremental approach to its responsibilities. He was tremendously innovative, at a time when BPOs were the focus of stiff criticism in the West, making sure that Tecnovate not only performed well but constantly kept us ahead of the competition. I think he would credit me with giving him the freedom to develop the business in his own way, to evolve his own hiring strategy and to take on responsibilities that others might not have permitted.

I would never have started up such an operation in a country that I didn't know well – Japan, for example, or Russia. It was a huge bonus to have someone like Prashant in charge, who I could trust completely, who was extremely well-qualified to run the business, and for the whole operation to be in a familiar culture, where I understood the customs and business environment. India wasn't a great country to sell to, but it was a fantastic place to employ people and put your back office.

Since we founded Tecnovate, BPO operations in India have multiplied enormously. In the aviation industry alone, companies like US giant Delta Air Lines have become customers – it started working with Wipro Spectramind in 2003, saving itself more than $12 million a year. Wipro has also worked with Boeing and lots of other airlines. By 2003, ebookers was saving around £5 million a year thanks to Tecnovate and the BPO operation itself was valued at $160 million. Not a bad return on £25,000 and a few shares three years earlier.

Chapter 9
Selling Ebookers

In 2004 we had three million people a month visiting our website. When you think that, at the time, only 10 per cent of European travel bookings were made online, this was a very big number. Sales were going like the clappers at $1 billion a year, our network of businesses in 11 countries was thriving, we had tied down a great selection of airline and hotel deals… what could go wrong?

From painful experience, we knew that there's a long list of things that can go wrong in the travel industry: recessions, terrorist attacks, wars and pandemics can shut down the industry almost overnight. But in 2004, besides the re-election of George W Bush as US President in November, there was little to trouble the global economy. Perhaps the most significant event was the launch of Facebook in February 2004, followed by its astronomical growth to 1 million users by the end of the year.

We knew that, like Facebook, American online travel companies were growing at breakneck speed. Up until this point, only a couple had ventured across the Atlantic: Travelocity and (particularly) Expedia, which had won a share of the market alongside us and Lastminute.com.

My original plan was always to sell ebookers to an American company. It made logical sense to me that an American business would look at Europe's 300 million consumers and recognise a market similar to its own: a relatively wealthy population, quickly embracing the internet and using it to book flights, hotels, hire cars and insurance, just as people had begun to do in the States.

As early as 2000, just a year after we went public, I discussed selling ebookers to Expedia. Travelocity looked at us too – I remember having meetings with the CEO, where I explained our situation. Our share capital in 2000 was around $700 million, so it would have been a smart time to sell, in retrospect. One always thinks that companies will carry on becoming more valuable indefinitely…

Buying 11 companies across Europe was central to this plan to appeal to US buyers. They wouldn't want to spend time and resources buying a series of European companies and then have to integrate them all, with their different languages, technologies and cultures. We did the hard work for them, they could buy a going concern covering the whole continent, with a website featuring 11 little flags to click on. In the US, 30 per cent of travel bookings were made online – triple the European number. American online travel companies figured that this European percentage would quickly rise, so they wanted to get a foothold in the market and capitalise on the growth.

In 2002 we'd bought a UK-based, traditional bricks and mortar company called Travelbag Holdings, owned by an Australian called Peter Wade, who wanted to sell so he could go back home where his family had made money from the Woolworths chain of shops. It was a long-haul specialist, like us, based in the English countryside, with a nice, profitable sideline of African safari holidays. I bought the company for £50 million in ebookers' shares, then sold the African safari business to Lunn Poly for £5 million. Travel Bag added to our attractiveness for American buyers – it broadened our brand and gave us greater credibility. Plus it was profitable, which was quite a rarity among travel companies.

The Americans were aware of us, partly because we'd listed on the Nasdaq exchange, which was almost entirely made up of US companies. Every three months, I'd tour the East and West coasts on roadshows, telling them how well we were doing, how we were delivering results. If we did indeed deliver, our share price went up.

Ringing the opening bell with Tani at the Nasdaq, 2004

Once we'd recovered from the nightmare of 9/11, survived the 2002 SARS health crisis and the First Iraq War of 2003, we entered relatively calm waters. Then in spring 2004 Tani said she was keen for us to sell. We figured that the American competitors in Europe were growing ever stronger, they were spending $90 million a year on marketing compared with our $18 million, the margins on flights were getting smaller and so investors became more interested in hotel booking companies. Airlines like Ryanair and easyJet were selling flights direct to customers over the internet, with others promising to do the same. We saw the writing on the wall and decided it was time to get out.

First of all, I had to persuade ebookers' independent directors that selling the business was a good idea: they looked after 60 per cent of the shares while I had 40 per cent. One director was David Gill, the MD of Manchester United, another was John Donaldson, the chairman of Thomas Cook travel company. They gave their blessing to the attempt to sell.

From April 2004 I became completely focused on selling the company. I appointed bankers in June, when the share price on the Nasdaq was $7 or $8, and then by the time we sold it had reached $12. When we went public in 1999 our market cap was $306 million and we sold at $471 million, so we did well. We built the business.

I appointed Credit Suisse as our bankers on the basis that they were a lazy bunch, but they were cheap. Then I made a list of five or six companies that might buy us and rang their managing directors to ask: "Are you interested?" All of them said yes, so they had to sign a memorandum of confidentiality. I invited them all to our data room, where they could look through our documents. Some of them were our competitors and the airline contract documents were very interesting for them. One was the private equity firm Bridgepoint, which generally invests in companies of our size, but soon decided they weren't sufficiently interested, compared with our travel industry competitors.

Alongside Bridgepoint, there were three big travel companies in the mix: Cendant, Priceline and Sabre Holdings Corporation. Cendant was the world's biggest travel business. It already owned Avis car rental, the Ramada hotel franchise and Orbitz, the second-largest online US travel business, which it bought for $1.2 billion earlier in 2004. It was clearly on a buying spree and had also bought the UK travel company Gullivers for $1.1 billion, which was weighted on hotel bookings. We were in line to become Cendant's European branch.

Cendant's biggest competitors were IAC/InterActiveCorp, which owned Expedia, and Sabre Holdings Corporation, which owned Travelocity. Sabre owned the software that we used to start ebookers, so there was an industry logic in the company buying us, particularly since Travelocity was aiming to expand in Europe and it could consolidate its market share. At that time, the Europe online travel market was dominated by us, Lastminute.com and Expedia.

Out of six, one fell away very soon, two spent a lot of time on the documents (we could see how long, because they had to log in and out of our virtual document room). Three others just looked at the deals and said no. I guess their deals with the airlines weren't as good as ours, so they went off to renegotiate them. For a while, we were down to two companies: Cendant and Priceline. But we could see that Priceline weren't seriously interested in buying the business, they were just looking at our contracts. Finally, there was one company left: Cendant. At this point, the serious, detailed and lengthy negotiations over terms and conditions began between us. One of the biggest issues was that, as a relatively young company, Cendant wanted to be reassured that we weren't going to collapse as quickly as we'd arrived. Selling a young company is one of the hardest things to do in business. You have to persuade the seller that the wrinkles they see in the business are just a function of its youth, rather than a problematic weakness. So your whole pitch is to sell based on the future potential of the business, rather than on its current situation.

All buyers are risk averse and have a desire for growth, so it's a matter of satisfying them on both of these scores, which is easy to say but very difficult to achieve. They asked us hundreds of questions, which we had to answer truthfully and transparently, but then we would keep talking and explain that any problems might not be as bad as they seem, and that the future growth in online travel bookings would be rich compensation.

The truth is that any fast-growing company is fragile. No managers have been in their positions for very long, the company cannot point to decades of performance or its experience of dealing with industry cycles. Of course, in the few years that we'd been operating, we had endured some dramatic events, like the dot.com crash and 9/11, which had caused some of our competitors to collapse. Even so, Cendant made it clear that it was taking a step of faith in buying us and we had to reassure them. We had to be honest and admit that, yes, we're a young, fragile company, but look at the future growth potential!

Cendant wanted evidence that ebookers was 'bomb-proof'. We couldn't give them exactly this guarantee, so we had to explain how it was on its way to this point. They wanted to know how ebookers would continue to acquire customers – one of the most important, and most expensive factors in any online business's success. They asked whether we had enough resources to compete in customer acquisition against our rivals. The only way we could answer this convincingly was to point out how we'd built the business in a very different way, based on our 20 years' experience in Flightbookers. Whereas other companies used large amounts of capital for customer acquisition, we understood the industry better than them, so we could convert a higher percentage of website visitors into customers.

I had faith that the company I'd built was resilient and solid. Earlier, we'd had marketing deals with AOL and Yahoo! which created a huge pool of customers who were familiar with the brand and likely to return to us regularly for their travel bookings. We now had hotel and car hire deals in countries across Europe, which were profitable and reliable. We had thousands of employees who were well-trained, hardworking and could execute our plans. And we had growing sales figures, thanks to successful marketing deals, with good momentum for the future. (This turned out to be true, because by the time ebookers was sold to Expedia in October 2015, its sales had doubled to $2 billion a year).

Our Tecnovate BPO division in India was highly productive. This by itself was a major selling point: my Indian background gave me a distinct advantage in this area, more than anywhere else. While US companies had long understood the potential of India as a way to achieve competitive gains, through wage differentials and India's huge reserve of highly qualified graduates, Europe was slower off the mark. Half of the Fortune 500 companies in the early 2000s outsourced some functions to India, whereas in Europe it was a rarity. We realised we could pay these graduates excellent local salaries and still make significant cost savings on equivalent business costs in the West. Communications technology in India had become cheap and reliable, so Tecnovate gave us a tremendous boost in our negotiations with buyers, saving us upwards of $5 million a year. Beyond even these savings, the operation promised to become a profit centre for ebookers, with the potential to offer its services to third parties and earn money from its training division, Travel Guru.

Across the whole of ebookers, we were efficient, our HR department worked extremely well: our supervisors and leaders sorted out personnel issues without having to involve me. And most importantly, we had these three million customers a month clicking on our website. This was the biggest carrot for our prospective American buyers. How else could they attract three million Europeans?

One fundamental debate was over our growth rate: were we growing sustainably, year on year, or were the peaks and troughs simply responses to events? Figures like sales projections, share prices and even a company's annual results are open to scrutiny and subjective analysis. The press liked to take a negative angle if they could find one, which might be something unrelated to our actual performance, such as releasing sales figures which (while excellent) were slightly lower than someone had forecast. You needed a certain amount of ice in your veins to deal with all these issues.

In fact, the whole process was pretty nerve-racking. Once you give people access to your papers, they start asking questions to your mid-management, so you lose control of how the deal progresses. People inside the company were leaking information to the press. You can't say anything if it contradicts what others have said and confuses the buyers. Cendant had the run of our offices and they spent lots of time with our people.

In the end, it came down to a series of negotiations on price: there wasn't much history to base the valuation on, because we were one of the first European online companies to be sold. We pointed out the multiples of earnings that they'd paid for Orbitz and we came to a compromise – $471 million, which equalled half of our annual sales. They wanted to show that they'd paid very little for the company, so their shareholders and the market (including the financial press) would be pleased and applaud the deal. They were buying our debt as well as the assets of the business, and they were keen to make it sound like a really good deal for them and a precedent for future deals. In most M&A deals, the buyer's share price falls, so they were trying to minimise how much of a loss they suffered on the stock market.

After we signed the deal, they imposed conditions on the sale, dictating how it was announced. I wasn't allowed to issue my own press release, only one that they'd approved. They put words into my mouth, with the final 2 December 2004 notice saying:

"ebookers has become a leader in European online travel and today's transaction represents a logical next step in the company's development. Within the Cendant group, ebookers will be well placed to take the business to the next level, building on our existing strengths in Europe, and excellence in value-add services such as long haul and hotels. This is good news for our customers, our shareholders and our employees."

If it was my decision, I wouldn't have used the phrase "and excellence in value-add services" which was almost meaningless and grammatically incorrect. But these are the minor compromises that can crop up in business deals. The main point was that we were happy, they were happy and we concluded 2004 with a signed, watertight agreement.

For their part, Samuel Katz at Cendant said that the deal "immediately strengthens Cendant's position as one of the world's leading online travel distributors and provides a foundation for significant growth opportunities in the fast-growing European online segment." (He also described us as a 'tuck-in', which was a casual phrase to use about a billion dollar a year business.)

In a similar way to how I'd set up ebookers in 1996 and gone public in 1999, selling the company was ahead of the rest of the market, at least in Europe. We were pretty much the first European travel agency to go online, the first to list on the stock exchanges and the first to sell. There are advantages and disadvantages in this leadership: you are testing the water ahead of everyone else, who then has the benefit of avoiding your mistakes, potentially getting a better deal and paying less for services and getting paid more when they sell. On the other hand, first mover advantage counts for a lot. We attracted early adopters to our website ahead of the competition, achieved a stock market listing just in time before the dot.com crash, and sold before online company valuations plunged after the 2008 credit crisis.

When you're first into the market, your brand gets an extra bonus: you're associated with something new, with being a pioneer, offering something that nobody else has thought of. Then, to make the company truly saleable, you have to work like a dog for 14 to 16 hours a day, put in the graft, try to get into an expanding market, achieve some sort of monopoly, buy cheap and sell expensive. You need access to cash, you need to be lucky, to be able to persuade Private Equity companies to give you money, sell to investors and to shareholders.

These were all important elements in building the company ready to be sold. It sounds complicated, but from a certain point of view it was easy. Thousands of businesspeople have followed the same pattern; all you have to do is repeat the process.

One of the things that I believe puts people off starting a business, or expanding it to a large scale, is hiring top advisers – lawyers, bankers and consultants. I'm acutely wary of wasting money, since experience has taught me that keeping costs down is the key to financial success, but you have to learn to distinguish between wasteful and useful investment in expert help. As my colleague Sanjiv Talwar, who co-founded ebookers with me and became group managing director, remembers from the early 2000s, we had lawyers coming out of our ears. We had lawyers for Flightbookers, ebookers, for our bankers JP Morgan, employment lawyers, acquisitions lawyers. There were more lawyers in the office than anyone else.

Each of these lawyers were expensive to hire, but they each added a layer of certainty to our operations. If anyone challenged us, or tried to defraud us, we could rely on this legal advice in any court case – or simply to warn other people not to mess with us. The same is true of bankers. It's tempting to dismiss bankers as unnecessary, or as parasites feeding off hard working businesses. My experience is that, so long as you choose wisely, they add a tremendous amount to a company and it's worth paying generously for good advice. Our lawyers and bankers had experience in areas like stock markets and acquisitions which we didn't have, so we could depend on them to guide us.

Cendant certainly relied on their lawyers to advise them. We worked out they must have spent $30 million on legal fees going through our documents.

Three weeks after we concluded the sale, I was in Thailand on holiday with my family, staying at the Chiva-Som health resort on the east coast for Christmas. On Boxing Day, we walked along the beach and the sea was way out, maybe half a mile further away from the shore than usual. Later we discovered that on the other side of the country, and in Indonesia, India and Sri Lanka and all around the Indian Ocean, a massive tsunami had devastated thousands of communities, killing 230,000 people. It was one of the strangest sensations I've ever felt. Animals that were tethered to buildings broke free despite injuring themselves and ran to higher ground, well before the wave hit the shore. A friend of mine was on a boat and the captain turned it around and went out to sea, because he could tell something was wrong.

The pain and suffering that the Boxing Day tsunami caused was tremendous and it had a long-lasting effect on the whole region. It was just the kind of devastating, unpredictable disaster that could destroy careful plans, not only of businesses, but of entire countries. I was thankful that we'd already sold ebookers and were no longer at the mercy of dreadful events like this, in a business sense at least.

There were other reasons why I felt relieved and grateful to have sold ebookers. Its valuation fluctuated wildly over the five years between stock market listing and sale, up as high as $750 million and down as low as $60 million. Our stock price on the London Stock Exchange went from 600p in early 2003, down to 140p in the summer of 2004, then back up to 320p by the time we sold the company at the end of the year. You could never be sure that the highs would last, or that you could recover from the lows, so selling at a valuation of $471 million, well above our IPO level of $306 million, was a blessing and a calming reward for years of hard work, not only with ebookers but with Flightbookers for 20 years before that. We'd become used to the quarterly routine of touring the States and presenting our results to investors, but this was another potential cause of concern – each quarter you were at risk of the company taking a sharp nosedive, if the results didn't look good. As long as you had two good quarters in a row, you were saleable.

By nature, I prefer to create and build things rather than to manage them, so once ebookers had reached a certain stage, my instinct was to sell it and move on, rather than to settle into a more pedestrian rhythm, keeping the business ticking over. Of course, part of the motivation was to make some money, but part was to move on to the next adventure.

How I Felt After the Sale

The money finally hit my bank account in March 2005, three months after the deal was concluded. Although everything had been signed and legally fixed, my policy is never to fully relax until the money enters my bank account. But what then? How was I going to spend the rest of my life?

According to my agreement with Cendant, I was supposed to spend nine months still working in the business. But when I called up to ask about where I should work, they told me it wouldn't be necessary. The same thing happened to a few dozen of my colleagues at ebookers: we'd put aside £4 million as bonuses for 60 of them, if they stayed for a year after the sale. Then we discovered that Cendant had paid them off ahead of time and let them go. They wanted a clean sweep. You can see the logic in this, but it still surprised me and I was sad to see the company's results suffer in the following years. I'll always feel somewhat responsible for ebookers, whoever owns the company, so I'd rather see it prosper.

Waking up in March 2005 with £100 million in my bank account was a surreal experience. I'd spent all my life trying to make money. Then, when you've made it, you don't know what to do next. It takes time to get into the 'giving' mode and think about charity work.

The point is about getting money is that you're not prepared, you're not qualified or expert in any other business, so you can't simply branch off at random. Property was the only thing I understood, other than the travel business (and my 10-year, £5 million non-compete clause meant I had to stay out of travel).

Meanwhile, there were a few projects going on, like renovating our Surrey home in Wentworth, west of London, on the golf course. Slowly, I gave up some of the things that I'd become used to paying for, like the contract for a private jet that took me to our European offices. Other than Tani taking her friends to Milan for shopping expeditions, I barely used it any more. When you live 15 minutes away from Heathrow, what's the point of driving to a private airport and paying thousands of pounds an hour to fly somewhere? I can only think of a couple of occasions where using the private plane saved us a lot of trouble: one was going to Biarritz in southwest France, which had no direct connections from London. The same applied to my apartment in Trump International Tower on Columbus Circle in New York. I sold that in 2014 or 2015.

With spare time on my hands, I began to play more golf and took up shooting, which was something my father enjoyed. I went to Purdey's in South Audley Street and paid a lot of money for a pair of guns. Really, I didn't know what to do with myself at first. You never think you're going to make serious money. You find yourself thinking: 'How did that happen?'

There are lots of things that I enjoy, which wealth brings you. Going to the semi-finals and finals at Wimbledon; playing golf at Queenwood; staying in the best spa hotels in the world. It's nice to spend money when you have it. After all, you're only *nouveau riche* once.

How the Media Reported Our Sale

Dealing with the press was a constant background factor in the sales process. Our early experience of media coverage in 1999 was overwhelmingly positive: journalists were excited by the novelty of the internet, by our rapid expansion and soaring sales figures, by our Nasdaq listing and acquisition campaign. Both in the UK and across Europe, newspapers, magazines, TV and radio stations were keen to hear from internet entrepreneurs. We were at the cutting edge of technology and it appealed to their readers, viewers and listeners. They could see how much time, effort and money we could save them.

Then since the dot.com bust of 2000 and 9/11, the whole online sector suffered from a press backlash. We regularly appeared on lists of 'doomed' companies who were about to collapse. The press reported on every shift in our stock price, speculating on whether this meant we were in trouble, or about to be acquired.

Media relations is a fine art. I had great support from my PR person, Oliver Strong, who was and is a good friend. He helped me to remain alert to press relations, partly because they influenced our stock price, especially at the time of our quarterly reports to the Nasdaq exchange, and six-monthly reports to the London Stock Exchange. Besides Oliver, we contracted out to two external PR companies, Cubitt Consulting for the financial press and Burson-Marsteller for consumer media.

Ever since ebookers and Lastminute listed on the stock markets within a few months of each other in 1999 and 2000, we'd been close rivals. This appealed to the financial press, who covered it in the style of Borg-McEnroe or *Beauty and the Beast*. With their appointment of Allan Leighton as Chairman, they had the ear of many City journalists, who dutifully wrote up their latest news as the darlings of the online sector. We were seen more as the plodders, so to speak. But in the long term, I'd say we got the better of them. The perceived rivalry in the media probably helped both of us, by pushing us to try harder.

Once it came to selling the business, the stakes were much higher than mere beauty contests between me and Martha Lane Fox. You can plot the progress of the ebookers deal through a series of articles, published between September and December 2004 in the *Financial Times*. First, it reported on 9 September that we were 'in talks with several interested parties' about selling the group. It noted approvingly that our share price (on the London Stock Exchange) had risen by 45p the previous day, following the announcement. We didn't say who was interested in buying, but the paper correctly guessed that IAC/InterActiveCorp and Sabre Holdings were 'potential candidates' while Lastminute.com wasn't interested. The article ended by saying: 'The shares rallied on upbeat interim results when Dinesh Dhamija, chief executive, said trading in July and early August was much stronger than before'. This sums up how subjective impressions can move the market.

More troubling coverage came on 5 October, when the *Financial Times* reported that InterActive had pulled out of contention for buying us. Our shares dipped by 17p, a move the FT described as 'fell sharply', on the news. The report was generally gloomy, talking about 'the investor caution that has overhung the company because of negative statements and profit warnings in the past two years.' It compounded this downbeat impression by saying that I was 'unavailable for comment', which was unusual for me. Journalists are by nature hungry for news and if the sales process was simply proceeding smoothly, there'd be nothing for them to write. Even the FT, which is perhaps the most sober and responsible of papers, isn't immune from this. It headlined the article 'Expedia's owner walks away from Ebookers auction'.

A month later, we were all smiles again. On 15 November the *FT* published a longer news story announcing that private equity firm Bridgepoint Capital was a prospective bidder for ebookers. It quoted me giving a highly optimistic forecast: "The recovery of the European mid and long-haul travel market looks set to continue throughout 2005," I said. "In addition, European customers continue to show increasing internet take-up for travel purchases." In a textbook example of how figures can be presented in different ways, this article praised how we had 'narrowed' our pre-tax losses, while turnover rose by 11 per cent. It noted how we were buying offline travel companies in order to put their business on the internet. "This shift has positive implications for growth rates and 2005 profitability as online channels have higher growth rates and are more profitable than the offline channel, primarily due to lower fulfilment costs," we told the *FT*. We were also investing more into profitable 'non-air' activities like hotel booking and car hire. "The push into hotel bookings is set to continue, with the recruitment of a dedicated hotel team and the launch of Hotelbookers.com by the end of the year," it concluded.

This article was very well timed for us. Whatever negative implications Cendant might have drawn from our pre-tax losses or our rising operating costs, they could take comfort from this barrage of positive messages, the ambitious plans, the 'excellent progress' that we convinced the FT to document and the presentation of future market developments as though they were established fact. The article uses the phrases 'looks set to continue' and 'is set to continue', which, to anyone who studies the financial press, is code for 'might or might not (but we're crossing our fingers)'.

Finally, once the deal was announced, the *FT* ran a news story to tell the world how Cendant, 'the world's largest travel group' had bought us as part of 'the consolidation sweeping the online travel sector'. It speculated that the deal would put pressure on IAC/InterActive to push on with Expedia's European plans. And as ever, it reported how the deal affected share prices: Cendant's shares on the Nasdaq fell by 0.7 per cent while ours rose by exactly double – 1.4 per cent.

Chapter 10
Philanthropic Giving and Human Rights

Jobs give people self-respect. The human instinct to be needed by society and to provide for one's family is crucially satisfied by employment. So I've always concentrated on ways to boost employment, both in my own business activities and in the companies that I've supported through mentorship, offering management advice or as a trustee. In my political work too, I've tried to raise employment, whether in the UK, in Europe or in India.

Wherever you look today, old technologies are replaced by new ones, causing a constant churn of jobs. Yet so many people who lose their jobs as a result are unprepared, with disastrous consequences. In response, I've contributed to educational and health charities which prepare people for work and sought to help businesses that provide employment. The point is for people to work and pay taxes, rather than being a burden on the State.

Naturally there are others who are unable to work, through misfortune, disability, or insufficient training. But my focus through my charity and philanthropic work has been on those who can work.

One of the things I'm most proud of in my years building and managing businesses was the thousands of jobs that I created. At ebookers, we went from zero to 2000 jobs in the space of four years. This was in the early days of the internet revolution and many companies have replicated this astonishing growth since then, using the power of digital technology.

By creating well-paying jobs, you extend people's horizons, train and educate them and add to the well-being of society as a whole. It was very satisfying to build businesses across Europe and in India. In London alone I employed more than 5,000 people over 25 years in business.

Since selling ebookers in 2005 I've mentored a series of companies with a unique USP or technology, with the potential to create many hundreds of jobs and improve people's lives. For example Thesqua.re provides serviced apartments to businesspeople when they're away from home, so they have somewhere convenient and comfortable to stay at an affordable price. It's basically an Airbnb for corporates. I've watched the CEO Sid Narang grow this company from modest beginnings to its current size, with more than 100 employees, managing 126,000 apartments in 300 cities. Plus he's transformed it into a technology company from its bricks and mortar beginnings.

At the non-profit group TiE (The Indus Entrepreneurs – originally an Indian-heritage group in Silicon Valley), I manage a special interest group on sustainability and mobility, which helps entrepreneurs embrace new ideas and adopt green technologies. TiE has been important for me in all kinds of ways, as I've mentioned elsewhere. Until 2020 I was vice-chairman of TiE Global and now I'm head of global fundraising. But as a charitable organisation, it helps thousands of people get a start in their business lives and promotes employment, which is how I think business can have the greatest impact on society. It shows people how to become (and stay) an entrepreneur, and has established an ecosystem to support them.

TiE started up in 1992 and has spread to 20 countries, with 3,000 charter members. It supports youth and women's networks, it's opening a university and runs pitching competitions. For example, in 2018 we promised to invest £50,000 in a fintech company and had 70 start-up companies pitching to us at the Lansdowne Club on Berkeley Square. You see the effects all over the world: we set up 30 Indian entrepreneurs in Nairobi, in Kenya, after they appealed to us for help. In February 2020 we were looking at 100 start-ups, working out which one to fund. One year five of us invested in a young company and each received £23,000 dividend after 10 months, when it was acquired by another company.

Entrepreneurs and senior businesspeople from an Indian heritage are hugely over-represented in the UK and the United States. If you look at the Fortune 500 companies, many of the largest are run by Indians (or people with Indian roots), including Google, Microsoft, Adobe, Pepsi, Nokia, Deloitte, Novartis, Mastercard, Diageo and NetApp. I think that what the University of Southern New Hampshire said about Indian managers, that they have a 'paradoxical blend of genuine personal humility and intense professional will' is something to do with their success. I also think that the drive to expand employment opportunities, so central to Indian businesspeople's motivations, is a big factor. Your employees instinctively recognise whether you value them, or whether they're simply working to please your shareholders.

It always gave me great satisfaction to see my employees develop, to take on more responsibilities and to bring others along with them. I always wanted to hire and retain the best people, to incentivise them and nurture their careers. Over the years, 11 of my UK-based employees became millionaires in ebookers.

In the UK, I admire the Winston Churchill Memorial Trust, which awards 150 Fellowships each year so that young British people can travel for a month or two, anywhere in the world, to research ideas by meeting experts, then pass on what they've learnt when they come back. It's an inspiring organisation and I've donated to support their work. It helps equip people for the workplace, broadens their horizons and helps them to see the relevance of education and training to their own futures.

I came to support the Memorial Trust through someone from a similar background to me. Shreela Flather is an Anglo-India campaigner and politician, the first Asian woman to get a peerage. She was voted Asian of the Year in 1996 and lives not far away from me in Maidenhead, where she used to be Mayor. She shares my commitment to raising people's aspirations and helping them to become productive members of society.

Tony Bourne, an old schoolfriend who was a partner at the merchant bank Hawkpoint for many years, and on the board of BNP Paribas, introduced me to the cerebral palsy charity Scope, and I ended up joining its advisory board. In Scope's case, it does extraordinary work assisting people who have tremendous challenges in their lives, whether in mobility, education or finding employment. I felt it was important to make a contribution in this way, as well as through supporting entrepreneurship. Basically, I believe it is the duty of businesspeople to make philanthropic donations.

On a similar theme, I support the work of Lepra, a charity helping people with leprosy and researching ways to prevent the disease. I joined as a trustee and was amazed at how widespread leprosy still is, with hundreds of cases diagnosed every day in India, Pakistan, Bangladesh and some African countries.

Although some of my charitable work and donation has happened since 2005, I was already involved in the voluntary sector in the 1990s, as our business began to grow. Some of this has been with spiritual-focused groups such as the Swami Narayan temples in North London and temples in India. My wife Tani is more involved in this area than I am, but I do recall one event which opened my eyes to a certain kind of spiritual energy.

I was at a London reception in 1978, in my late 20s, with a cigarette in one hand and a glass of Scotch in the other. An older woman said to me: "Come here, and get rid of the whisky." She instructed me to sit on the floor with my back to her and then put her knee in my back and clicked my shoulders. It all happened quite quickly and I was sceptical that anything had changed. One of her followers was at the party and saw what had happened. "You'll give up smoking and drinking," he told me. "No way!" I replied. "Nobody tells me what to do!"

Sure enough, a couple of weeks later, cigarettes began to taste stale, so I threw them away. And since I wasn't doing very well financially, I decided to give up both smoking and drinking for a while. I didn't drink again for 36 years, until I succumbed back to the poison in 2014 when I became involved in politics, where non-drinkers are viewed as deviants. And I've still never smoked another cigarette.

It turned out that this lady was Shri Mataji Nirmala Devi, who founded her own branch of yoga – Sahaja – and addressed the United Nations several times on ways to achieve peace. Her philosophy is that everyone has the power to heal themselves and can heal others. If your chakras are open, then your energy makes you balanced. And the moment you're balanced, then you can heal people. I later discovered that she had turned hundreds if not thousands of people away from alcohol – a great service to humanity in my view.

Just to the south of New Delhi, the Guruji Temple at Bade Mandir welcomes 20,000 people every day and more than 100,000 on special occasions, feeding everyone with a traditional langar vegetarian meal, no matter where they are from or whatever their religion or background. Together with Tani, we made a substantial donation to this temple, so that it can heal people, both spiritually and mentally. There's ever more demand for this kind of sanctuary, where you can escape the madness of everyday life. I think that temples and churches play an underestimated role in nurturing people's mental health.

At Bade Mandir, we knew the spiritual leader Guruji in the 1990s, but there were few visitors to his temple in those days. Now, although he died in 2007, his movement has become phenomenally popular: other people have donated and thousands have benefited. I like to take a focused 'rifle shot' rather than a scattered 'shotgun' approach to charitable giving, choosing a target like this and making a meaningful donation. Guruji's foundation is also very active in the UK, where the congregation visit elderly people to comfort them and provide company and langar food for gurdwaras in London.

In London, I visit Hindu temples in Ealing and Neasden, particularly on special occasions. But overall, I like to think that wherever you are is your temple. Attending a temple, or church, is good for the spirit. In fact I think that spiritual and mental healing is why temples exist.

In 1999 I decided to establish a charity of my own, called Chikitsa – a Sanskrit word meaning 'medicine' or 'therapy'. I based it in Gurgaon, 36km south of Delhi, where massive construction projects have transformed parts of the city into gleaming skyscrapers and ultra-wealthy residential colonies. But in Old Gurgaon [now known as Gurugram], thousands of people lived without running water or sanitation, with little public infrastructure or services. The population of Gurgaon has more than tripled from around 850,000 in 2001 to 2.7 million today: there are more than 12,000 construction companies listed in local directories and hundreds of building projects under way. The phenomenal pace and scale of India's urbanisation leaves many victims in its wake. In 2020 you could see the mass of migrant workers as they left Delhi during the coronavirus lockdown.

The first priority was to offer free primary healthcare to communities where many are unable to afford it. I founded it together with my father-in-law, General OP Malhotra, who had retired after a distinguished career as head of the Indian Army, ambassador to various countries, including Russia, and Governor of Punjab. He was able to recruit a number of retired army doctors to volunteer for Chikitsa and had already held senior roles in major Indian charities for blind and deaf people and as President of the Equestrian Federation of India (where he once demonstrated the sport of 'tent pegging' to the Duke of Edinburgh).

All we asked from patients was a one-off fee of Rs10 – about ten British pence – towards their medical history paperwork. Everything else is free. And for the past 21 years we've treated more than 120,000 people each year through 15 clinics in the poorest areas of Delhi, Gurgaon and Manesar, where we look after the health needs of construction workers and their families among others. Whenever there is a healthcare crisis, we are quick to respond. For example, we cured more than 1100 tuberculosis patients in Delhi National Capital Region and have worked hard to help people affected by the coronavirus pandemic. We founded a specific Vector Borne Disease Prevention programme in Sangam Vihar, New Delhi, in 2017, to combat the rising incidence of malaria and dengue fever in the city.

We also offer mobile clinics which can visit rural or poorly-served communities: many people are so ill that they're not able to travel to get medical help. Each bus costs £20,000 to equip and they're very narrow 'Maruti' buses, so they can drive through the tight streets of poor villages. (Maruti, by the way, started in 1982 as a joint venture between Suzuki Motor Company and the Indian government and makes upwards of a million cars and trucks every year, maintaining a 55 per cent share of the Indian market despite fierce competition from Tata and other importers.)

One side-effect of a massive construction programme is that many workers lose limbs. So we started a service offering free artificial limbs, orthotics and prosthetics and a clinic in Gurgaon. This, along with the whole of Chikitsa's work, helps relieve the pressure on the overcrowded and overstressed Indian healthcare system.

When I was in India setting up Chikitsa, I approached the local drugs companies and asked them: "When drugs are six months away from expiry, can you sell them to us?" So we get a lot of discounts. Retired doctors and medical people come and work for us for a few hours at a time. There's so much need here.

These initiatives have helped Chikitsa win all kinds of awards for good governance and CSR performance from Indian and international groups, which is very pleasing. After my father-in-law passed away in 2015, his son (my brother-in-law) Ajai Malhotra, who was an Indian ambassador like his father, took over as a trustee of the charity, together with Ajai's son Udai.

In 2002, I grew determined to offer something more to the thousands of children in Delhi and Gurgaon who faced a troubled future, growing up in these unregulated, neglected ghettos with parents working for low pay in construction. So along with my father-in-law I founded a second charity, Shiksha – meaning 'education' in Sanskrit. This offered high standard, free schooling to local children, at Education Centres where we provided books, notepads, uniforms and a nutritious mid-day meal.

The predicament that faced thousands of children was bleak. Few had official documentation, which prevented them from attending government-run schools; they had missed out on early years education, so they were behind their peers; many were children of rural migrant workers, so they faced social isolation; and the majority of families had meagre resources for living expenses, never mind education. You see kids in the dirt and their mothers are carrying bricks on their heads, walking up and down ladders. I thought it would be a good idea to offer to take the children away from their families during the daytimes, so they could get a school education.

We provided both regular courses, following the national curriculum for children, then vocational training for young people, teaching them tailoring, beautician work, English language skills and computer training for example. We also run a special school for blind students, where they are taught using Braille.

Within months of launching, we were invited to adopt a government primary school in Indira Colony at Jharsa village in Gurgaon. It was extremely basic and under-resourced: there were 40 students and one teacher, but no running water, electricity or toilets. Once we took over and upgraded the facilities, soon 300 children began attending regularly. We adopted similar schools in Jacobpura and Rosewood City, improving and modernising them before handing them back to the Haryana government.

This relationship with government schools threw up some challenges. We found that government-funded teachers had very low motivation and were poorly educated – they didn't even have teaching qualifications. They would sit around in the courtyard smoking cigarettes and drinking tea, and when they delivered milk to the children they'd dilute it and keep some back for themselves. The headmaster was unable to do anything about them, so I wanted to close the school. My father-in-law OP Malhotra argued that the kids had nowhere else to go and that they depended on us for their education, so in 2006, we rented premises at Mohyal Colony in Jharsa village and established our own Education Centre, closing down the old school. We then built this Centre up to the point where we now have more than 1100 students, many of them progressing on to further education or into paid employment – something that I'm very pleased to see.

In 2016 we set up a Computer Training Centre in Sangam Vihar – a suburb of Delhi – which is one of the largest unauthorised colonies in Asia. Two years later the Centre was accredited to the National Institute of Open Schooling, recognising its role in helping children who are left out of the formal education system get mainstream schooling.

One of the schools that we fund in a modest way is Isha Vidhya in Coimbatore, Tamil Nadu state. A pupil there called Sivasankari scored 86 per cent in her 10th grade exams and went on to study at the Kovai Kalaimagal College of Arts and Science in Coimbatore and now plans to become a teacher. Another, called Kouthama, had barely any English when he joined the Isha Vidhya school in Salem. But after a few years of hard work and persistence, he scored 1107 out of 1200 in his final year examinations and went on to study civil engineering. This is a tremendous result for a student who came from an underprivileged background and goes to prove how much a good education can change someone's prospects.

In Gurgaon, many of our pupils came to the city with their parents, who migrated from the countryside and now work as rag-pickers or as labourers. For example, we had a pupil called Sonu Kumar whose parents came from a village in Bihar, in the northeast of India. At our Education Centre in Wazirabad, a suburb of Delhi, Sonu really flourished at his studies. With the encouragement of our teachers, he won a scholarship to the elite St Paul's School in Gurgaon, one of the best schools in the region. He is consistently top of his class and plans to become a computer engineer.

Other students have excelled at sports, winning regional trophies, or taken up courses in design, maths and medicine. When Roshi arrived at our school in Gurgaon she was malnourished and reclusive, refusing to speak to anyone. After her teacher noticed an interest in drawing, she held up Roshi's artwork as an example for the rest of the class. After that, her confidence built and she is hoping to become a doctor: "I want to do well and bring light to my parents' name," she said.

Since the outbreak of the coronavirus pandemic, the level of need has shot up. There are hundreds of thousands of labourers going back home with no work to look forward to and no payments coming in. My friend Firdaus Ruttonshaw is a Parsi, who has family in Pune. His family were asked by the government to look after 12 people during the outbreak and his first cousin asked Firdaus if he could send her some money. "I've had 200 people turn up, I've got rid of 80 of them, but I still need to feed 120 people," she told him. She had raised the equivalent of about £500, which really wasn't going to go very far. So Firdaus gave her about £5,000 which would last her at least a few days. For people who are focused on charity, it's a very big issue. They feel that they're letting down the people who have built India. During the pandemic, Firdaus's brother died, leaving a valuable property as inheritance. Firdaus told his cousin to use the proceeds of the sale to feed the people, so she's carried on doing this every day.

The coronavirus pandemic is exposing many world leaders who have pursued isolationist or nationalist policies up until now. Of course the pandemic forces countries to isolate, but the response in the end has to be global rather than local. Former President Trump, with his withdrawal from the Paris Accords, from engagement with the World Trade Organisation and the World Health Organisation, was just being a brat and a bully. He lacked the brainpower to deal with this situation: he was just a businessman and there are so many elements of global society which aren't run as businesses. He bashed China, but it's a losing fight. China is spending more on research and development than the US and I think by 2030 it will be the world's largest economy. The US has to make an accommodation, but that wasn't in Trump's character.

It may seem hard to believe, but in 1991 India's GDP was equal to China's, whereas now it's less than a quarter the size. How come? I think it's the communist system, which has been able to raise a billion people out of poverty through harnessing their energies, promoted enterprise and fostered an outward looking approach to the global economy. Whereas China only banned foreign companies in order to grow their own industries, like Alibaba or Tencent, India's civil servants took an easier route, giving licences to the devils they knew, rather than creating competitive champions. For example, Coca Cola withdrew from India in 1977, after the government insisted that it reveal its formula. The Chauhan brothers introduced their own Thums Up cola, which then dominated the market until Pepsi arrived in 1991, followed by Coca Cola in 1993, which acquired Thums Up and invested in the brand – it's now the market leader among cola drinks.

India's system of licensing businesses through government departments made some ministers very powerful. If an industrialist got to know them well, it would result in monopolies. On top of that, most Indian family businesses are conglomerates. Once you have a licence to sell shoes, you can get a hotel licence, for example. Especially in manufacturing, this created a whole ecosystem of monopolies, as civil servants wouldn't give licences to anyone other than these family firms. It's not a very consumer-friendly environment and has contributed to India's poor economic record in the past.

The old Indian social system which used to condemn poor 'untouchables' from lower castes is slowly breaking down and being replaced by a more meritocratic society where hard work and persistence can result in worthwhile employment and a good standard of living. But it is a slow process and India is still reluctant to engage with the wider global community. The legal system, for example, is hopelessly outdated and inefficient. I hope that Chikitsa and Shiksha have contributed to the growing meritocracy and encouraged productivity, in however small a way.

For my own part, I benefitted enormously from my education in both India and England, thanks to my parents' determination that I should study at a good school and university. For an Indian immigrant to England (or from anywhere, for that matter), education is one of the best ways to overcome prejudice and discrimination. Things are much better today than they were in the 1960s and 1970s, when I would get racial abuse. So I'm grateful to the Mayo College in Rajasthan, St Xaviers in Delhi, King's School in Canterbury and to Fitzwilliam College, Cambridge, for the start in life that they gave me.

I donated to all of these institutions, to help them fund places for people who could benefit from a good education. At Fitzwilliam, I joined the fundraising committee alongside the former UK Chancellor of the Exchequer Norman Lamont, investor and Lord Lieutenant of Greater London Sir Ken Olisa and President of the Royal Television Society Sir Peter Bazalgette. We were all undergraduates at Fitzwilliam and each put in (or raised) at least £100,000. We then raised £20 million within seven years, before the college disbanded us.

We were very active in those years, contacting alumni, organising dinners, getting people to put endowments into their wills. Ken Olisa gave the college £2 million for a new library and they named it after him. It's the sort of thing I might possibly do in the future.

I think the system of private funding for university colleges works well, and Cambridge is one of the best at it. The colleges have an 'a la carte' approach, where you can have a ceremony at the cenotaph if you donate £1 million, or you could have two ceremonies for £2 million, one for you and one for your wife. I think that the more a college can become independent from government, the better. On one hand, the government gives Cambridge £2 billion a year and has every right to demand that it should accept more state school pupils. On the other hand, the colleges need to have a degree of academic freedom rather than simply follow government instructions. Harvard is the gold standard for this: it gets billions of dollars a year through fundraising and can offer scholarships to 70 per cent of its students.

Meeting the Queen, 2012

Giving immigrants a better chance in life, whether they've migrated from a rural Indian village to the slums of Delhi or from developing countries into England, is close to my heart. You have to distinguish between immigrants and refugees, however. Refugees have little choice in their predicament and protecting their welfare is a social service to the world. Of course their rights need to be protected. Immigrants, by contrast, are usually moving to another country in search of work, often attracted to a place because their relatives have already gone there.

Many immigrants are prepared to fill jobs that local people don't want to fill, whether because they are too menial or because of geography. You'll find that there are vacancies for nurses in Scunthorpe, but nurses in London won't want to relocate to Scunthorpe, because their children are in school, so an immigrant can do that job. This is one reason that immigration is good – it is an efficient way of allocating human resources.

Immigrants face discrimination in the UK and in Europe, in much the same way as immigrants do in any country in the world. India is one of the worst in terms of prejudice against people with a darker skin colour. What we need to remember is that immigrants are overwhelmingly good people, strong, hard workers who are desperate to earn a living and to prove themselves to those they've left behind. They want to show themselves off. And immigrants are far less likely to take the dole, they're usually more resourceful. I would always employ an immigrant over a national, because they have nothing to fall back on except hard work.

Of course, their rights need to be protected, whether they're refugees from war or despotic regimes, from persecution or natural disasters. In some cases, as with the Ugandan Asians in the 1970s, accepting them brought enormous benefits to the British because they came with expertise, skills and often with a lot of money. The same is true of Syrians and Iranians – I would take anyone who's qualified, perhaps using a points-based system.

If you compare the British system with many on the continent, we are far more relaxed about immigration: the Dutch and Germans insist on immigrants living in their countries for years before they offer social security or free healthcare. Indeed this is EU law, across the continent. It's just that the UK never implemented it.

As someone whose family comes from the Punjab, the region of northern India and Pakistan to the northwest of Delhi, I've always paid close attention to the effects of the 1947 partition which separated the two countries, causing floods of immigration in both directions, as Muslims in India fled to Pakistan while Hindus to the north sought sanctuary in India.

My family were among them, as my paternal grandparents lived in what became Pakistan and fled on bullock carts to India, accompanied by guards to protect them from pillage and rape. So the plight of communities in the subcontinent today, especially in regions such as Kashmir where ethnic and religious tensions still run high, are always concerning to me.

In the European Parliament, we had a series of debates over the policies of Indian Prime Minister Narendra Modi of the Bharatiya Janata Party (BJP – which translates as the 'Indian People's Party'), especially relating to Kashmir. In 2008 there was a wave of almost two million undocumented migrants from Pakistan and Bangladesh – mainly Christians, Sikhs and Farsis – into India, pushed out by discrimination from the Muslim majority. Modi made a distinction between these persecuted migrants, offering them Indian citizenship after six years of residency, and the Muslims who came with them, who could seek citizenship after 11 years. His reasoning was that Muslims could not face persecution in their home (Muslim-dominated) countries, so they were only coming for economic reasons.

Critics of this policy argued that people would be left stateless and living in refugee camps, and that some communities, like the Hazaras – who are Muslim, but nevertheless face persecution in Pakistan – would be left unsupported by anyone. My view was that India had the right to document anyone who arrived at its borders, and I (along with others) won this vote in the European Parliament.

Kashmir is another problem altogether, as it has been since before partition in 1947. The state has such a high degree of geo-political importance, from its actual position adjacent to China, Pakistan, Afghanistan and India, from the wealth of its water resources which supplies much of northwest India, and from its role as a microcosm of regional relations, teeming with religious and political tensions as India and Pakistan vie for supremacy.

The colonial view is that Kashmir is an Indian state, since the King of Kashmir in 1947 – Hari Singh – opted to accept India's armed forces and join India, while the Muslim Nawab of Junagarh opted for Pakistan. Every kingdom in Kashmir could choose whether to join India or Pakistan. A temporary constitution was agreed, with the promise of a plebiscite in 1949 so the Kashmiri people could decide whether to unite with India or Pakistan. However, US Admiral Chester Nimitz (who led the US armed forces to victory in the Pacific in World War II) ruled out a plebiscite, because the Pakistani forces refused to move back to the western borders of Kashmir, and so for 70 years the status quo has been a temporary constitution and an unresolved statehood.

Narendra Modi pointed out that, after 70 years, you can no longer describe the Kashmiri constitution as 'temporary' and proposed updating the law to get rid of things like child brides and the law whereby men can divorce women simply by saying 'talaq' ('divorce') three times. Kashmiri women who married outside Kashmir would lose rights to any property they held. These were clearly outdated and Modi won a lot of votes from Muslim women as a result. He had previously removed the 'talaq' rules from the whole of India, which helped him to beat Congress in the national elections because there are 200 million Muslims in the country.

What I felt about the Kashmir situation, as an MEP, was that we Europeans had no right to dictate what a democratically-elected government of another country should do. If there is violence, we can send peacekeepers, if countries are not strong enough to deal with it, but if politicians don't meet each other, then making statements about another country's policies is a waste of breath. It's just 'playing neo-colonial politics', as I said to the European Parliament. You can try to twist their arms, and hope to strengthen relations through trade deals, but otherwise you just make enemies. And what's the point of that?

I've tried hard to promote trade deals between the EU and India, and between the UK and India, as a way to boost employment across the board. Removing tariffs would have a tremendously positive effect in both Europe and in India: a deal could create up to a million jobs in the EU and three or four million in India at a stroke, by doubling trade.

There have been unintended consequences of my philanthropic giving: as head of the India desk at the European Parliament, I was pleasantly surprised when Indian government ministries gave me immediate appointments for meetings – something that would typically take weeks to arrange. It smoothed the way to meeting people I wanted to meet. (It's always good if you're giving something and you get a blessing of some sort.)

The relative poverty of Indian society means that every dollar invested has a far greater beneficial effect over there, just as every dollar donated can do more good for humanity in India than in the West. That's a big reason for me concentrating my philanthropic giving on India, especially my three charitable initiatives – Chikitsa, Shiksha and the temples – which helps hundreds of thousands of people.

Basically, there are two good things that one can do in India: take a holiday and visit the spas and luxurious hotels and sites, or donate to charity. Your money goes so much further.

Responsible Capitalism

I think that looking after employees is a good thing. By training them, you increase their horizons, and if you can motivate people it will pay dividends. At ebookers we always tried to look after employees. As the saying goes, if you pay peanuts, you get monkeys. I wanted the best people, to incentivise them. At our Indian company Tecnovate, we had a lower turnover than other BPOs (Business Process Outsourcing companies). We were settled, a known enterprise, and number one or two in our industry. It was a badge of honour to work for us.

I'm not sure what we did differently, but with 11 European companies, employees could move around the continent if they wanted, or between Europe and India. When I set up Tecnovate, the Indian embassies in Norway, Sweden and Finland had never issued work permits for India before. There were lots of firsts, from lots of points of view. There were all kinds of incentives if you worked for us.

Every company has good and bad sides but I think we did well, because we were at the forefront. People were attracted to us, they'd never seen things like this in their previous bricks and mortar companies.

Treating customers well is also very important. Customers are kings, they're always right even if they're wrong. It's better capitalism to be responsible, to make more out of every situation, to make more money but also to be sustainable. The point about sustainability is that if you misjudge it, you're dead. If you're too generous, or you cut corners, people are a great resource, but they're also fickle.

We used shares as incentives. When we sold the company, we put £4 million away for 60 people in a separate bank account, which buyers couldn't touch. Each one of the 60 original employees was allocated an account, which they could get if they stayed for a year. For example, the CFO got £400,000.

Chapter 11
My Passion for Golf

Since I was a teenager, golf has been one of my life's greatest pleasures. As a pupil at King's School Canterbury golf was a passport to acceptance by my peers; at Cambridge it provided friendships that have lasted a lifetime; in work, it fostered good relations with clients and customers; and in more recent years it has kept me fit and entertained, spending time with tour professionals, former sportspeople and ardent golfers at my local club. In my view, it is the prince of sports.

Here are my ten favourite English clubs. It's not a definitive list, just those courses I've played which have a special place in my sporting memory.

My Top 10 English Golf Clubs

1. Queenwood, Surrey

A few minutes' drive from my home, Queenwood is my favourite local club. It's famously exclusive: just a few hundred members paying well into six figures to join, which means that you can just turn up and play. Half the time there's nobody else within sight. The service is exemplary, worthy of a world-class hotel.

There are 15 tour pros among the members, people like Graeme McDowell, Justin Rose and Adam Scott. One time I played 18 holes with Ernie Els. There are footballers like Andriy Shevchenko and Alan Hansen, who both play off very low handicaps, and actors like Hugh Grant and Michael Douglas. You can end up paired with them in tournaments and socialising in the clubhouse.

Queenwood is a young club – it only opened in 2001 – but the landscape feels ancient and natural, fringed with gorse, full of delightful rolling greens, with a stately clubhouse in the background.

2. Wentworth, Surrey

My home sits next to the 17th hole of Wentworth's West Course, the best of the club's three courses. The annual PGA Championship is here and it hosted the 1953 Ryder Cup. Golfing connoisseurs call it 'the English Augusta' and there's definitely a grand sweep to the fairways, picturesque vistas of shrubbery, woods and water, and echoes of the world's best golfers performing sporting feats of genius ever since its launch in 1924.

Richard Caring kept the place in good standing during his ownership, but the standard of food has risen since Chinese investors Reignwood bought it for £135 million in 2014. I go there more for the food than the golf: you can also laze around the health spa, pool and gym.

3. Royal St George's, Kent

Rated number one in England by some, the Royal St George's links course in Sandwich, on the Kent coast, is one of the toughest tests in the sport. It's hosted the British Open 14 times since its foundation in 1887 and was due to welcome the 2020 event before COVID intervened.

For some reason, I've always played well at Royal St George's: even when the wind is blowing at 30 miles an hour, I get a good feeling. Sometimes your eye is set and you just like the way a course plays. Even the bunker on the 4th hole, apparently the highest in Britain, holds no fear for me.

James Bond author Ian Fleming was a member here and based a scene in Goldfinger on it, although the scene was filmed elsewhere. No doubt he appreciated the 'challenging golf holes, beautifully crafted greens and bunkers, a character of its own, and stunning scenery,' as one golf writer put it. For me, a visit to Royal St George's gives me a chance to catch up with my old university friend Tim Dickson, the club captain, a wonderful writer for the Financial Times who has his own publication, Golf Quarterly.

4. Sunningdale, Berkshire

Another beautifully-landscaped gem around the corner from my home, Sunningdale has an Old and a New Course, designed in 1901 and 1923, each as lovely as the other, though the New Course is tougher. They're a visual feast, with heather, pine, birch and oak trees, sandy bunkers and rolling fairways leading to expansive greens and a gorgeous clubhouse. If you get a chance to play them one after the other, it's possibly the best day's golf in the world.

There's a relaxed, 'old-money' feel about the club. Its conditioning and the clubhouse facilities are all first rate, as they have been for all these many years.

Look out for the sausage, bacon and brown sauce sandwich at the halfway house after the 10th hole, where the Old and New Courses meet.

5. Royal Worlington, Suffolk

This was the course we would escape to every week from Cambridge to practice. And what a course! Designed during the golden age of English golf course construction from the 1890s to the 1920s, it's a stern test of skill, with tight fairways, sloping greens and various water hazards to catch the unwary, especially on the treacherous fifth hole.

Golf writers like Leonard Crawley at the Daily Telegraph judged Royal Worlington the finest nine-hole course in the world, which is some compliment, given that the landscape is largely flat and the acreage limited. It shows what a master designer can achieve with imagination and patience.

6. Ganton, Yorkshire

Three miles southwest of Scarborough on the North Yorkshire coast lies Ganton Golf Club, one of the finest inland courses in Britain. It hosted the first post-War Ryder Cup match outside the US, in the days when only British and Irish players took on the Americans. Gary Player and many others loved the testing course, with its deep bunkers, gorse-fringed fairways, savage rough and frequent stiff winds.

In 1974, during my final year at Cambridge, the University team beat Oxford by nine matches to six at Ganton. So that confirmed the course as a permanent favourite in my mind. Playing for the second team, the Stymies, we were two holes down with three to play and still managed to halve the game, much to the annoyance of the Oxford Divots.

7. Brancaster, Norfolk

Officially known as the Royal West Norfolk Golf Club, Brancaster is hidden away between a tidal marsh and the North Sea on the Norfolk coast, miles from any urban distractions and one of the finest private clubs in the country. To get in and out of here, you have to watch the tide, since the road becomes impassable.

Once out on the fairways, Brancaster offers an unspoiled links course, breezy conditions and frequent water hazards including the marsh itself. Once your round is complete, settle into the mahogany-panelled clubhouse next to a roaring open fire and watch play on the 18th, with waves crashing softly in the background.

8. Westward Ho!, Devon

Another venue for the Oxbridge match, Westward Ho! In North Devon is a spectacular course by the sea, with a wide beach to the west and sandy links undulating across the landscape. Amazingly, it's the oldest course in England, created in 1864 by a vicar whose brother was a member of the Royal & Ancient in St Andrews.

Playing for the Stymies, we beat the Oxford Divots here in 1972, despite the quirky course with its local regulations. Rule number eight – a result of farmers having the right to graze their animals on the fairways - states: "A ball which lies in or touches heaped or liquid manure may be lifted without penalty, cleaned and dropped."

9. Saunton, Devon

A couple of miles north of Westward Ho! across the River Taw, Saunton is set deep into the sandy Devon dunes, challenging golfers with its pot bunkers, blind tees and lengthy fairways: there are eight par fours of more than 400 yards and a par five of 530 yards. The test is worthwhile, though, as you're immersed in a marvel of the natural world, recognised by UNESCO as a precious environmental site and home to 500 plant species.

It takes upwards of six hours to get here from London, whether you drive or take the train, which limits the crowds and makes it even more special and memorable, especially if you play both West and East courses during the day.

10. Hunstanton, Norfolk

My final pick is the links course at Hunstanton on the Norfolk coast, not far from Brancaster but with a subtly different atmosphere and challenge. The tightly-mown fairways mean you can play a 'running' game – keeping the ball low to the ground rather than lofting it into the air – which counters the fierce breezes. There's one par three hole where you'll play a nine iron if the wind is with you; a two iron if it's in your face.

In *The Golf Courses of the British Isles*, George Darwin wrote: "Hunstanton is very amusing golf" and I agree. There are frequent surprises and delights here.

My Top 10 International Golf Clubs

As a young boy living in Delhi, I first picked up a golf club at the age of four or five. The game appealed to me right away and I was soon playing nine holes, encouraged by my father. In Mauritius, where my father worked for the Indian High Commission, my game quickly improved and I came second in the under 16 tournament at the age of 10.

This set the scene for a lifetime of golfing enjoyment: there are marvellous courses in just about every country on earth, so once you are confident to play a decent round, you are guaranteed a few hours of sporting pleasure wherever you go.

Here are 10 of best international courses I've played:

1. Pine Valley, Philadelphia, United States

Rated number one in the world by many golfers, this course sets the highest standards and takes no prisoners. "It's a monster, but it's beautiful," said Robert Trent Jones, one of America's great golf writers. "Pine Valley fills you with dread and delight." The course was designed in the 1910s on sandy pine forested land outside Philadelphia by George Crump, after a tour of the great clubs of Britain and continental Europe, and has captivated golfers ever since with its breath-taking scenery and fiendishly difficult holes. It was an honour to play at this exclusive private club, where you might see former presidents and professionals out on the fairway.

2. Pebble Beach

Bang on the Pacific Ocean in Monterey in California, Pebble Beach has amazing views looking out onto Carmel Bay and is among the very best courses in America. It's hosted the US Open six times, starting in 1972 when Jack Nicklaus won it.

Pebble Beach is an awesome course. Sometimes you're standing at a tee and all you have behind you is the Pacific Ocean, with the surf crashing on the shore. All the holes are scenically wonderful, but the 18th caps them all. It has a magnificent cypress tree in the middle of the fairway, a 100-yard bunker and uninterrupted ocean views for the whole 550 yards of the hole.

3. Spyglass Hill

The sister course to Pebble Beach on the Monterey Peninsula, Spyglass was named after a place in the novel Treasure Island by Robert Louis Stevenson, who visited in 1879. All the holes are named from the book, so the 4th is Blind Pew, the 10th is Captain Flint and the 14th is Long John Silver.

The 16th ('Black Dog'), is a notoriously difficult par three, where you have to go across the sea to reach the green. When I played it there was a fresh breeze in our faces so I used a driver for the 230-yards. Out of 36 of us, only three made the green, and two of those were me and my son.

4. Delhi Golf Club

This is where it all began for me, back in the 1950s when I would play here with my father and brother. Laid out in the 1930s as the Lodhi Golf Club, it was renamed in 1951 after independence and granted special privileges by Prime Minister Jawaharlal Nehru. After that, civil servants like my father joined up and today it has a waiting list measured in years and hosts Asian tour matches like the Indian Open.

There's no rough to speak of, only bush, so accuracy is at a premium. But the average age of members is 80, so you have to be patient. Most members only come for the food.

A nice feature of the course is the Lal Bangla mausoleum, housing the graves of Lal Kunwar, mother of Shah Alam II, and his daughter Begum Jaan. Shah Alam II was one of the last Mughal emperors. He ruled Delhi when my ancestor Jassa Singh and his army over-ran the city in 1783 and subjugated him.

5. Muthaiga, Kenya

Counted as part of the European PGA Tour, the Muthiaga Golf Club on the outskirts of the Kenyan capital Nairobi can boast winners like Seve Ballesteros and Ian Woosnam. It winds through the woodlands of the Karura Forest, decked with flowering bushes and magnificent trees.

This was my last international outing in 2020 before the pandemic struck and I'd love to go back one day with my Cambridge buddies for a Hawks tour. It's just the sort of place they would love.

6. Ooty Golf Course, Tamil Nadu, India

High in the Avalanchi mountains of Tamil Nadu, sitting at a heady 7200 feet altitude, Ootacamund Gymkhana Club – known as Ooty – is a relic of the Raj, a hill station where British army officers and civil servants would come in summer to escape the heat of the Indian plains. The wooded course is thick with eucalyptus, oak, rhododendron and fir trees, while the ball travels further than it would at sea level, which gives your game a lift.

Today the Indian army has an officer training base here, so they're often seen out on the bumpy course, which takes some stamina to complete, with its regular uphill hikes. The winding, undulating fairways with several blind tees mean you're well-advised to hire a caddy.

7. Quinta do Lago, Portugal

The Algarve in Portugal has just about the most perfect conditions for golf: 300 days of sunshine per year, warm winters, verdant, gently rolling hills and valleys and a spectacular coastline. From the 1970s and 1980s onwards British golfers have flocked to its fairways – there are now at least 80 clubs, including several championship courses.

My favourite is the Quinta do Lago near Faro, which Ryder Cup captain Paul McGinley redeveloped in 2014. The venue is simply fantastic: 2000 acres next to the Atlantic and a natural park, five golf courses, tennis courts and a Michelin-starred restaurant. Golf World puts Quinta do Lago in its top five European resorts.

8. Valderrama, Spain

The 1997 Ryder Cup was one of the great golfing contests in history. Seve Ballesteros captained the Europeans, playing on the continent (rather than in the British Isles) for the first time. Tiger Woods made his debut Ryder Cup appearance alongside Phil Mickelson and on the European side were Colin Montgomerie, Nick Faldo and Ian Woosnam. After a scintillating three days, Europe triumphed 14½ to 13½.

To follow in these footsteps is every golfer's dream. You have the Sierra Almenara behind you, the Mediterranean Sea in the distance and a beautifully designed course, challenging, impeccably manicured. A piece of golfing magic.

9. Airlie Beach, Queensland, Australia

There are some lovely courses at Airlie Beach, on the Queensland coast about 500km southeast of Cairns. I spent time there as a guest of the Queensland Travel and Tourism Corporation and British Airways in the early 1990s and always felt that the golf we played helped me get a deal with BA. It's not that you agree anything specific out on the course, but it's a genteel, amiable sport and helps you get to know people, to form a bond. I remember going round one of the courses at Airlie Beach in four over par – it really suited my eye.

10. Lost City and Gary Player Courses, Sun City, South Africa

Sun City began in the late 1970s as an oasis of leisure, sport and shopping in the South African bush. By 1993 there were two major golf courses here, both designed by the great Gary Player – the Lost City course and the Gary Player course. They're both magnificent, carved out of the rocky landscape with mountain views and waterside fairways.

The standout hole is the 13th on the Lost City course, with its elevated tee. You drive across a water hazard full of two-meter-long crocodiles! No chance of retrieving your ball from there.

19th Hole – Legend Golf and Safari Resort

Up in the north of South Africa near the border with Botswana, this golf course has one of the greatest holes in the world: the 19th. Players take a helicopter ride to reach the tee, which sits 400 yards above the hole on a precipitous cliff-edge. The green itself is enormous and shaped like a map of Africa, giving you a sporting chance of hitting it, even from this vertigo-inducing height.

This is one of the few courses where you can fit in a round during a safari: even walking along the fairways, you'll see herds of giraffe, zebra and antelope. Several of the other holes are modelled on the greatest examples in world golf – par threes in Augusta, St Andrews and Royal Troon.

Chapter 12
Investment Strategy

Did you know that the sun delivers more energy to the earth in one hour than humanity requires over the course of a whole year? Or that in the Middle East, using fossil fuels to generate electricity costs fifty times more than solar energy? Fifty times more! These are the kind of statistics that make my investment antenna start bleeping.

Since selling ebookers, I've spent a lot of time looking out for investment opportunities. Technology changes, like the ones which we harnessed to put the business online, are one important criteria: so the falling price of solar energy technology attracted my attention. Political change is another big factor. For Flightbookers in the 1980s, political support for an entrepreneurial culture was important. For ebookers, the way that the internet overcame political and national borders was a massive advantage.

In 2005, once the ebookers sale was complete, I took my family for a holiday to Romania, to visit my wife's brother Ajai, who was the Indian ambassador to the country at the time. One of the 'non-compete' clauses in the deal for ebookers was that I couldn't invest in or run a travel business for 10 years. So I was looking for opportunities where I could benefit from other developments. Soon it emerged that Romania was an amazing option. This was a relatively poor country with big ambitions. It had spent the previous 15 years modernising and growing, with help from Western Europe, as it recovered from its post-War communist history under the Soviet Union until the revolution of 1989, when dictator Nicolae Ceauşescu and his wife Elena were executed by firing squad on Christmas Day.

When I arrived, 16 years later, preparations for Romania to join the European Union were going strong. Its neighbours Poland, Hungary, Czech Republic, Slovakia and Slovenia had already become EU members in May 2004 and Romania was an official 'acceding country'. It had joined NATO earlier in 2004, so there were few doubts that, alongside Bulgaria, it would soon become a full EU member, with all the investment and commercial opportunities that came with it. Sure enough, accession happened on 1 January 2007.

Within a few months of this first visit, I'd bought quite a lot of land in Romania: 900 acres of farmland and 475 acres of forest near the capital Bucharest, 22 acres in the middle of the city, which I'm planning to turn into a logistics centre, and a number of holiday properties including a resort on the Danube Delta with thirty villas, overlooking a lake full of wildlife.

Altogether, I invested €50 million in Romanian projects, mainly land and property deals. I have 16 special purpose vehicles to manage everything. I'm really committed to the country; I think it shows tremendous promise. Besides joining the EU, Romania can draw on its history as a major European nation. In the 1920s, Bucharest was known as the Paris of the East, and it is still hugely important in the region: it has a young, educated population of 20 million people (second only in Central Europe to Poland, with 37 million); the port of Constanța dates back to Roman times and is the only land route for EU goods and people to reach the Black Sea; and Romania's land is incredibly fertile, more than five times as fertile as Germany's land, I've heard. Under communism, Romania and Ukraine were the breadbasket of the Soviet Union.

What's become even more exciting to me is that Romania has 2110 hours of sunshine per year. To make a solar energy plant profitable, you need 1400 hours a year. So the maths is compelling (and of course, sunshine is free). It will take a major piece of investment: according to our pre-feasibility studies, we'll need at least €220 million. I've already invested €15 million in the agricultural land where the solar plant could be built. My partners and I will put in 30 per cent of the total and the whole sum is already raised. So this is how I've approached the project so far:

I researched the solar industry and how it fits into Romania's economic priorities. The government has received €750 million from the EU to close down its coal-fired power generation plants, so this space will be filled by solar and other renewable sources of electricity, particularly in the south of the country. At the moment, Romania imports 30 per cent of its energy, and the government is keen to reduce that percentage to lower the security and economic risks. So far, Romanian solar generation hasn't been very effective – their largest plant is just 56MW, compared with mine, which will have 330MW – but the technology is improving all the time. In the past two years, productivity from solar panels has gone up from 12 to 21 per cent. You can buy 620W panels instead of 330W panels. It's a huge increase. During the pandemic, stockpiles of Chinese-manufactured panels are stacking up in warehouses, bringing the price down even further. Another German company claims that it can increase the electricity yield from panels by more than 100 per cent.

China is behind the most important developments in solar energy: of the top 10 solar panel companies, nine are in China. Their research and development capacity is amazing, the way they've brought costs down. Chinese companies are willing to come to Europe and build solar plants from start to finish.

If China is the future, the best profits are still in the United States. I've been watching presentations from Singularity University, the online group set up by Peter Diamandis and Ray Kurzweil, to look at how technology will shape the future. A recent renewable energy paper talks about the prospects for solar power, how productivity of 20 per cent is now a possibility and how new transparent solar panels could one day harvest energy from our buildings, windows, car windscreens and mobile devices. With improved battery capacity and performance, solar energy could satisfy the world's needs. For my project in Romania, I'm considering growing shade-loving crops such as jalapeño chillies underneath the solar panels – a practice known as agrivoltaic generation. (Singularity University has been making futuristic prognoses since its foundation in 2008. Co-founder Ray Kurzweil predicted that he will live to 125 and has already reached 72 years old. He claims that around 80 per cent of his many predictions – such as the widespread adoption of the internet – have come true.)

At an ever-faster pace, governments are responding to the promise of solar. Romania passed new laws on power purchasing agreements, meaning that solar power companies can sell to the French railways, or to Amazon for example. They now offer 'contracts for difference', so that if the spot price goes below your cost, they'll subsidise you to make it up. This push in Romania for solar energy happened in May and June 2020.

From an EU point of view, solar energy also fits right in with its agenda to promote sustainable green development. There's a €1 trillion fund to develop renewable energy across the continent by 2040, including closing down fossil fuel plants such as those in Romania. There are numerous EU infrastructure grants available in Romania, to build new roads and increase its trading potential, adding up to tens of billions of euros.

The country has come such a long way since 1989: in many ways, it's drawing close to the Western European standard of living and the reliability of its legal system. Even so, there are challenges. The bureaucracy sometimes reminds me of India, with long delays for permissions or legal decisions. Corruption is lower than in India, but more than in Western Europe or the US. And it suffers from a brain drain, as the educated elite are tempted by higher salaries and living standards to live and work overseas. I find the Romanians more Mediterranean than Slav and have found them to be hard-working, intelligent people.

It's hard to raise money in Romania, or for Romanian projects, because there's less history of large-scale investment here for people to benchmark against or to reassure themselves. But solar energy is booming all over the world: recently an Algerian company put out an international tender for a 70MW scheme. Mine is 270MW, so I should do the same thing, with a consultancy like KPMG showing me how to do it. A banker friend is putting me in touch with some family offices and private equity investors who are into sustainable development.

So far, I've drawn up a business plan, calculating the cost of the electricity generation as €50 per megawatt. I've drawn on my various personal and private networks – LinkedIn, Facebook, CEO, Young Presidents Organisation, Singularity University. Through Singularity I was introduced to the PV Network, for photovoltaic technology. It reminds me of when I was putting together ebookers, with contact lists and calls to make introductions, assembling teams and raising investment. The lady who runs TiE London, who used to be at KPMG, introduced me to the senior partner and then the person who does solar deals. He's raised €30 billion for solar investments.

I've hired a solar energy consultancy to research the opportunity. They're based in Bucharest and I'm paying a great deal less than I was quoted by an Italian company. The consultancy is certified by the Romanian Solar Energy Association, so they know what they're talking about.

This company did legislative, topographical and CV yield surveys along with a mapping grid and began a discussion with the Romanian grid operator. I estimate that it will cost €106,000 to get operator licences for the solar plant, and up to €3 million for the entire preparation, not including construction. I'm now looking for a partner who is knowledgeable about these kind of projects, so the cost will come down: I'm de-risking myself.

Once it's up and running, with a reliable income stream, pensions funds will be queuing up to invest, so it should be easy to sell. I reckon that I can sell my part of the project at a good profit. At worst, I might lose the €3 million development costs and go back to renting the land to farmers, growing wheat and sunflowers. On the plus side, Romania welcomes foreign investment, its energy plans are bang in line with mine, the EU supports us and there's a general appetite for sustainable energy investment, especially now that the costs have fallen so dramatically and the awareness of the damage climate change is doing has increased in parallel. The pandemic has only increased the political will to drive green energy. A host of voices, including the

International Monetary Fund, are urging national governments to invest in renewable energy resources as a means of spurring economic activity, tackling climate change and saving money at the same time.

I've remained committed to Romania despite a couple of disasters. In 2007 I invested in a real estate company called Copper Beach Capital, which then built a 16-storey apartment block in Bucharest called Blue Tower. But the company went into administration in 2009 following the 2008 recession, before the building had finished, because the Greek bank we'd borrowed from stopped lending and cancelled its future lending commitments to us. The block was eventually sold to a Romanian bank in 2013. I lost €6 million because of that. So instead of an office with 24 people in 2009, we just have a small operation now, with accounting and legal services outsourced.

A second disaster – in retrospect – was refusing an offer from a Mayfair-based hedge fund to buy 30 per cent of one of my Romanian investments for €80 million in 2006. That would have given me my investment back on the deal, while still owning 70 per cent. A couple of years later, the whole valuation collapsed due to the recession. That sort of missed opportunity annoys the hell out of me, but with the money I've made, it's a question of 'when is enough enough?'

On the various plots of land that I bought, I'm planning to build an international school, a hospital, solar farms in Puchenii Mari and Bucşani within a 25km radius of Bucharest, and a hotel in Suceviţa in the north of the country overlooking a 15th century monastery with frescos painted on its walls. This is a UNESCO global heritage site and, as a European Bank of Reconstruction and Development executive explained to me "just the sort of place in Romania we're trying to promote, we'd love to work with you." At the moment, all I have is land that I paid €800,000 for in 2010, and the approach road keeps being washed away by rainstorms, but the prospects are excellent for the future, once the economy recovers from the pandemic.

In the Danube delta, where the river spreads out into a broad series of wetlands to the east of Romania, I bought the Delta Nature Resort in 2007 shortly after it was built. Since then, I've invested to upgrade it and added facilities for corporate events, weddings and so on. It's a fantastic place to go for birdwatching or just soaking in the scenery. (The only problem is the mosquitoes, so we installed air conditioning in the rooms.)

After 25 years in the travel business, ten years in charity and five years in politics, I'm ready for new challenges, which is why the solar project in Romania appeals to me so much. It's complex, it's challenging, the barriers are high but the rewards are also high and – most important to me – it's a chance to do some good while making money at the same time. I'm absolutely committed to green energy, as government subsidies are no longer needed and it's the best way for the world to go forward. Solar energy is going to be abundant and prices are going to keep falling, making it profitable versus fossil fuel plants and without subsidies.

When I was running for the Lib Dem London mayoral ticket, I was horrified at the statistics for how many people died from air pollution – ten thousand every year in London alone. If all vehicles were electric and ran on renewable energy, it would save countless lives.

Investing in the Future

Wherever I invest, I'm always looking to the future. Now that the 10-year non-compete clause that I signed on selling ebookers is over, I've been free to invest in online businesses since 2015. Some opportunities have worked really well: for example, a competition for young businesses that we organised through TiE attracted loads of entries. The winner was a fintech company and, after I put £10,000 into it, I received £23,000 back 10 months later. Nice return.

I firmly believe that, in the future, all companies will be online and will be software businesses. There's a driving logic which leads every form of enterprise towards digital technology. So I'm constantly on the lookout for businesses which demonstrate this, by digitising processes and sectors which have been slow to catch on.

Also, as the price of smartphones comes down and everyone gets one, they're taking over more and more of our business and social lives. So everything has to be designed around mobile technology and the businesses I invest in are often mobile-centred. What alarms me is how little mobile expertise and innovation there is in Europe. Although Nokia and Eriksson are great companies, and have something like 21 per cent of global 5G patents in telecoms, they're not national champions in the way that Huawei is in China, or Apple and Microsoft are in the US. We need to build a European infrastructure champion and partner with governments. That would be a smart investment, especially in a country like Spain, where 80 per cent of physical connectivity is through fibre.

I'm always curious about 3D printing investments. In the United States, 17 per cent of the economy is logistics – by truck, rail, ship and plane, hauling vast amounts of goods around, a sector worth $3.2 trillion. If 3D printing can reduce this giant bill, through delivering everything from aeroplane parts to sections of buildings, then you have a huge added value that can go to other parts of the economy, not to mention the environmental savings from lower emissions and pollution. When you watch Donald Trump lowering regulations on pollution and emissions, while Silicon Valley invents new 3D printing applications, you wonder which way the country is heading. When the price of 3D printed goods is demonstrably lower than goods that have been trucked across America, I guess people will vote with their wallets.

Now that Tesla has made high-performance luxury electric cars available, I'm an enthusiastic owner. For a few years after selling ebookers, I was seduced by the idea of supercars like the McLaren F1 with gull wing doors. But when I took my son to a showroom to have a test drive, we couldn't fit our bums into the seats, so I bought the Maybach (a Mercedes version of a Rolls Royce), that they'd sent to pick us up, for a discounted price and a Bentley Convertible instead. Once Teslas appeared, though, I pretty much left those cars in the garage. Tesla exemplifies what I like about new technology: the cars are clean, efficient, great to look at and literally take your breath away when you accelerate from 0 to 60 mph in three seconds. The Model X even has gull wings. It makes sense to me that Tesla has just replaced Toyota as the world's most valuable auto brand, despite never having made a profit.

I invest in lots of small businesses. Not complete start-ups, but companies with a good risk profile and excellent management. That's the key thing for me, it's all about people. I invest in an apartment rental company for corporate clients called www.thesqua.re which lets out flats to banks, for example, where their staff can stay, with hotel-level services but much cheaper. I invested in Karan Bilimoria's Cobra Beer because I liked his business plan, the way he'd researched the market and pitched his product to fulfil a need.

Generally, I don't invest directly in the stock market. Whenever I've tried to do this I get the timing wrong and lose money. If you look at the main indexes, those are often worth tracking: if you'd put money in the FTSE in 2009, you'd have tripled your investment within ten years. Brokers won't advise you to buy the index because they don't make any money from it – they only make money when you switch stocks. And to me, stock market investing feels too close to gambling for comfort.

What I look for in a business is good management. I look for a track record, evidence of being able to manage people, being able to execute a plan. Seeing a husband and wife (or equivalent couple) partnership always reassures me. It reminds me of how I started out with Tani and how a good team is bigger than the sum of its parts. Typically, I put in between £30,000 and £100,000 into growing businesses, because I like their management and risk profile. I want to be able to go in and talk to them anytime.

When I look at a travel website, there's a whole list of things that I want to see. I want customisation, a 360-degree view of a hotel room, details of rainfall and humidity, Wi-Fi strength, electrical plug details, things that are so important to visitors but which are often left out. If you need a visa, there should be details of a company that can get one for you. The functionality of our website at ebookers was very important to me: we included a flight tracker so you could see whether your flight would leave on time, or what time someone else's flight was going to land. We had more sophisticated customer service options than our competitors, we responded more promptly to messages and paid more attention to the data we collected from our offices.

Looking back to my experience with ebookers, one of the important keys to success was upselling: how to encourage or persuade our customers to add car hire, hotels and insurance to their flight bookings. The best solution is to give customers the feeling that they're in charge, they make the decisions. Just like Dell computers give customers a choice of monitor screens, memory and storage, if you leave these choices up to the customer, it means you can never be wrong. And it takes away a lot of work.

So these are the things that I look for in an investment:

- What's the unique selling point, what's the competitive edge?
- Does the business have an edge in its use of software?
- I'm looking for companies that think global, rather than those who are limited to their city or country.
- Is the business in a 'land grab' situation where it has the prospect of first mover advantage and a monopoly position?
- Do changes in national or international laws and regulations favour the business?
- How will the business adapt to the new pandemic realities? For example, I'm not planning to invest in any travel businesses for some time. But manufacturers can adapt their production lines to make ventilators; gym instructors can do online sessions; online retailers are likely to thrive.
- Is the enterprise environmentally aware? This is no longer just about corporate social responsibility and reputation, it's about financial realities and future-proofing the business. You want to mitigate any carbon emissions, do power purchase agreements with green energy producers, build offices to high environmental standards and have your premises next to rail stations and cycle routes.

I foresee that the whole investment landscape is going to change dramatically over the next couple of years. It's not only business sectors like travel or retail that will have to transform, but the length of investment horizons. Private equity investors typically go for deals lasting between three to ten years, with their rewards coming in the final couple of years. Those timescales won't work anymore.

We're also going to have to get used to China as the world's dominant commercial power. Already, 90 per cent of all the goods in Walmart stores (the world's largest retailer) come from China. The country's ecommerce market is now worth $1.2 trillion, compared with $650 billion in the United States.

The changes we're facing now are just as profound and rapid as those that catapulted ebookers into the FTSE250 at the turn of the millennium. It's a scarier time, because the world faces a devastating public health crisis, but the opportunities are just as promising, the rewards for success just as enormous.

What are you waiting for?

Green Energy – the Way Forward

I became really interested in solar electricity generation when I saw the European Union promising to invest a wave of money into green energy. It appeals to me as a way to spread wealth and freedom since renewable energy is uniformly distributed around the world. With every percentage rise in energy production, a country's GDP rises in parallel.

Green energy is an area where you don't have to be first, but you have to be in the game. It gave me the idea to use assets in 2020 and onwards that I'd bought in 2008. There are two potential uses for solar power that I'm investigating: green hydrogen and ammonia, and cloud computing.

BUSINESS 2: Green Hydrogen and Ammonia

To decarbonise the entire industrial system, we need to produce energy which, like electricity, releases no CO_2 into the atmosphere. But we also need to produce it in a CO_2-free way. It's no good making electricity using coal-fired power stations.

Solar energy can power water electrolysis to produce hydrogen, which then reacts with nitrogen to create 'green' ammonia, with no CO_2 emissions. According to the latest research, the market for green ammonia will expand by more than 700 per cent by 2030 to $852 million. It can replace conventional fuel oil in ships, vehicles and even planes, since it burns in standard internal combustion engines.

So far, green hydrogen only accounts for 1 per cent of total hydrogen production. The rest involves gasification of coal or lignite, or using natural gas or methane as feedstock, all of which produces CO_2 emissions. But green hydrogen also has a great advantage over electricity in that it's storable: you can transport it by ship or keep it in a warehouse and convert it into energy later. By contrast, transmitting electricity along cables is expensive and wasteful. As one electrolysation specialist put it: "All the renewable energy companies [realise] they've got a new product. They can now supply renewable molecules to the gas grid and industry."

Now that the US has re-joined the Paris Climate Accord under President Biden, there is renewed impetus to achieve its aims and reduce carbon emissions. Hydrogen production is rising up the global agenda as a viable means to this end: new projects that fit desalination and electrolysis equipment to offshore wind turbines, producing hydrogen, are taking shape in Scotland, Germany and the Netherlands. One scheme will pump hydrogen back from the turbines along former natural gas pipelines.

The cost of green ammonia is currently higher than fuel oil, but experts predict it will fall below oil in the coming years, as electrolysis equipment becomes cheaper and more widely available. The Dutch government has made green hydrogen a central part of its energy policy and launched a national programme, aiming to reach 4GW of installed electrolyser capacity by 2030. Portugal announced a €7 billion national hydrogen strategy in 2020. 'Big oil' companies like Shell and BP are investing in renewable green hydrogen production, which will further reduce its cost and increase the market size.

Green hydrogen is central to the European Union's trillion-dollar Green Deal: it's part of the wholesale shift from carbon-based power, in which gas will have a major role to play. "We cannot electrify everything," as the CEO of WindEurope Giles Dickson said recently. "Some industrial processes and heavy transport will have to run on gas. And renewable hydrogen is the best gas. It is completely clean and it will be affordable, with renewables being so cheap now." Of all the world's markets, Europe is likely to become the focus of green hydrogen and ammonia production. So I'm keen to play some part in this development.

BUSINESS 3: Cloud Computing Storage

Big tech is under increasing scrutiny: governments feel they should pay more tax; liberals and conservatives both claim that they censor free speech, that they promote violence, harm mental health, stifle small businesses, kill the high street, outsource jobs.

In need of positive PR, big tech can at least claim the high ground in green energy use. Between them, Amazon, Google, Microsoft and Facebook are now the world's largest corporate purchasers of clean energy. In total, the companies use more than 45 terawatt-hours per year, equal to a country like New Zealand. (One terawatt equals a trillion watts).

Over the past five years, these companies have competed to see who has the greenest energy use. Microsoft says it will be 'carbon negative' by 2030, Google plans to operate on carbon-free energy by 2030, Amazon's operations will be powered by renewable energy by 2025 and reach net-zero emissions by 2040, Facebook is already net-zero for operations, and aims to be net-zero across its supply chain by 2030, and Apple aims to cut emissions by 75 per cent by 2030 across its supply chain, having already powered its operations from renewable energy sources.

These are lofty ambitions, given the exponential rise in energy use they're all going through. Facebook's energy usage quadrupled between 2015 and 2019 as it powered global video consumption, while Google's electricity demand tripled between 2013 and 2018. The biggest energy consumer of them all is Amazon, with its power-hungry Web Services division storing the world's data on the cloud, along with fleets of trucks delivering the world's goods.

Although late to the green energy party, Amazon has made up for lost time by becoming the world's largest corporate buyer of renewables, operating more than 150 renewable energy projects in Australia, Europe and the US, enough to generate 6.5GW of sustainably sourced energy. It took some employee activism to get there: in 2019, Amazon staff joined their colleagues at the other big tech firms in a climate strike, coming out in sympathy with the message of Greta Thunberg to the United Nations in New York. Jess Bezos has also pledged $10 billion to combat climate change through his Earth Fund.

For me, the relevance of all this green energy activity by big tech is the growth of demand for cheap, renewable electricity.

The land in Romania where I plan to build a solar electricity plant could also house a cloud storage facility, with computers working day and night making Bitcoins, for example. I already have investors ready to commit to this project. All I have to do is give them a piece of my land and get a 20 or 30 per cent stake in the project. If it works, this could be worth a lot of money.

Chapter 13
Entrepreneurship

As Winston Churchill famously said: "You should never let a good crisis go to waste."

Economic conditions in 2020 were the worst in a generation. When I look back almost 50 years to the situation in 1974, the UK was in a terrible situation. The FTSE was down at 146 (compared with 6000 now) and the global oil crisis, together with a miners' strike brought down the Conservative government of Edward Heath. There were electricity blackouts and GDP fell by almost 4 per cent in a year. Six years later in 1980, when I was working at IBM, unemployment was soaring and inflation hit 22 per cent and factories were closing all over the country as Margaret Thatcher tried to bring inflation down.

What kind of a fool would give up a secure, reasonably well-paid job for a multinational corporation and strike out on their own, at a time like that, or a time like now?

Here are 10 reasons why starting a business during a recession is a great idea:

- Everything is up in the air. People are jolted out of complacency and become more receptive to new ideas. They need to save money, so if you can offer them a better deal, they'll give you a chance.
- Employees are easy to find and cheap to hire. When times are tough, people are more grateful for jobs, they work harder and they're more resourceful. You can find exceptional candidates, with high educational standards and good experience, who would at other times be out of reach or uninterested in working for a new business.
- You are yourself more motivated to succeed. When your back is against the wall, it's easier to start an enterprise: your outlook is 'nothing ventured, nothing gained' and you can commit wholeheartedly to making the business work.

- You can benefit from government incentives. In any recession, there will be public funds available to kick-start the economy, whether in the form of subsidies for employing staff, tax exemptions or investment grants. Look for these and figure out whether they suit your business.

- You can surf the wave of the recovery. Few recessions last longer than a year or two, and even during deep recessions, there are always people who are willing to invest in new ideas, to promote or buy novel goods and services. By standing out against the crowd, showing a confidence in your abilities and your product, you can leapfrog existing competitors and win new markets.

- Great entrepreneurs go against the crowd. So if the crowd (aka the market) is subdued, lethargic, retreating, you can create a strong impression by appearing to be the opposite. Your energy and drive, optimism and determination will stand out from your competitors and win you new business. People will feed off your enthusiasm, in the belief that it will spur their own growth.

- Partnerships are easier to find and secure. In a crisis, there is more of a spirit of collaboration between companies, as erstwhile competitors battle against an external enemy, whether high inflation, falling consumer confidence, rising unemployment or a terrible new infectious disease. This gives you a chance to benefit from industry platforms and to promote yourself to a wider customer base.

- Promotion and marketing can be easier, cheaper and more effective. For example, advertising rates are lower in a recession. Newspapers and other media are more receptive to 'good news' stories, because everything else is so grim. Tell editors how your company is going to change the world for the better.

- You'll naturally keep a close eye on costs, because in a recession, every penny counts. As the business grows, a good entrepreneur will maintain this focus, giving you an edge on your competitors. By contrast, businesses launched in a time of plenty, with lax spending limits, may struggle once times get tough. Iron is stronger when it's forged in the fire.

- Psychologically, it's better to be active than passive. An entrepreneur takes hold of their own destiny, refuses to be controlled by circumstances or fate. A recession may put millions out of work or force them to accept jobs they'd rather avoid, but if you can start your own business, you've taken a different route. It's a mixture of schadenfreude and relief, and it's a potent fuel for any entrepreneur in the midst of a recession.

*   *   *

For many years, I've mentored entrepreneurs. Some of them relatively new, working on start-up ideas, some of them with more mature businesses which are seeking to expand into new markets or scale up. What I can offer isn't only the fruit of working on Flightbookers and ebookers, but from decades of attending courses and seminars run by Harvard Business School, the Young Presidents Association, TiE (The Indus Entrepreneurs) and various other groups.

From early on in my business career as an entrepreneur, I treasured the lessons that I could pick up from these groups: learning first hand from your peers is so much more valuable than reading press reports or even books (though I hope you find this one helpful!). By the time a new idea has made it into the press, it's generally too late.

Here are some principles of entrepreneurship that I've found are timeless and helped me in my career.

Marketing and Promotion

Everyone needs a good website, but that's a relatively minor expense compared with marketing costs. What you want is to be number one on Google for your preferred search term. You should invest in this both through search engine optimisation (SEO) to get natural search results and also through advertising with Google.

My biggest attribute is that I understand growing businesses: I'm a born marketer. So I like to advise people and companies on how, when, why and at what rate to grow. You should aim to grow by enough that you give sufficient work to the new employees that you hire, but not too much more. Say you had three employees, you might aim to grow to nine employees within a year. So you'd look to keep the six new people busy, rather than winning business for 20 new employees.

It's good to hire public relations agencies. Not only can they get your business covered in the media, they can win you new business by talking to people. They know where to market you and how to represent you on social media. Don't worry about being too small for them, they handle all kinds of clients.

Growing your Business

As a start-up, the first thing to do is to establish your sales channels. Without sales, there's nothing. So be clear what the size of your market is and how quickly you plan to expand. Then develop a core team, which should comprise finance, logistics, marketing and yourself, who should understand all the different functions.

Look carefully at what your competitors are doing and what companies like Amazon have done in your sector. Can you offer something similar, which replicates the distribution advantages of digital media companies? Can you scale up, or digitise your business to absorb some of the commerce that is still offline?

If you're a service enterprise, think about expanding like a law firm: the senior partner wins new business, then hands it on to more junior colleagues. The business itself takes on the work, not the individual. Too many entrepreneurs try to build a 'job' for themselves, rather than a sustainable business which can thrive with or without them.

More than any other factor, growing a business comes down to hard work. You have to be ready to work up to 16 hours a day, keeping on top of everything: the accounts, the marketing, staff issues, dealing with suppliers, paying the rent. If you look at economies in the Far East today, this is what sets them apart from the West. They work incredibly hard, with the same tools and knowledge as everyone else. That's why they do better.

The Winning Mentality

Entrepreneurship is about taking risks, but it's also about how you react to failure. If you're disheartened by failure, running a business may not be the right thing for you. There are exceptions: if your business idea crashes straight away, maybe try a different idea rather than persevering with the same thing. In the digital world, Mark Zuckerberg's motto "Move fast and break things" is useful to bear in mind. At ebookers, we were aiming to break the grip that traditional travel agents had on the industry. We moved fast, captured a giant market share and succeeded. More recently, we've seen the limits of this approach, when Boeing tried to become a digital disruptor and its products – airplanes – literally crashed. The relevance of this mentality in 2020 is that many businesses are likely to fail during the pandemic. Quitting too soon is a major cause of business failure. You need to develop resilience, keep costs down and be persistent to succeed.

Above all, I'd say that entrepreneurs need a positive outlook. Of course there will be setbacks and failures, but optimism and living without regrets are vital. As partners, Tani and I were fortunate to share this mindset. We were able to live in the moment and embrace things as they came to us. We allowed ourselves to fail and to succeed. We brought with us from India an attitude of self-reliance: with virtually no safety net from social welfare, India forces entrepreneurs to take risks and to make their own way. We were congenitally averse to living on government handouts.

*   *   *

Each year for 18 years I attended week-long Harvard Business School courses in the US. After nine of these, you're eligible for an executive MBA. I found the experience highly motivating and informative: it helped me take decisions as an entrepreneur and business owner, putting things in perspective and giving me excellent tools. The same goes for Young Presidents Organisation (YPO) courses.

Here are 10 things I learnt from Harvard and YPO:

- Listen to what the best people in your field have to say. Joining groups like YPO or Harvard Business School gives you access to some of the sharpest minds: they will analyse current challenges and lay out their predictions and solutions. Once you hear these messages repeatedly, they set in your mind and help you to make decisions.
- Look at what the mavericks are doing. People like Richard Branson at Virgin or Stelios Haji-Ioannou at easyJet. They're expert at spotting gaps in the market and innovating before the multinationals have creaked into action. Often, like Stelios, they've come from one country and set up in another, using a fresh pair of eyes to create something new.
- Watch out for whoever is creating 'alpha' returns. If the whole market rises by 5 per cent, a company that delivers 5 per cent growth is classed as 'beta' – it's basically treading water, treating business as though it were the civil service, using intelligence but not really creating wealth. If someone delivers 12 per cent growth, that's alpha.
- Prioritise. There will be a hundred distractions a day, competing for your attention. Learn to focus on those issues that matter, the ones that advance your agenda and yield results. Delegate to others.
- Understand your market. Work out where the opportunities for margins are, where you can get competitive advantage through bargaining with suppliers, selling to new customers, reducing prices. Keep an eye on new entrants and how the market is changing.

- Use digital technology, artificial intelligence, algorithms and cloud storage to help you grow. There are ever more digital tools, which began as highly specialised solutions but are now available off the shelf at low cost. Cloud services allow you to increase storage at a minute's notice, whereas at ebookers, we had to buy large physical computer servers to increase our capacity.
- Professional services companies can help you, even though they're expensive. Banks, legal and accountancy firms are important pillars for your business. Your next-door neighbour may tell you that he's good at maths, but if you take his accounts to your bank, they'll say it's unprofessional and throw you out.
- Don't be afraid to ask for what you want. The world admires leaders who know their own mind and pursue their vision. You'll be surprised how often you get a positive response to a genuine request.
- Set ambitious targets. Why settle for selling to your city or even your country? The fantastic thing about the internet is its universality: sell to Australia, to India, to China, to Brazil. There are far fewer barriers than you may imagine.
- Find something that you're passionate about, whether it's the product, the industry, the opportunities or the market. Other people will respond to your enthusiasm and follow your example. People (your employees) are your greatest asset, so nurture and inspire them.

One thing I really liked about the professors at Harvard was how many of them actually invested as well as taught. It gave them more authenticity, because you felt that they really believed in what they were teaching.

$$*\qquad\qquad*\qquad\qquad*$$

There is an undeniable thrill about starting a new enterprise. The fascination and magic of watching a business grow, take on a life of its own and prosper, is second only to having your own child. Even after 40 years of entrepreneurship, I'm still captivated by the process and am now engrossed in starting up a solar energy business in Romania. There are many risks and many potential rewards, but the greatest thing is that I enjoy it, and it stands to make the world a better place.

It's tempting to think that starting a business was easier in the past and that the obstacles of the present day are more daunting and harder to overcome. Put that out of your mind. Starting a business is never easy, at any time in history. It only seems more difficult today if you haven't done it.

Chapter 14
Entering Politics

When Nigel Farage's UKIP party won 24 seats in the 2014 European elections it caused a political earthquake. It was the first time any party other than Labour or the Tories won the most seats in a nationally-contested election for more than 100 years and it sent a chilling message to the Prime Minister David Cameron. He came under tremendous pressure to hold a referendum on EU membership and in response, he pushed the Conservative party to the right, hoping to win back those he feared were defecting to UKIP.

This was too much for me. I'd always voted Conservative up until this point. The party felt like the best option for a self-made entrepreneur, supporting free enterprise, lower taxes, international trade. And throughout my adult life, it had stood for Britain being part of Europe, with all the benefits that I enjoyed, whether that meant travelling on the Eurostar to Paris, employing European nationals in London or running 11 companies across the continent. Being part of the European Union was central to my concept of doing business; it was a crucial part of how I'd developed, grown and sold ebookers. Why on earth would the Tory party forsake this fantastic institution, which brought so much peace, prosperity and employment to Britain?

Cameron's rightward shift in 2014 was a wake-up call. You could say that it politicised me. Whereas before I had political opinions, but put my energies into business, investment and philanthropy, this act of betrayal (as I saw it) motivated me to put not only time and effort, but resources into the battle to keep Britain in Europe.

Some of my friends were Liberal Democrat supporters, including Sudhir Chaudhrie who invested $8 million into ebookers and served as a non-executive director. He joined the Liberal Democrat party in 2004 and donated generously to them over the years. In 2014, after meeting various Lib Dem figures including their treasurer Ian Wrigglesworth, I decided to join the party and donated £550,000 to help them in the 2015 election, following five years of coalition between the Tories and Lib Dems with Nick Clegg as leader.

Much good it did them. The party went from 57 seats down to eight in a night of almost complete disaster. Even the leader Nick Clegg lost his Sheffield seat as the electorate punished the party (unjustly in my view) for capitulating on student fees and generally not standing up to the Conservatives during the coalition.

My own feeling was that the Lib Dems achieved a great deal in coalition. In our 2010 manifesto we proposed the Green Investment Bank, to promote renewable energy and a sustainable economy. Nick Clegg as Deputy Prime Minister and Vince Cable as Business Secretary helped implement this idea and it launched in 2012. We put forward the idea of an extended tax threshold, going up from £8,000 a year to £12,000. That was another good policy – it appeared in our election manifesto in 2010, not in the Tories' – but somehow they claimed credit for it and the electorate only focused on our position on student fees. We can look back and say that this was a mistake: it certainly cost us lots of votes, and at the time of the original policy, we could have counted on Labour votes to defeat student loans legislation. Nick Clegg saw it as an issue of leadership: he wanted to show that he could make unpopular decisions for the sake of political unity. But if it hadn't been student loans, it would have been something else. People say that being in coalition killed us, but what's the point of politics if you can't go into government?

Overall, I thought that Nick Clegg was an excellent politician but a poor manager. He neglected to promote the party during his time in charge; there was no marketing, which was what killed us in the 2015 election. He put Paddy Ashdown in charge of the election campaign and he was totally inadequate. You could see that from election night, where Paddy responded to the forecast that we'd get eight or nine seats by saying: "If that happens, I'll eat my hat." If he'd done enough market research, he'd have known that in advance.

It was a shame, because I liked Paddy. As an ex-military man, he led from the front, rather than letting the troops go in and sitting back. He made mistakes, but he was well respected, right across the spectrum. The test of politicians is how people from other parties view them once they've left office and Paddy was very popular. In contrast with those politicians who are elected simply because they've put in the hours, but don't know how to lead, he comes out very well. The worst cases are when people are so fearful of messing up that they delay taking decisions. One has to be aware of the huge risks that one faces all the time, but one still has to make choices.

From a financial point of view, if you compare the Lib Dems' approach to the Tories, you can see big differences. The Tories appoint businesspeople as treasurers, in charge of fundraising. They can speak to donors in a language they understand and they run the campaign in alignment with business. As a result the big donors, who can put in tens of millions of pounds, support the Tories.

In 2015 new Lib Dem leader Tim Farron appointed my friend Sudhir to strengthen ties with India. Soon afterwards, Farron approached me and asked me to become a Lib Dem advisor on enterprise, which I gladly accepted. Like Sudhir I've also donated substantial amounts to the party, adding up to more than £1 million over five years, though never as much as on that first occasion in 2015. I must admit it felt like a waste of money.

After the chastening experience of coalition with the Tories, the Lib Dem membership was eager to move leftwards, which accounted for Tim Farron's leadership. His position on the left of the party pleased many activists. But it was his religious beliefs which caused his downfall in the end: as a committed Christian, he couldn't bring himself to support gay rights or women's rights to choose abortion. These were red line issues for many members, and he only lasted two years as the LibDems gave a very poor showing in the 2017 elections, going from 8 seats to 12.

Meanwhile, Farron appointed me deputy treasurer of the party in 2017, so it became part of my job to attract new donors. By this time, David Cameron had pushed the UK into the European Union referendum and lost, causing a civil war in his own party, and Labour was struggling with its own European schisms under Jeremy Corbyn, with a remainer membership and a secretly pro-Brexit leadership.

As a member of the only party fully committed to staying in the EU, I became increasingly devoted to the Lib Dem mission. So in 2018, I put my name forward for selection as the party's London mayoral candidate for the 2020 election, seeking to replace the incumbent, Labour's Sadiq Khan. This really crystalised my political beliefs: once you have to stand on a stage and debate the issues in front of an audience, it's no good hedging your bets. You have to decide which side you're on.

My platform stood on four main arguments: crime, housing, a clean environment and transport. I'd expand community policing, so that there would be more officers on the streets. Under Boris Johnson and Sadiq Khan, City Hall closed down London police stations, putting them further away from communities. It saves a lot of money, but local officers no longer know what's going on in local communities. They don't know the families, they can't spot who are the bad eggs. My vision is that you should recruit police officers from within communities: wherever you have a family of three siblings in a tough neighbourhood, one of them would be a police officer. This would help deal with knife crime and gang violence.

Meeting a Lib Dem supporter while door knocking, 2018

We could easily house more people in London, given the political will. If you took 3.7 per cent of the green areas of London, within 10-15 minutes' walk of a tube or overground railway station, you could build a million homes. It's hard to overcome people's instinctive reaction when you mention the word 'green', but there are lots of ways to increase housing density without spoiling the environment, like allowing four storey buildings to go to five storeys, or building on brownfield sites. Boris Johnson and Sadiq Khan both made extravagant promises of how much new housing they would deliver: Khan said 82,000 homes a year but has only built 5,000 a year. There's a desperate need for more housing, hospitals and schools.

Cleaner air is also a massive issue in London. Pollution causes around 10,000 premature deaths a year in the city, particularly from vehicle emissions. There are five or six areas that are so bad, they're way above EU limits for air quality. This policy tied in with my ideas for transport improvements, to promote electric cars by offering free parking and charging points, along with electric buses, expanded cycle routes and pedestrianisation.

There are also some easy wins to release funding in transport. Each year, thousands of tourists buy Oyster cards and only use part of the balance on them, leaving more than £330 million dormant. I'd propose to capture that money by saying, if you don't use it within 18 months, you lose it. We could then employ it to improve London Transport, to electrify more trains and harness green energy sources. Since I've spent the past few years researching renewable energy generation in Romania, I could put that knowledge to work for Londoners.

The fact that Sadiq Khan's family came from Pakistan, and that his father was a bus driver (as he often points out), proved that Londoners were happy to elect politicians from ethnic minorities, so that was a useful precedent. My view on BAME integration is that more effort needs to go into English language skills. There are far too many first- and second-generation immigrants who don't speak good, or any, English, years after moving to the UK. This makes integration almost impossible, especially for women who rarely leave their homes.

Looking back on my own experience of coming to the UK, learning good English was absolutely vital to my education and career. Without that, I couldn't have progressed beyond the administration work my school careers advisors suggested for me. In the UK, the top of the immigrant population is well-integrated but the bottom end still struggles. It means that we lose out on a lot of talent. By learning English and speaking it in the right way, it makes you much more accepted and you feel like you're part of the community.

Running against me for the Lib Dem candidacy were Siobhan Benita, who stood for the mayoralty as an independent in 2012, humanitarian aid consultant Lucy Salek, who was a Lib Dem candidate in Lewisham in the 2017 General Election, and an economist called Rob Blackie. The lead up to this selection decision was eye-opening to me. It was clear from very early on that Siobhan Benita was the 'anointed' candidate – the Lib Dem leadership were firmly behind her and did her favours at every opportunity. This was not only frustrating to me, it bordered on illegal practice, as far as I was concerned.

The party leadership announced that there would be a meeting for all candidates to present their case on a certain day. There was no flexibility offered; either we came to this meeting or we lost our place. Siobhan said: "I've booked a holiday, can I have my meeting earlier?" and they gave in to her. Then we were given a specific deadline for our campaign spending, to promote our candidacy for the selection. I set about assembling a board of Lib Dem supporters, and advisory board, a PR company, getting speaking engagements and interviews in the press, including a full page in the Evening Standard.

Then, with a single day's notice, the leadership moved the deadline forward by a month to 28th September. It meant that several of the formal contracts I'd taken out had to be cancelled, even though I couldn't get any refunds. It meant that I lost about £30,000, but more importantly, it meant that I couldn't put my candidacy in front of London-based Lib Dem members. This decision was clearly aimed at knocking out my candidacy, because all the others were already well-known to London members. This was infuriating and I protested to Vince Cable's office, to Baroness Doocey of the Lib Dem English Party, who was overseeing the process. She said that the person responsible apologised, but that was little help to me. I told the party that if this sort of sharp and dishonest behaviour happened again, I'd sue.

In the end, Siobhan won the election and I tied for second place with Rob Blackie before second choice votes were counted, when I dropped to third, ahead of Lucy Salek. Siobhan was always a strong candidate. She came from Anglo-Indian parentage and she did quite well, even if she kept coming to me for money.

(To my surprise, in late July 2020, Siobhan decided to withdraw from the mayoral election, which had been delayed due to Covid-19 from March 2020 until 2021. This meant that – if I was still interested – I could take part in a re-run of the election, with Siobhan's votes re-distributed to me and the other candidates. It's an amusing turn of events – although sad for Siobhan that the delay has proved fatal to her ambitions – but I've decided not to compete for the position. That ship has sailed.)

After Tim Farron resigned after our poor showing in the 2017 election, Vince Cable took over the party in July 2017. Vince was far more the sort of leader who appealed to me, even though he came from the left of the party (he started out as a Labour supporter). We shared an educational history – like me he studied at Fitzwilliam College, Cambridge – before gaining a PhD in economics, writing widely on politics and economics and shaping the coalition's economic policy as Business Secretary. He was a heavyweight political figure who gave the Lib Dems the best grounding and reputation they'd had since Sir Menzies Campbell was leader.

In the May 2019 local elections, Vince led us to a historic result of controlling 18 councils (ten more than before) and 1352 councillors (706 more than before), then to similarly excellent European Parliament election results. So he went out on a great high. People complained that he was too old to lead the party, but he was only 73 – both of the candidates in the 2020 American presidential election were older than that.

After falling short in the mayoral selection process, I decided to have a second go at selection, this time to get to become a Member of the European Parliament (MEP). Once again, there was a short-list of prime candidates and once again there was fierce competition to get to the top. This time, my main rivals were a Harvard-educated German human rights lawyer with the grand-sounding name of Irina von Wiese und Kaiserswaldau and Luisa Porritt, who had just become a Lib Dem councillor the year before.

There was a party policy, stating that any London candidate of BAME descent, with a disability, or from the LGBTQ community would automatically rise one place in the voting table. Yet after voting had closed (and before the votes had been counted, and I came second to Irina von Weise by six votes) the party suddenly changed the rules. They said: "We're not doing it because of complaints from the West Country".

I was convinced that only one of us would be elected, so once again, I was beside myself at this sleight of hand, which seemed directly aimed at preventing my election. How could they change the rules, after voting had finished? It's like seeing a football team score a goal, then saying that the goalposts were in the wrong position.

So I took the Lib Dem English Party to the High Court and lost on a technicality, on gender equality grounds. My lawyers urged me to appeal, but I decided I'd leave it there. In the end, all three of us were elected because there was a huge surge towards the Lib Dems, in reaction to Brexit. Plus Labour and the Conservatives didn't bother to contest the election, because they figured it wasn't worth taking up the seats for the short time until Brexit happened, so we had an easy run. I'd say that our slogan – Bollocks to Brexit – was another factor in winning so many local council and MEP seats.

With Michel Barnier, 2019

From July 2019 until February 2020 I was working in Brussels, going to around five events and meetings a day from Monday to Wednesday, then voting on Thursday. Compared with the way the UK parliament votes, it was a model of efficiency and speed. Instead of trooping through the lobbies, which takes ages, we had a choice of three buttons to press: yes, no or abstain. It took seconds, so we could rattle through multiple votes in no time.

Besides leading the India delegation and taking part in the South Korean delegation, I was on the Single Market committee, looking at gambling, air fares, 5G telecoms, mobile phone chargers. The charger issue really caught my imagination, because it was a great example of corporate waste and obstinacy. Apple, Samsung and other manufacturers all produced different plugs and adaptors for their chargers, costing around €25 or €30 each. The same company would even produce a different charger for a new generation phone. It meant that chargers for the 50 million phones sold annually in Europe were heading for landfill.

We were determined to deal with this issue and force them to adopt the same standard charger, saving consumers money and protecting the environment. Apple initially refused to compromise. They said: "Our plug is totally different to anyone else's." Then we discovered that, for some products, they'd used a Samsung type of plug. So we told them: "You have to change." And eventually they did. I found out a lot about how the single market could become more efficient than it is.

We had a similar argument with the aviation industry. We worked out that, because every European country has its own air traffic control system, this adds 10 or 12 minutes to each flight, on average. With hundreds of flights a day, that adds up to more pollution, higher costs to the airlines, meaning lost time and higher costs for passengers. I found that ridiculous. So we invited the aviation industry lobbyist to speak to us. He said: "There will be a new system in 2024, with only three or four control points, and by the end of the decade there will be only one." I said: "Why not immediately?" They were delaying to protect jobs across air traffic control. (They were quite glad to see me leave).

I was also on the Budget Committee, because I wanted to find out how much we paid into the EU, so I'd have evidence when tackling Brexiteers. We paid £8.2 billion a year, which compares with £12 billion a year that we pay on overseas aid (or did, until the Department for International Development was abolished by the Tories in June 2020).

Making a point in EU Parliament, 2020

There was room for me to pursue projects which had a personal significance: I hosted an exhibition along with the British Embassy in Brussels, on banned wild animal products from sale in Europe, and a yoga and meditation exhibition. I attended a parliamentary Ayurveda day, based on Indian allopathic medicine. That attracted a lot of interest: the Indian Ambassador to the EU came along.

For the 2019 UK General Election, I gave another £220,000 to the Lib Dems. Not much next to the £8 million that David (Lord) Sainsbury gave us, the biggest political donation in British history. Sadly it didn't achieve his aim of preventing Brexit and it didn't even keep our leader Jo Swinson in her seat. She lost, and although our vote share went up to 3.6 million votes, we lost a seat and came down to 11 seats in the election.

Jo is an amazing person but not a leader. She lacked gravitas during the election. My choice for leader was Ed Davey, who was to the right of centre in the party. I thought he would be a better person for the job, but he still needs to prove himself and the first chance he had was at the May 2021 local elections, where the Lib Dems won an extra council and eight new seats, so that was an encouraging start.

From where I stood, the Lib Dems had some problematic internal contradictions. As the country's 'liberal' party, they proclaim their support for ethnic minorities, people with disabilities, LGBTQ, saying that they're more tolerant and inclusive than the other parties. But in its composition, it's a white, middle-class party. So the argument is very different when it comes to choosing its leaders. There were people who had worked for them for 30 or 40 years. They weren't prepared to see someone who donates money go above them. They'd say: "We hate money." And I'd reply: "I made it myself, it's not from my family. If I give £1 million, isn't that equal to 30 years working in the party?" Every party has to be a broad church if it wants to win big.

There's always an ambivalence in the party about whether we're tending towards the right or the left. In the 2019 election, we were caught on the horns of this dilemma. Labour had a large remain constituency, and many people urged us to stand down candidates in favour of Labour, to maximise the remain vote. But many natural Lib Dem voters are on the right of the spectrum, and they would have hated us to do deals with Corbyn. They detested him and his fiscal policies, his embrace of the militant left and his air of incompetence. Then there were the five million Tory remainers, who were desperate for a political home. If we had signalled that we'd do a deal with Boris to quash Brexit, if we held the balance of power, and ruled out agreeing to Corbyn's fiscal policies, they might have come over to us.

My proposal was to target the most promising 60 seats in the country, especially those half dozen where the ethnic vote could go our way, and try to swing those seats to us. We think we're a national party, but we lost our deposit in 136 seats in 2019. Not as bad as the 375 seats of 2017, costing us £187,500, but still a dreadful waste of time, money and resources. What's the point of sending candidates out to knock on hundreds of doors in constituencies where you're polling in fourth or fifth place, with 3 per cent of the vote? We should study the 2019 local election results and pour resources into those communities, recruiting businesses, individuals, NGOs, getting them to see the world how we see it. From our current 11 seats, if we went for 60, we might get up to 35 or 40. One absurdity is that within the party, there's an omerta over which seats are our best hope, because we don't want other parties to find out! It reminded me of building ebookers over two or three years. People thought we would fail because everyone would know our fares. Let them come and find us so that we can have a straight contest.

When it came to the 2019 election, Jo Swinson and the Scottish Nationalists triggered the ballot, not expecting that Nigel Farage would stand down in 317 seats, handing victory to Boris Johnson. The election came too early for Jo, she was an inexperienced leader and hadn't worked out where she could make alliances or influence the debate. At one stage, she truly believed she could become Prime Minister in her own right, with a majority in the House of Commons.

From a marketing point of view, the 2019 election was a disaster for the Lib Dems. We raised £17 million but our ratings kept falling. Our central office managers were like rabbits in headlights, watching Boris seduce the nation and Jo turn voters away. There was no alignment between the time and money spent, no agility or imagination. Barely anyone would open their doors to us when we were out canvassing. It's a dying form of electioneering, rapidly being replaced by social media posts and email campaigns.

Having Jeremy Corbyn as leader of the Labour Party caused us problems: whenever Labour moves to the left, it means the Lib Dems are squeezed out of the equation. It polarises the electorate – either you're a militant socialist determined to bring down capitalism or you're a committed Tory, fighting against the Red menace. When Labour has a more centrist leader like Tony Blair or Kier Starmer, there's much more room for Lib Dem views.

In the UK, 50 per cent of people work and pay taxes, while the other 50 per cent are children, pensioners, non-working parents or else they can't work for some reason such as disability. Society has to decide how to move money from these taxpayers to those who need support, with all the infrastructure of the NHS, social services, schools and hospitals that goes with it. Most people understand this and are grateful that we live in such a society and share the Lib Dem view of redistribution. The right-wing media, on the other hand, presses the case for stripping away public services and letting the free market decide.

With Tony Blair, 2006

As we've seen from the United States, this approach leaves millions in poverty, without affordable healthcare, eating junk food and suffering from obesity, opioid addiction and – most recently – the world's highest coronavirus death toll. Today, 69 per cent of the US population has less than $1000 in the bank. There's a huge and growing divide. In my political life, I've fought to prevent these trends developing in the UK and Europe. Promoting enterprise is crucial, but it must come with a social conscience and the wealth created must be distributed fairly. The Lib Dems best represent my views on these issues.

For the future, the Lib Dems have to rebuild their position starting from the grassroots. They're good at local politics because their activists are very earnest, they make sure the rubbish bins are collected, so they can do well. That's our mentality, trying to do the smallest things for everyone. I don't think local communities ever regret voting Lib Dem councillors in.

When it comes to regional or national politics, it's a different story. Somehow, we lack the national leadership and organisation that we enjoyed under Paddy Ashdown, the charismatic SAS soldier, or Charles Kennedy when he opposed the Iraq War, or Nick Clegg in coalition in the 2010s, which brought us a lot of new supporters.

What the Lib Dems have to do in future is to make any coalition offer contingent upon Proportional Representation (PR). Not to offer a referendum, as we did with David Cameron in 2011, which resulted in a 67 per cent defeat, but a firm commitment to enact PR into law, which the government could then pass, since it would have a majority in parliament. Either that, or the Labour/Conservative leader would have to call another election and risk losing power. Of the world's advanced democracies, the only ones without PR are the United States, India and the UK. I think PR would result in better decisions and a more just distribution of wealth.

By the next UK election in 2024, the Tories' lead will probably have fallen from 10.5 per cent to more like 5 or 6 per cent, so if Labour has a pact with the Lib Dems where they agree not to stand against one another, that could be decisive. There are 80 seats where the Lib Dems came second to the Tories: if Labour stood down in those and we stood down where Labour have a good chance, it could redraw the British political map. I think with Kier Starmer as Labour leader, there is a good chance of this happening. The two parties have to follow the example of Nigel Farage, when he stood down 317 candidates contesting seats the Tories could win, presenting them with a large majority in 2019.

A 2020 report from lobby group Compass pointed out areas of policy agreement between Labour, the Lib Dems and the Greens, including renewable energy investment and welfare reform, and urged Kier Starmer to build bridges with his fellow leaders. There's very little chance that, on its own, Labour could achieve a 10.5 per cent swing against the Conservatives, but in combination with other progressives, it could be possible. The promise of PR would energise Lib Dem activists and could win the 60-odd seats where a progressive vote would overturn the Tories.

A lot depends upon who business supports: my priority is to get people with resources to join the party. Lib Dem activists are great, they're evangelical, but they don't have two pennies to rub together.

When you compare our situation with the United States, BAME people have more opportunities to thrive politically. There are now 20 people of Indian heritage in the White House under Joe Biden. They're judged not by their colour but whether they're good or not. They can earn their spurs easily if they're good: it's not so easy here.

If you look at Kamala Harris, she's half Indian, half Afro-Caribbean – the perfect combination; she was an attorney and a senator. It's a great story and raises the stock of all Indians in America. There's a long-standing history of achievement. The Indian education system at a junior level is very competitive, and when people move overseas they have to be very good to succeed, because they don't have much money.

To an extent, the same thing is happening in the UK, with the high profile of people like Rishi Sunak as Chancellor and Sadiq Khan as Mayor of London. I'd love to see that continue and accelerate.

The British Parliament

For the next couple of years, Boris will be fine because he's still a relatively new leader and anyone would have been thrown by COVID. He's very good at rallying people around him, so the public will forgive him. By 2024, though, the electorate will have seen through him: when your economic market contracts from 500 million to 68 million, it has a knock-on effect. We're used to getting our tomatoes from Spain etc. Once the price of everything in the supermarkets has gone up and real incomes gone down, there will be a massive swing away from the Tories. I predict a landslide against them, along the lines of Tony Blair's victory in 1997. It's too early to judge how Kier Starmer will perform in an election, but he has to be better than Jeremy Corbyn.

What's worrying to me is the calibre of people in Johnson's cabinet. All the intellectuals, like Dominic Greave (Magdalen College Oxford) and Oliver Letwin (Trinity College Cambridge), were Remainers, so they're out of the picture. When you look at Pritti Patel as Home Secretary, you have to be concerned about a lack of substance. My philosophy would be to enhance the economic position of everyone in the country. This Tory government has allowed politics and 'sovereignty' to trump economy and trade.

In line with its xenophobic Brexiteering, the government introduced a 'National Security and Investment Bill' in late 2020, meaning that it could more easily disqualify foreign takeovers of British companies, even five years after the event. This was aimed at Chinese investments such as Huawei, but will hit buyers from any country. Why would anyone want to invest in the UK, when the deal could be cancelled years later?

Once British people start asking 'Where's our extra independence?' in return for higher prices, restricted travel, delays and bureaucracy, they'll want some answers from Boris and his motley crew.

Chapter 15
The Tragedy of Brexit and the impact of COVID-19

As an immigrant to Britain who built a Europe-wide company employing thousands of people, then represented London in the European Parliament, Brexit feels very personal to me. Throughout my career, I've seen the enormous benefits that Britain has reaped from membership of the European Union: the boost to trade, the decades of peace following centuries of war, the cultural cross-fertilisation that improved everything from food to football, to the freedom of movement which broadened everyone's horizons.

Brexit threatens to return Britain to the insular, declining nation that it was in the mid-20th century, after World War II removed the last vestiges of Empire. Brexit was the reason that I entered politics and donated more than £1 million to the Liberal Democrat cause; it was a direct contradiction of all the lessons I'd learnt from business, from politics and from life.

Let me explain.

Brexiteers argue that once we have 'taken back control' of our laws and regulations, Britain will be better able to thrive in a global marketplace. My response is that, as a $3 trillion economy, Britain is hopelessly outclassed in international trading negotiations with the United States ($20 trillion economy) and China ($15 trillion economy). As part of the EU, we were part of a $19 trillion economy which could punch its weight on the global stage. Alone, we will be bullied and forced to accept inferior trading terms. The additional cost of all the customs checks and administration will hamper the UK's economic growth for years to come.

They say that British firms will do better without 'unelected bureaucrats in Brussels telling us what to do'. Besides the fact that European Members of Parliament are all elected and instruct bureaucrats just like British MPs instruct civil servants, the percentage of UK laws that come from Europe is very small – only around 13 per cent – and most of these are common sense, progressive rules like paternity leave and minimum wages, or ones with clear benefits to consumers like reduced mobile phone roaming charges.

The idea that Brexit will somehow return sovereignty to British people is misguided, in my view. In trade, we either subscribe to the EU's rules, giving us access to a market of 515 million people and 60 hard-won trade deals with countries worldwide, or we subscribe to World Trade Organisation rules, which means tariffs on our exports, higher costs and prices and – most likely – a sharp decline in the economy. Trade deals are hugely complex to negotiate, they typically take six to ten years to agree, because there are so many issues to resolve, both financial and political. Brexiteers promised that they would conclude dozens of deals at breakneck speed. Just one of their many undeliverable promises.

Besides the WTO, we already subscribe to the European Court of Justice, to the European Court of Human Rights, to the United Nations and its many agencies. The notion that we can split ourselves off from international treaties and agreements is a fantasy. The closest that any nation currently comes to full sovereignty is North Korea and I don't think we want to copy them. Since voting to leave the EU in 2016, the UK has already lost representation on the International Court of Justice in the Hague, with the judge replaced by one from India. The UK had a seat on this court from its foundation in 1946, until now.

What everyone is looking for is a better standard of living for themselves and their families. The way to achieve this is through fewer laws, more freedom, more single markets and more trade. Because Brexit will mean duplication of many of the regulations agreed across Europe, it will only add to the bureaucracy that people and companies face, it won't remove it, as Brexiteers wishfully imagine. According to the latest estimates, the UK will have to complete an extra 215 million new customs declarations, costing £7 billion, each year as a result of Brexit. This money will have to be paid by the British people, not by the government.

Years ago, if you took £100 and travelled to 10 European countries and changed your money at every border, you'd come home with nothing. Who would make money? The banks and currency exchanges. How does that help us? The same thing applies with trade tariffs across borders, the UK is bound to lose most. It will also lose privileged access to the massive supply chain resources across the EU, which makes up a high proportion of UK manufacturing. That's one reason the auto industry is so upset about Brexit, and why manufacturers like Toyota and Nissan are shifting operations out of the UK, along with hi tech firms like Sony and Panasonic. They only came to Britain in the first place because they knew they could export tariff-free into the rest of Europe. Without that, they'd rather be in Slovakia alongside Volkswagen and the rest of the European auto industry.

People say that we'll be able to trade globally, to become 'Singapore on Thames' and take advantage of digital technology to trade with India and China. There are logical problems with all of these ambitions. The Singapore on Thames concept will fall down if Britain tries to attract companies with a low-tax environment. Countries and blocs like the EU are moving towards taxing companies where their services are delivered, rather than where they're headquartered. The Americans are resisting this measure: they don't want Amazon, Google and Facebook to be charged for what they deliver to Europeans, but that's exactly the kind of pressure you can exert with a $19 trillion economy behind you, where you also fund NATO. The UK couldn't do that on its own, with its $3 trillion economy.

Even if we agree a mutually-beneficial trade deal with the United States, government figures show it would add just 0.16 per cent to the UK's GDP. Free trade agreements with Australia and New Zealand would be worth even less to us. Part of the reason is that trading in goods is far more expensive when they have to travel a long way: it's known as the gravity factor. Brexiteers are either ignorant of these laws of physics or somehow believe they don't apply to them.

In their dreams, Brexiteers believe that the UK will be free to create 'world-beating' companies once it is free of the shackles of the EU. This is another idle fantasy. The truly global giants of the 21st century like Amazon, Google and Facebook reached their current size thanks to the 330 million consumers in their back yard. They now spend billions of dollars a year on marketing, putting themselves far out of reach of UK competitors. What's needed is a Europe-wide determination to create industrial champions, along the lines of Airbus, which (until COVID-19) had earned a competitive advantage over America's Boeing.

Whatever new inventions we come up with in Britain get so much money thrown at them by US-based private equity investors that they're forced to relocate to the US: tech companies go to Silicon Valley and biotechs to Boston. In the travel industry, where I worked, a company like Booking.com spends $5 billion a year on Google advertising. How is a UK business going to compete with that? The only way to do it is in collaboration with European allies.

During my time as a business owner, I wanted Britain to be an order giver rather than an order taker, to dictate how commercial relationships developed. This worked out well for me, because the British as a whole, in my view, are better entrepreneurs than the Europeans. We used European customers to make money in the UK. You can see a similar pattern between Western and Eastern Europe: the EU dishes out funds for new infrastructure in the East, but that's nothing compared to what the West gets in return, through selling German and French products to their populations.

Without industrial champions, you get situations such as the tussle over 5G, where China is promoting Huawei and the US is issuing threats to stop Europe adopting its technology. If Nokia and Eriksson merged their 5G capabilities, with support from the EU, the continent could have a global player of its own. At the moment there's no chance of competing against US and Chinese marketing muscle. Amazon is using European consumers as fodder.

In July 2020 the UK government had to bow to US pressure over Huawei's role in 5G, just a few weeks after it had announced that the Chinese company would be allowed a limited role. Boris Johnson was given no choice. He wasn't persuaded to drop Huawei, he was told to, or else the US would apply sanctions to British trade. Would the US have said the same thing to the entire European Union, at the risk of getting sanctions on US trade in return? I don't think so. That's just one example of where, as a so-called independent nation, we are now powerless to resist the strong-arm tactics of other states.

What I found in the European Parliament was that it constantly tried to remove the barriers to free trade. We opened up the mobile phone market, so people no longer had to pay extortionate roaming charges. We fought against vested interests like city mayors who made money from taxi franchises; we supported Uber, Lyft and Halo coming in. We urged countries to merge their air traffic control operations, to save time, money and fuel. Everything was heading towards greater efficiency, towards frictionless trade and higher productivity.

Without these benefits, following the Brexit vote, the UK will already have forfeited an estimated £200 billion by the end of 2020, according to Bloomberg Economics. This, it points out, is close to the entire amount paid by the UK into the European Union budget over the past 47 years. The analysis found that the British economy is already 3 per cent smaller than it would have been if we had voted to remain, and will shrink further still. The Conservative government Treasury figures show a 5 per cent fall in GDP lasting until 2035. Is this really what people voted for? Of course, it will be blamed on COVID-19 rather than Brexit.

A frictionless, efficient, highly productive economy is what the United States has had for 150 years, since it resolved the North-South conflict in the Civil War. Without some similar cataclysmic drama in Europe, it may take several more generations before we reach this economic nirvana. Brexit could be one step along this path: future Europeans will look back and see how Britain suffered as a result (or else decided it had made a terrible mistake and pleaded to be re-admitted).

The idea that the United States will offer us some kind of sweetheart deal, based on our 'special relationship', is just as fanciful as the rest of Brexiteers' fantasies. Did they listen to President Trump's America First, transactional rhetoric? Do they expect the US to put caviar and steak on a plate for us? People use these emotional arguments to justify their positions, whereas I'm simply being realistic. The US will not make life easier for us because we speak the same language. They'll bully us and force us to accept inferior conditions because they can and because it enriches them.

Although Britain is transitioning from a manufacturing nation into a more high-tech, services-based economy, after the 2016 referendum, London soon began losing its crown as Europe's prime tech hub to Berlin. Amsterdam and Stockholm also gained ground. The thing with software engineers is that they're a very fluid resource. If they're stuck in the UK, needing permits, needing visas, they're likely to move to the continent where they have more freedom and job opportunities. Politically, the whole thrust of Brexit is anti-immigrant, whether from the EU or from elsewhere. When Theresa May was Prime Minister, she went to India and met with Narendra Modi. He asked her how many software engineers she would allow into Britain and she replied: "None."

My view is that a points system for immigration would work very well. It's worked for Canada, for Australia and for the United States. At the moment, people like me are seen by Brexiteers as brown-skinned, we're looked down upon by the Conservative government, despite so many senior figures like Rishi Sunak having Indian heritage. The same thing applies to EU countries like Romania. There are thousands of highly-skilled Romanians who were educated in their own country and want to come to the UK. It's a disaster for Romania because their best and brightest people want to leave. But British businesses consider them too much of a risk, because they equate Romania with gypsies and crime. In my experience, Romanians have superb technology skills. Like many Eastern Europeans, they're tremendously hard-working, resourceful people. They just want to earn a living, proving to their friends and relatives that they made a good decision, then go back to Romania, buy a plot of land and retire.

The UK Office for Budget Responsibility (OBR), having calculated the effect of Brexit on the UK economy, estimated that Britain's borrowing costs will rise by £1 billion a year in 2024, as a result of restricting the flow of low-skilled EU labour into Britain. The country stands to lose £1.5 billion a year in lower tax receipts, due to lower immigration, while saving only £500 million through lower welfare spending. When asked about the 'economic opportunities' flowing from Brexit that the government is keen to stress, Michael Gove could only point to the 50,000 customs agents that will be needed to fill out forms, as British firms grapple with the new trade complexities.

When I was campaigning for Remain with Nick Clegg, we found that opposition to immigration was the number one issue on the doorstep. This was true of immigrants themselves – 40 per cent voted for Brexit, not because they were stupid, but because they thought their jobs were under threat from Eastern Europeans. But the fact is that immigrants perform the jobs that British people can't or won't do, either because they feel the jobs are too menial for them, or because of geography. It's hard for British nationals to uproot their families and move to a remote part of the UK, whereas immigrants are grateful for a chance to work. So Indian nurses will take jobs in Scunthorpe, for example, which English nurses who live in London might refuse.

The Conservative government is clearly hoping that the productive, entrepreneurial leaders stay in the UK post-Brexit and build a New Jerusalem on England's green and pleasant land. But why should they stay, if there are greater incentives, better conditions and a larger market on offer in Europe? You might think that necessity is the mother of invention, but for today's bright young businesspeople, the world is their oyster. At least gaining some of the three million Hong Kong residents is some kind of light at the end of the tunnel. I'd like to see their entrepreneurs come over here.

The largest UK-based companies in the FTSE100 do most of their trade outside the UK and they have the resources to deal with Brexit. For exporters, who do 44 per cent of their trade with Europe, they'll have to overhaul their costs or else move their offices to Dublin or Amsterdam, which will be expensive. They'll do it, but it means their companies will no longer be British and our jobs will go to the continent. In a competition between an Amsterdam-based company with a market of 450 million people and a London company with a market 68 million, there's only going to be one winner. The bigger offices, in Europe, won't employ British people.

The idea that we have greater economic and fiscal flexibility outside the EU is another myth. During the Brexit debate, nobody was telling Britain that it had to join the euro, just as nobody forced Gordon Brown to sell half the country's gold reserves for $250 dollars an ounce in 1999. (In July 2020, gold was selling at $1800 an ounce). What I can confidently predict is that the euro will appreciate relative to sterling, because it's traded by 450 million people in Europe compared with 68 million British people trading in pounds. When China switched out of dollars, they didn't buy pounds, they bought euros – it's the new global reserve currency, second only to the US dollar.

Along with a weak currency, Brexit promises to devastate many traditional industries. If we're trading under WTO rules, there would be tariffs of 10 per cent on car exports and 30 per cent on dairy products. Look at the Welsh sheep farmers: they voted overwhelmingly for Brexit, but 90 per cent of British lamb goes to Europe. If tariffs go up, imagine what's going to happen to them. The same applies across the UK: the regions that were suffering the most, after years of austerity imposed by successive Conservative governments, voted most emphatically for Brexit. Already, these same regions are in trouble. A report by the Centre for Competitive Advantage in the Global Economy, published in July 2020, showed that: "Areas of the UK that voted to leave the EU have suffered the biggest economic hit since the 2016 referendum," as the Financial Times reported. Places like the West Midlands, which rely upon manufacturing. They were bitter that the metropolitan elites in London were prioritising finance and services at their expense. But blaming Europe for the sins of Westminster is like demolishing your roof because your windows are broken. Blaming immigrant workers is even less logical: they are a net economic benefit to the country, draw upon less welfare payments and haven't cost the country anything to train and educate.

What Brexiteers really wanted was political: to 'take back control' of immigration policy after decades in which the monocultural whiteness of British society had been diluted by people like me. Never mind that we contributed far beyond our share in raising the economy to its current heights, that we gave the country its Chinese takeaways, its Indian curry houses, its kebab shops and its French bistros; that 3,268 foreign soccer players from 111 countries have made the Premier League the world's best since 1992 (and that British schoolchildren can now pronounce their names); and that BAME people, from Shirley Bassey to Freddie Mercury to Stormzy, from Nasser Hussain to Marcus Rashford, from Mo Farah to Kelly Holmes, have made their nation proud.

Brexit is an attempt to deal with the UK's problem of uneven income distribution, which will not address its causes or provide any real solution. If anything, it will make these problems worse, as the country's economy suffers and there is less to go around. Both small and large businesses in the UK will suffer: small ones will find it harder to expand, because they'll be limited to one country instead of 28; we'll go back to an era of small bespoke British businesses that stay forever in start-up mode, never fully able to scale. This cannot be an engine for job growth. Manufacturers will find it harder to be competitive as they pay tariffs on their supplies and components from Europe and are then hit with more tariffs when they export goods back into Europe.

What's especially painful for me, as someone who benefited enormously from the European single market when I built and sold ebookers, is that a new generation of British entrepreneurs will be denied these opportunities, just as students are losing the chance to study at European universities that they've enjoyed for many years. Most of all, as the Financial Times put it in July 2020, Brexiteers' economic arguments are 'a costly and damaging sham'.

We'll live to regret this decision. Still, I'm now committed to getting the best version of Brexit possible.

What I think that the UK needs to do now is to get thousands of software engineers to move here, using an Australian-style immigration points system and encouraging people to come. There's more and more competition for this kind of talent: Lisbon has launched a scheme to attract tech entrepreneurs, including refugees from Brexit, with low taxes and special visas. Portugal has a flourishing venture capital sector. Within weeks of Brexit in January 2021, Amsterdam had already overtaken London as the share-dealing capital of Europe. Berlin and Tel Aviv are two other cities competing hard for software professionals.

The fear of immigration which underpinned Brexit is liable to stifle the UK's economic recovery if we're not careful. We're already having trouble filling the jobs that immigrants used to do, like seasonal farm work and nursing. Most of all, we need to tap resources like Romanian workers, who are among the best software engineers in the world.

Post-Brexit, we're already seeing small fishing companies and other food producers going bankrupt because they can't export their products to Europe. Boris Johnson had to do a deal by the end of 2020. He didn't care much about fishing, or any other business – 80 per cent of the UK economy is in services and there was nothing about these in the deal, not even financial services, which contributes more than £130 billion to the economy and supports 1.1 million jobs. He really delivered on his threat to 'f*** business'.

The EU's attitude to Britain in early 2021 is a taste of what's to come: we chose to leave, so we can't expect any favours from them. And their market is seven times the size of ours, so they have the upper hand in any negotiations. Tough luck.

As an entrepreneur, paperwork has never really bothered me. You deal with it to get what you want. But why put in these extra layers of bureaucracy? Jobs are now moving to the continent. Many service businesses are setting up

EU offices, we've seen 350 companies in a queue waiting to be dealt with by the Dutch Development Authority.

The impact of COVID-19

Brexit coinciding with the COVID-19 pandemic was terrible timing in many ways, because it dampened global economic activity and caused eruptions of nationalism, even from the normally collegiate Europeans, as when Ursula von der Leyen tried to ban Northern Ireland from importing vaccines. Together with the dreadful loss of life, the effects of 'long-COVID' could also be horrific: by some estimates people could lose up to 10 years from their lifespan.

I'm optimistic that the UK's economy will recover quite quickly. We seem to have a bottomless pit of money to support businesses and stave off recession and the government wants to win the next election of course. The other impact of the pandemic is how it has advanced all kinds of technologies: videoconferencing apps like Zoom and Teams have improved tenfold since the beginning of 2020. There are fewer and fewer reasons to spend hours traveling into cities. You can submit documents online and do all kinds of things that save time and money. I have to say that's great.

Whereas pre-COVID, extroverts had the best lives, now introverts have come into their own. You adapt to different circumstances. As Darwin said: "It is not the strongest of the species that survives, nor the most intelligent, it is the one most adaptable to change." COVID has forced change on all of us in the most dramatic ways.

For businesses, COVID has made it easier to hire employees from anywhere in the world. If we're communicating online, there's no great reason to hire UK-based employees. As long as they're self-motivated, national boundaries are irrelevant. These days, when I log on to international business and science conferences, there might be five out of 50 people from Harvard, but the rest from everywhere else in the world – people who could never have afforded to attend such meetings before.

I've bought an Oculus Quest 2 headset and enjoy experimenting with it. There's a programme which makes you feel as though you're floating through space, even when you know your feet are planted on the floor. I can see that in future, meetings will use this technology. You just need one of these headsets costing something like $250 and you can see everyone in 3D, rather than in 2D from a videoconference.

During the pandemic they're becoming very popular. People are cooped up and virtual reality can take them to distant lands – you can visit the Great Wall of China from your living room. It's good for exercise too. You can have a tennis racquet in both hands and hit virtual balls that are flying towards you, with dance music on the soundtrack.

As a business idea, it's taking off in a huge way. There's a New York-based virtual reality company called Spatial.io co-founded by Anand Agarawala which expanded its sales by 130 times in 2020. Companies like Ford and Pfizer use his technology to get 3D versions of Zoom or Slack and it's had millions of dollars in venture capital funding.

For the business travel sector, the pandemic is an absolute killer. People will still want to visit the Costa del Sol for the sunshine and beaches, but if I'm working for you, would you pay for me to fly, take taxis, stay in a hotel, eat in restaurants, just so I can have a meeting which could take place on Zoom or Teams for free? There will be mass unemployment in business travel, people will have to retrain. The model is broken.

What the pandemic has accentuated is business models changing much faster than ever before. The pace of change in 2020 was up to five times quicker, everyone had to adapt. In some ways the pandemic reminds me of the 2001 September 11 attacks on the World Trade Center in New York. The whole travel industry shut down overnight and for us, it was a near-catastrophe. Customers suddenly wanted their money back and ebookers' valuation fell from $770 million to $60 million. At the time, people commented that I seemed to be unperturbed. I was quoted saying: "I just couldn't do anything about it. Sometimes you just have to weather the storm and get through what life throws at you." I think the same is true of the pandemic. We're all in the middle of a terrible storm, and the best advice is to 'stay calm and carry on', as Churchill said.

Chapter 16
Passage from India

In the 1960s, my father owned some land in Delhi which the government seized, to build Jawaharlal Nehru University. Naturally enough, he sued the government for compensation. That court case is still running today!

This tells you an awful lot about Indian bureaucracy and how difficult it can be to get anything done. Over the decades, we've received some payment for the land, but very little, compared with its market value. My father passed away in 1999, so together with my brother, we've taken on the lawsuit, fighting with more than a dozen other freeholders, leaseholders, government representatives and an army of lawyers who have spent almost 60 years making money out of the case.

It's one reason why India is a $3 trillion economy whereas China's is $14 trillion, despite them being the same size back in 1992. For all its faults, China has encouraged commercial enterprise and devised a system that lifts millions of people out of poverty. India is the world's largest democracy, but has 400 million people living without sanitation or electricity.

Conditions in India, from its bureaucracy to its bathrooms, are what have kept me in Britain all these years, since arriving as a schoolboy in 1968. Although I was born in Canberra, Australia, as the son of a diplomat, my identity is firmly within the Indian diaspora. Most of my relatives still live in Delhi and elsewhere in India. My company thrived partly because of its amazing back-office operation based in India and I founded two charities that provide medical and educational help to thousands of Indian people. Nevertheless, I live in England, I'm a naturalised British citizen and have no plans to move. This is my home.

Why haven't I moved back to India, where people celebrate my successes almost as though I were a Bollywood movie star?

Well I grew up in India, went to school there, so I do know the country. And besides living in Mauritius, Afghanistan, Prague and Holland with my parents, followed by England, I've spent an awful lot of time in the United States. From all these experiences, I've concluded that I love England – and

Europe – the best. Europe has the greatest literature, the finest culture, the profoundest civilisation in the world. I could spend weeks in the lap of luxury in the finest spa hotels in India, but it wouldn't be the same as living there day to day.

If you compare how easy it is to start and grow a company in England compared with India, the differences are enormous. In some areas, like getting electricity connected and getting credit from banks, conditions in India have improved dramatically. In the World Bank 'Ease of Doing Business' rankings, the country jumped from 77th in 2019 to 63rd in 2020. But in terms of actually starting a business, registering property and enforcing contracts, India lies near the bottom of world rankings, below 150 or 160 other countries. If you want to buy somewhere in India and the solicitor says 'The property is fine, I've done checks', you have to be really careful. Due diligence is very sketchy, whether for property or for businesses. Most large companies are family conglomerates that emerged when the left-of-centre Congress Party was in power, and civil servants would seek to profit from dishing out business licences. As they developed, these firms became considered as personal fiefdoms. Even when they listed on stock exchanges and the family owned a small minority of shares, they were still considered the personal property of the family, with ex-government officials controlling majority stakes through government investment funds and propping them up. It's common for large business owners to siphon off money from investors for their own projects, while muzzling the press by threatening to withhold advertising. Corporate governance is still pretty lax in India, compared with the UK.

Under the BJP government of Narendra Modi, freedom of speech has suffered in India. Until he became prime minister, many of the press were intelligent and well-travelled. They knew what was going on in the US and the UK and would give suggestions of how to improve things. On the other hand, he's taken some brave decisions to bring the economy into the 21st century, to root out corruption and get people to pay their fair share of tax, and to tackle the religious persecution of Hindus in Pakistan and Bangladesh. Modi has done more than any Indian politician to alleviate poverty.

In the European Parliament I was head of the Indian delegation and had to deal with a number of issues thrown up by Modi's decisions. The first was when he homogenised the laws of Kashmir with the rest of India. Pakistan and the Green Party and human rights advocates immediately went on the offensive, saying this was a travesty of Kashmiri rights. At first I was ambivalent, but I suspected Pakistan of making trouble, because they claim part of Kashmir's territory, so I delved into it, went through speeches and read the constitution. In the end I fell squarely on the side of India.

On human rights, it was not that Kashmir suffered, but that its people gained new protections, rather than lost them. There were 40 laws in India to safeguard human rights, such as forbidding men from divorcing their wives simply by saying 'I divorce you' three times (the 'triple talaq'), which is unfair to women. Second, you could marry a child bride in Kashmir, as young as 12 or 13. And third, women could own a home, but if they married outside Kashmir, they lost the property. Wildlife laws that applied in India didn't apply in Kashmir. So I warned the EU parliament about how these old laws infringed human rights and we won the vote not to censure India.

For Modi, these were smart political moves. His opposition to the triple talaq and child brides was widely known and gave him the votes of millions of Muslim women, which helped swing the election in the BJP's favour and away from Congress. I think that, overall, he's done a better job than his Congress predecessors in running India. The Bharatiya Janata Party (BJP) has only run the country for 12 out of the 73 years since independence in 1947 but of course the COVID-19 pandemic has put everything back a great deal. India is still way behind China economically and it needs to be far more disciplined if it's going to get anywhere.

The second issue we had to deal with at the EU parliament was Modi's response to refugees. There was a forced mass migration of 1.9 million people from Pakistan and Bangladesh to India in 2008 – Christians, Sikhs, Parsees – and Modi promised that if they'd faced persecution, India would give them citizenship after living in the country for six years. He also specified that Muslims would still have to wait for 11 years (which was the original period of time) since by definition they would not be escaping religious persecution if they were fleeing Muslim countries, but rather moving for economic reasons.

There was a further outcry over this, because it was seen as religious discrimination against Muslims, and also because Ahmedia and Hazara minorities coming from Pakistan and Bangladesh weren't counted as Muslims by their previous countries, but neither were they granted sanctuary through the six year citizenship rule by India. My view was that India had the right to document people arriving at its borders and we won this vote too.

It was a tough experience, because the Lib Dem group in the European Parliament was corralled by a Muslim MEP into voting against India – he deliberately didn't invite me to a crucial meeting, despite me being chair of the Indian delegation for the entire parliament. So I had to appeal to the Conservative and Labour blocs, who fortunately agreed with me and we carried the vote against my own party's wishes.

Meanwhile, I did everything I could to promote a trade deal between the EU and India. At the moment, there are a series of tariffs on trade between the two sides, along with all kinds of side agreements and sector restriction, dealing with everything from used cars to generic drugs. Despite the lack of a Free Trade Agreement (FTA), the EU is nevertheless India's largest trading partner, making up 11 per cent of trade (as much as India has with the US and more than with its neighbour China).

All the main indicators of trade between the EU and India have flourished over the last few years. Since 2010 trade in goods has soared by 72 per cent and the EU's share of foreign investment into India has more than doubled, making it the largest foreign investor; and there are 6000 European companies working in India, employing 1.7 million people.

After attempting to agree an FTA in 2007, the two sides called a halt to negotiations in 2013 over what the Europeans called a 'lack of ambition', mainly over India's reluctance to include social, environmental and human rights clauses in the agreement and a failure to agree on ways to protect investments and intellectual property.

Talks started again in 2018 and when the FTA came up for discussion at the European Parliament, these same issues cropped up. The Greens were adamant that an agreement had to commit India to limiting its CO_2 emissions. So I did some research and found that India's CO_2 emissions are 7 per cent of the global total and Europe's are 9 per cent, even though India has 2.5 times as many people. So that shut them up. The other issues were human rights in Kashmir and the treatment of refugees, where I also managed to win votes, so that talks could progress. Narendra Modi was due to visit Europe in March 2020, but cancelled due to the Covid-19 pandemic.

As well as protecting investment and intellectual property, the EU wants 'investor-state dispute settlement' provisions. At the moment, foreign investors have to spend five years trying to resolve their problems in Indian courts – and, as we know, these cases can drag on forever. I think the Indian government would be prepared to budge on this, in return for a guarantee of more visas for Indian workers in Europe. But against the backdrop of the current European refugee crisis, with thousands of migrants queuing on the continent's borders and landing on its beaches, this is a tricky issue.

The rewards, though, are so enticing that I'm convinced that it is worth persevering. At a stroke, the current €125 billion worth of trade with the EU could be doubled, leading to the creation of a million jobs in Europe and two or three million in India. In my view, this boost to employment would be more valuable to India than getting visa regulations relaxed. This has always been my mantra: jobs bring prosperity.

In 2021, I think there are good signs of the relationship between the UK and India developing well. Both countries have applied for membership of the Comprehensive and Progressive Agreement for Trans-Pacific Partnership (CPTPP) and I think both sides will show flexibility in how they create new partnerships, which is what you need.

The best thing for the UK would be to get 10,000 Indian software engineers to come to Britain, that would be gold for us. We're expecting to get an influx of people coming from Hong Kong, which would be helpful, because like the Ugandan Asians of the 1970s they're entrepreneurial and they have money. But attracting some of India's millions of IT professionals is the bigger prize.

It was a shame that Boris Johnson had to cancel his scheduled visit to India in January 2021, where he was due to be guest of honour at the Republic Day parade. As the press noted at the time, he has a personal connection with India, since his ex-wife and mother of his four children Marina Wheeler is half-Indian and he often visited her cousins in Delhi and Mumbai. Among these cousins is veteran Indian journalist Rahul Singh, who reckons Boris will translate his warmth for India into action. "He is totally at home in India and Indian businesspeople like him. He said to me that because he was married to someone half-Sikh, all the Sikhs in Britain would vote for him," said Singh. "I think he will bring out policies favourable to India." As I write this in early 2021, Boris has promised to visit India later in the year and has invited Narendra Modi to the Cornwall G7 Summit in June.

On a broader scale, I would love to see India clean up its bureaucratic corruption. Even in 2021, administrators routinely demand extortionate bribes just to make simple transactions. Of course this dissuades the international business community from trading with India and holds the country back from developing as it should.

In China, by contrast, the authorities are ruthlessly stamping out corruption: if someone demands a bribe, they're taken out and shot or hanged in public. That's the difference between an autocracy and a corrupt democracy. India suffers from what's known as the 'politician-babu' (or 'babu-neta') nexus, where politicians, civil servants and big business leaders are complicit in corruption, each shielding the other from prosecution. If someone has to collect a payment of Rs 10,000, they'll demand Rs 15,000 and keep Rs 5,000 for themselves. It's known that 40 per cent of politicians in the Lok Sabha – the lower house of the Indian Parliament – have criminal records. So they oblige their civil servants to cover for them, which means the civil servants become crooks themselves. It's a decades-long problem: people just learn to live with it. In my view, there should be more summary justice in India.

The problem goes back to the days of the Raj, and the layers of bureaucracy that the British installed in India as a way of dividing and ruling the Muslims and the Hindus. Its destructive legacy is still with us, entrenched in society. The Congress Party, which ruled for most of the late 20th century, was fairer to minorities but couldn't work out how to make the country prosperous. It would give loans to poor farmers, then forgive them on the verge of an election.

The BJP, in power since 2014, is trying to reform the country but it's tough and slow. The bureaucrats depend on the system so they can afford their golf and gymkhana club memberships. The party has a nationalist fringe: it's quite open about saying Hindus were discriminated against for hundreds of years under Muslim rule. Now the Indian intelligentsia complain about Hindu superiority, but they don't cry about the stock market rising or wealth increasing. When the BJP cracks down on black money, house prices begin to move down from their inflated levels. So I'm a supporter of the BJP from the point of view that people need prosperity. It's a scandal that China has moved so far to abolish poverty while half a billion Indians lack running water or electricity.

There is a fierce debate going on in India over the BJP's direction, which makes for gripping entertainment when viewed from a distance. In February 2021 one firebrand MP from Bengal, Mahua Moitra, accused Narendra Modi of creating a fascist 'police state'. She accused him of choosing 'brutality over morality', in the BJP's repression of journalists and critics. Sometimes the law seems harshly administered: the highly-respected politician Shashi Tharoor, who made a famous speech at the Oxford Union castigating the British history of colonialism in India, faced prosecution in early 2021 for supporting a farmers' protest. Modi successfully persuaded Twitter to suspend hundreds of accounts critical of his government.

Mahua Moitra's attacks are one thing. When it comes to British people criticising India, they can easily fall into the trap of neo-colonialism, with one side assuming superiority over another. To me, the question is simple: is the Indian government doing a good job of lifting people out of poverty? The Congress Party was in power for 60 years and didn't make much economic progress. Now the BJP has had 12 years, achieved a lot, but gets flak for putting down dissent.

There are certainly some stupid laws in India, especially relating to investment. For example, non-resident Indians – me included – cannot buy agricultural land. How stupid is that? Am I going to put the mud over my shoulder and take it to London? Once in government, politicians have no time to learn. So that's one reason that rotation of power is a good thing.

For the UK-India relationship to thrive, people have to show imagination and flexibility. When Theresa May visited India in 2016, aiming to present the new open face of Brexit Britain, she promptly shut the door on any additional UK visas for Indian nationals. What she should have said was: "How many do you want? And in return I want such and such trade conditions for British firms in India." Almost five years later, we're not much further on, although there is a deal to be done. At least overseas companies can now own 74 per cent of insurance or legal firms in India, thanks to a BJP-sponsored privatisation drive.

By 2030, India will be the third largest economy in the world, behind China and the United States, whereas today it's behind the US, China, Japan and Germany, pretty much equal with the UK and France. What's extraordinary about this list is the GDP per head: for Americans its $65,000, for the Japanese, French, Germans and British its around $40,000, for the Chinese its $10,000 and for India – just $2,000. India will have to increase personal prosperity by more than 30 times to reach the wealth enjoyed in the States.

The Indian Diaspora

If you look at a list of the world's largest and wealthiest companies, an incredible number of them now have CEOs of Indian heritage. Google, Microsoft, Pepsi, Mastercard, Diageo, Nokia, Adobe... the list goes on. It's a 21st century phenomenon, and it's symptomatic of a global rise in the status of Indian technocrats. In the United States, Indians' average income is $90,000 a year, compared with $50,000 overall. They're more often college educated, they work hard and contribute to society. The stereotype of Apu the Indian shopkeeper in the Simpsons cartoon is way out of date, it is about time they dropped it.

Many Indian companies have also done incredibly well recently, so it's not just those who have left the country: Reliance Industries' market cap is close to a trillion dollars, with Tata Consultancy Services and HDFC Bank well over $500 billion each. But despite this, for most Indians, the pot of gold remains very small in India, compared with what they can aim for elsewhere. For decades now, Indians have spotted that the rewards were largest in the United States and headed over there. For me, the east and west coasts of US are fine, but I'd never want to live there, especially in the mid-West, where levels of education are often low and there's a lack of culture.

Indians are by nature and by circumstances very entrepreneurial people. They have to be, since there's virtually no welfare safety net. They have to get off their haunches and do something if they want to make any money. And it's a very young population – 60 per cent of the country is under 35.

If you look back 300 years, India was the wealthiest country in the world, earning 23 per cent of global GDP. Once the East India Company gained control of the country in the early 18th century, the wholesale rape of the country began and continued for 250 years until independence in 1947, when India represented 3 per cent of global GDP. The 'master-servant' relationship with Britain didn't work out very well for India.

What I like is being part of the Indian community in England. It's something that I've become closer to in recent years. When I was a student and starting out in business, I kept the Indian community at arm's length: I wanted to make it on my own terms, building an international enterprise rather than selling to a specific group. After selling ebookers, I spent more time working with TiE, short for The Indus Entrepreneurs, which supports and promotes (mainly) Asian businesspeople all around the world, including London. I was president of TiE London from 2014 to 2017 and built it up from just a handful of charter members to 83 by the time I stepped down. We got some great speakers to come along, like Manish Madhvani, senior partner at GP Bullhound, the leading European technology bank which spotted eight unicorns [companies that have topped $1 billion in valuation] and invested early. We had Luke Johnson, who built Pizza Express from 12 restaurants to 250, and the Indian yogi Sadhguru Jaggi Vasudev, who has spoken at the World Economic Forum in Davos and has 25 million followers. After that, I became a trustee of TiE's global board in Silicon Valley, then vice chair of the organisation worldwide until 2020, putting in a few words here and there. In 2021 I took on the role of global head of fundraising.

While Indian men focus on business in the United States, a number of Indian heritage women have risen up the political ranks and achieved prominence. On the Republican side, Donald Trump appointed Nikki Haley Ambassador to the United Nations in 2016, while for the Democrats, Kamala Harris became a Californian senator in 2017 and is now Joe Biden's Vice President.

Indians have succeeded across business and politics in the UK too: the Hindujas and the Mittals are among the wealthiest families in the country; Rishi Sunak is Chancellor, Priti Patel is Home Secretary, Lisa Nandy is Shadow Foreign Secretary and Sadiq Khan, whose family is from Pakistan, is Mayor of London. Such a spread of wealth and power was unthinkable a generation ago.

My roles in business and politics put me at the centre of both of these worlds, something I'm very grateful to have experienced. Although my achievements weren't the direct result of support from fellow Indian businesspeople or politicians, the fact that Indians are now very widely accepted in positions of great trust and responsibility means that my path was made slightly easier, just as I hope to have made the path easier for future generations of Indians as they make their way through life.

How Narendra Modi has Transformed India

Since his landslide election victory in 2014, Narendra Modi and the BJP have remade Indian society and its economy, giving the country a newfound pride in itself and an enhanced role in global affairs. Despite criticism for his role in the 2002 Gujarat riots, when he was governor of the state and hundreds of people died, and for his seemingly impulsive orders banning high denomination banknotes in 2016 and locking down the population overnight in 2020, he has kept an amazingly high percentage of Indians on side. His approval rating at the height of the pandemic in July 2020 was 74 per cent.

Like other 21st century leaders, Modi has succeeded in using social media as a powerful tool to bolster his leadership. His army of followers deflects blame for any disasters or poor decisions onto state governments or onto Indians themselves, including the Muslim minority. He managed to put responsibility for the deadly clash with Chinese troops in the Himalayas onto the previous Congress party government. The national press gives him an easy ride because he controls government advertising spending, which pays their bills.

In May 2020, Modi announced a $266 billion stimulus package to boost the domestic economy and attract investment into India. He wants to make the country an alternative to China for the US, Japan and Europe, just at the point where more and more people are growing wary, or even hostile, to China and its overbearing influence. Xi Jinping's decision to impose new security laws on Hong Kong in July, and America's refusal to allow Huawei access to 5G contracts, have convinced many countries that China can't be trusted. If India can win the trust of the global community, this could indeed be "India's century" as Modi likes to say.

Looking again at the World Bank's Ease of Doing Business rankings, with China in 30th place and India in 63rd, I find it hard to understand why India still struggles with these categories – fulfilling contracts, or getting building permission. There are so many intelligent people in India, you'd think they'd be able to work together and achieve better progress.

With Modi, you can draw parallels with a leader like Vladimir Putin in Russia: he is adept at personal myth-making, for example disappearing into a remote Himalayan cave to meditate after his 2014 election victory, and refusing to hold press conferences or live media interviews. Many Indians now regard him as their saviour, someone who has given up the trappings of wealth to fight for them (echoing Mahatma Gandhi's lifestyle). They see Modi as a national messiah who will return the country to national greatness, which has a less wholesome ring of Donald Trump. Personally, I think he's doing a good job in very tough circumstances and wish him every success.

Chapter 17
My top 10 Indian
Business Leaders

1. Narayana Murthy – Infosys

Narayana Murthy stands head and shoulders above other Indian businesspeople in my view. He pioneered the current generation of Indian software companies, taking Infosys to global leadership – it was the first Indian company listed on the Nasdaq – and introducing the Global Delivery Model of software development. Basically, he popularised tech outsourcing from Western economies to India, where he recruited thousands of highly qualified software engineers to work on the problems of American banks and multinational corporations. This has worked very well for 20 years, but is now under threat as America becomes more nationalistic and other countries like Vietnam and Indonesia are starting to compete with India in this field.

What I most admire about Murthy is that he combines commercial genius with a human regard for employees and a strong customer focus. Infosys isn't just about making money, but making the world a better place. These qualities have won him many friends, along with the Legion d'Honneur from France, the Padma Vibhushan from India and countless other awards and honours.

In the UK, we're often reminded of Murthy because his son-in-law Rushi Sunak is Chancellor of the Exchequer and is growing famous for showering the country with money, as if he was as wealthy as Murthy himself.

2. Lakshmi Mittal – ArcelorMittal

Born just two months after me in 1950, Lakshmi Mittal proved that Indian business leaders could dominate a global industry. He developed a way of turning loss-making, government-owned steel factories into hugely profitable private businesses. First in Indonesia, then in the Caribbean and subsequently in the United States, Romania and elsewhere. He's a captain of free enterprise who became the third-richest man in the world, worth $45 billion in 2008.

I admire his ambition, his imagination and how he's invigorated the companies he bought. It's also good that he's donated so much to educational and medical charities, including Rs100 crores ($13 million) to a fund helping people in India affected by COVID-19. As someone who loves sport, I'm also impressed with how he inspired and funded Indian athletes, including Abhinav Bindra, who won the country's first ever individual Olympic Gold Medal, for shooting. It's this kind of recognition on the world stage that the country needs.

Mittal is a man of grand gestures and expensive tastes: he paid $128 million for a house in Kensington Palace Gardens in London, decorated with the same marble used in the Taj Mahal, and hired the Palace of Versailles for his daughter's wedding. Even if it's a bit over the top, you have to admire Mittal's ambition and confidence.

3. Ratan Tata – Tata Group

Ratan Tata has for years been at the very top of the Indian business tree. He's considered very honest, very credible, a generous donor to charitable causes and someone who took the Tata Group from its Indian roots onto the world stage. In his 21 years in charge, Tata's revenues grew by 40 times and its profits by 50 times, giving the $113 billion conglomerate a leading role in the global auto industry, steel, real estate, technology and plenty more.

It's a giant company with 722,000 employees, so its success is down to a lot more than just Ratan. Even so, he's made Indian businesses into reliable partners. For example, through buying Jaguar and Land Rover in 2008 and successfully investing in the joint brand, he improved India's international business reputation.

In his philanthropic work, Ratan reminds me of Bill Gates. He really studies what will make people's lives better. Rather than simply feeding the poor, he figured out that inadequate hygiene and sanitation caused a lot of hunger, so his trusts invested in water purification and education. In fact, the Tata Foundation struck up a unique partnership with the Bill & Melinda Gates Foundation to tackle diarrhoea in India, with great results.

4. Surinder Arora – Arora Group

A Punjabi like me, Surinder came to England as a teenager and (again like me) spent time as an insurance salesman, where he learnt the art of persuasion. Spotting an opportunity to develop hotels for airline staff at Heathrow, he won a contract with British Airways to accommodate crews in nearby houses in 1999 – making his way once again in a similar industry to me.

He worked night and day to build his business, holding down multiple jobs including shifts as a hotel waiter, while raising a family. Surinder's big break was to win the franchise for the Accord Sofitel brand in 2004. Soon he had both the Sofitel London Gatwick and Sofitel London Heathrow hotels, with 1100 beds between them, including the Renaissance London Heathrow hotel in 2012. Since then he's added another 4000-plus rooms in Hiltons and Holiday Inns, plus the Savill Court Hotel and Spa in Windsor and a share in Wentworth golf course. His net worth topped £1 billion in 2019.

He hit a rough patch between 2008 and 2010, after the credit crunch, when US hedge fund Davidson Kempner demanded repayment of an Allied Irish Bank loan and, when he couldn't pay it immediately, took over two of his Heathrow hotels. This was a lesson in how merciless international financiers can be: he wasn't struggling to make interest payments and his business was healthy, but they forced him out of these hotels anyway.

Besides his amazing work ethic and talent for managing people – his employees are famously loyal and stay with him for years – Surinder is a model corporate citizen. His charitable foundation has donated millions of pounds to medical, education and disaster relief causes. As a human being, he is modest, warm and engaging. You couldn't wish to meet a nicer man.

5. Arjun Waney – Restaurateur

As someone who loves good food and great restaurants, I'm in awe of Arjun Waney. He revived the Arts Club in Mayfair and made it one of London's best places to eat; he's founded stellar restaurants everywhere from New York to Dubai to Bangkok. And he's a thoroughly decent man who has saved countless people from blindness in India through his charitable foundation.

Arjun is like an Indian version of Richard Caring: he made his money in home furnishings (Caring was in fashion), then transferred his energies and talents into food and entertaining by creating amazing places to eat and socialise. He really understands food culture: his restaurants are world class, whether they serve Japanese, Italian, French or even Peruvian food.

He managed the exceptional feat of serving Michelin-starred quality food at scale: more than 500 people a day ate at his Japanese restaurant Zuma in Knightsbridge, with 170 more failing to get a booking. I've always enjoyed the atmosphere, company and food at the Arts Club and I'm sure that Arjun's personality and talent are the reason.

In 2013, Arjun sold 50 per cent of his restaurant business to Turkish conglomerate Dogus, that had money to invest from selling its telecom shares.

I think he got $400 million for his shares, while keeping control of the company. I was really impressed: that was one heck of a deal.

6. Nat Puri – Purico

Cricket-loving Puri, who once paid £50,000 to Virender Sehwag for becoming the first Indian batsman to hit 300 runs in a test match, is a fixture of the English Midlands business scene. Since arriving in the country from India in 1967, aged 27, he rose through the ranks at an engineering company, formed his own consultancy Purico in 1975, bought his old employer in 1983 followed by a string of UK and German auto component manufacturers, and now distributes hundreds of thousands of pounds to schools in India and Nepal.

He grew up on what became the border between India and Pakistan, like my parents, and learnt the value of maths at an early age. "If you can't read and write, it's OK," his uncle told him. "But if you cannot add, subtract and multiply, you are an idiot." At the University of the Punjab he added psychology to his study of maths: "In negotiations, if I understand what they want, and can satisfy them, then I can get a better deal," he worked out. Everyone says he's a very good businessman.

7. Yusuf Hamied – Cipla

In India, most people lack the money to pay for expensive foreign medicines, so the government allows drugs companies to develop generic versions and sell them at low cost. Yusuf Hamied and his company Cipla took this concept and extended it far beyond its Indian roots, developing life-saving treatments for AIDS, tuberculosis and many others. Up until 1995, his company did 90 per cent of its business in India, 10 per cent overseas. Now it's 60 per cent international, 40 per cent India, as Cipla's antiretroviral therapy for HIV sells for 20 cents per day, treating 6 million people.

Hamied learnt his chemistry at Christ's College, Cambridge, and funded the Yusuf Hamied Centre at the college in 2009. His mission to break the stranglehold of the multinational pharmaceutical companies on vital drug treatments is one of the most inspiring Indian business stories in recent times. He placed the well-being of his fellow human beings over profits, while running a hugely successful business.

8. Anshu Jain – Cantor Fitzgerald

While there are now many Indians in high-powered business positions in the United States, it's rare to find the same thing in Europe. Anshu Jain is an exception: from his roots in northern India he went to study in the United States in 1983 then joined Merrill Lynch and, in 1995, Deutsche Bank.

Basically, he was hired by Deutsche Bank from Merrill Lynch to add financial market muscle to the bank as it tried to compete with Barclays, Goldman Sachs and JPMorgan Chase. This worked for a decade until the credit crisis of 2008, when Deutsche Bank and Jain came under fire for selling toxic mortgages and manipulating the Libor rate in London. In 2011 he was appointed joint chief executive of the bank and stayed until 2015, enduring a turbulent couple of years when the bank was in trouble with the US Department of Justice.

Since then, Jain has been president of Cantor Fitzgerald and I think he's doing an excellent job there. We play golf together from time to time, when he's not in the Caribbean directing his teams via Zoom calls.

9. Mukesh Ambani – Reliance Industries

If this was a list of the richest Indians, Mukesh would be number one. His worth is currently around $72 billion, placing him sixth in the global rich list and first in Asia. But since we're talking about all-round qualities, he makes it on to the list through his extraordinary financial success rather than his personality or good works (although he does donate generously to philanthropic causes).

Mukesh's story is that he works with Indian conditions: he deals with whatever is necessary. We can't say that "This isn't the way the world should be," it's just how things are in India. Standards of corporate behaviour are not as high as in the West.

What's remarkable about his history is how he fell out with his brother Anil over the inheritance from their father. Today, while Mukesh is worth $72 billion, his brother is worth something like $500 million – he's almost bankrupt by comparison. Mukesh built Reliance Industries, which is the largest retailer in India and has a giant telecoms business. He's a flamboyant businessman: he owns sports franchises like the Mumbai Indians cricket team, and built a 67-storey tower called the Antilia Building in Mumbai, worth $1 billion, with three helicopter pads and parking for 160 cars.

The point is that Mukesh really knows how to do business in India. You really don't want to come up against him. Compared with someone like Ratan Tata, they're poles apart.

10. Anil Agarwal – Vedanta Resources

The original rags to riches story, Anil Agarwal started out trading scrap metal in Mumbai, then progressed on to manufacturing cables, followed by copper and aluminium. After listing on the London Stock Exchange in 2003 – the first Indian firm to do so – he had the finances to invest in mining. So he bought copper mines in Zambia, then Anglo American's zinc mines in South Africa, Namibia and Ireland. Finally, he went into oil production, buying India's largest private oil company, Cairn India.

Anil is a tough operator who showed great courage and imagination to list in London. He admits that he barely spoke a word of English at the time. "Everyone would say, I am from Bihar, I eat paan," he told the Indian business paper The Economic Times. "I ran and went to London. There I wore a suit and tie and was able to get something by just saying yes and no."

What he got was £100 million to spend on acquisitions, which he nurtured for the following 17 years, so that – via his Vedanta Resources business – he's worth $3 billion and is regarded as a kind of folk hero back in India, partly because of the $36 million a year that his foundation donates to education and health projects. "Though I live in London, I have not come out of Bihar," he said. "I eat with my hands, I sing local countryside music, and no matter how much I am trying to improve my English, the same accent comes out."

Conclusion

As I look back on the past 40 years, since Tani and I set out in business together, with barely any resources, yet with incurable optimism that we'd succeed, the challenges we faced along the way seem trivial compared with the situation facing the world today.

For every recession we survived, this current economic crisis threatens to be twice as deep. Compared with 10 per cent in the 1980s, countries are now stricken by unemployment higher than at any time since the Great Depression of the 1930s. The crises that hit the travel industry, from 9/11 to the Gulf War, look like picnics compared with the impact of COVID-19 and the way it has grounded airlines and imprisoned populations.

My strong feeling is that entrepreneurship is the answer to these challenges. It is the bedrock of every economy, because it changes everything. Every week, companies die and others are born, each one offering something new to society and to commerce, each with its own USP. With the impending tsunami of global unemployment, the capacity of enterprise to suck the jobless millions back into the productive economy and rebuild global trade will be crucial.

All over the world, the pandemic has exposed governments and leaders who are stuck in their dogmas. Those who insist that free markets solve everything, that this virus is a political conspiracy, have found themselves brutally exposed, with horrifying death tolls. The countries that responded most effectively followed the science, acted early and did not prioritise political or economic expediency over public health.

Likewise, entrepreneurs have to be responsive and study the data. The one thing that you can rely upon in business is that conditions are constantly changing, forever throwing the unexpected at you. You have to be able to pivot on a sixpence. This is a quality that sets entrepreneurs apart from civil servants or even from captains of industry: both are political creatures, who can work their way up a hierarchy, but create little real wealth.

Property values may suffer in the months and years to come, especially commercial property as millions choose, or are obliged, to work from home.

Cities will transform, as people stop living on top of one another and flee to the suburbs and the countryside. On the plus side, online retail and tech services like video conferencing will thrive, and as the cost of renewable energy continues to fall, its competitive advantage against fossil fuel-based energy will grow ever more convincing and persuasive.

From the point of view of entrepreneurs, the global economy is at a crossroads, where the way ahead seems unclear and troubled. But generations before us have stood in a similar spot: they've been guided by confidence in their own abilities, determination to work hard and the imagination and talent to find new solutions to the problems of their day.

As a virtually penniless immigrant in a foreign country, in the middle of a deep recession, I built a business and made £100 million, employing more than 5,000 people along the way. I hope this book has given you some insight into how this happened, what succeeded, what failed, what gave us competitive advantage, and the thought process behind it all.

A prosperous future depends upon millions of people building their own enterprises, getting up off their haunches and creating something new for themselves and for society.

Good luck.